THE
NO-BRAINERS

*Your panic-free guide to AI
and the modern good life*

Jacob Eliza

Published in 2024 by Foxx & Sisler

ISBN 978-90-834691-5-7 (paperback, first edition)
ISBN 978-90-834691-2-6 (ebook)

Production: preparetopublish.com
Proofreading: Stephanie Stringham

Visit the author's website at www.jacobeliza.com.

CONTENTS

People are thus able to maintain the illusion, and it is often just that, that they are after all the decision makers.
– Joseph Weizenbaum, *Computer Power and Human Reason*

PREFACE

Managing the Expectation Machine

Hey, it's the author here. I would love to have three minutes with you before we dive into this. You can time me.

I am sure you have certain expectations for this book. They may be high, they may be minimal, they may be vague, they may be specific. You may have heard something from a friend, or you may have been enticed by my publisher's brazen promotion tactics. However, no matter where you started out, it is likely that your expectations are already shifting ever so slightly based on the sentences you are reading right now. Think about it – is this the opening you were looking for?

We can't help ourselves: Our brains are well-honed expectation machines. We use probabilities to predict outcomes based on prior knowledge and adjust these predictions as soon as new evidence comes in.[1] As a practical consequence, we are on happy autopilot when the world sticks to its script and things go as planned. However, we snap into conscious, active mode when unexpected events come our way. This conscious state is fun when expectations are surpassed; it is very stressful when expectations are violated.

---

1 Here is where I could tell you that the mathematical underpinnings of this "expectation machine" date back to the 18th century and that ChatGPT, Spotify, and Netflix are also expectation machines. However, let's save that for the actual book, not the preface.

This means we are not happy when our pricey Airbnb beach abode doesn't look anything like its glamorous photo gallery and those five-star reviews suddenly seem very suspicious. We are not pleased when our boyfriend shows up two hours late for the Tame Impala concert and he suddenly sports a purple weave.[2] And we don't like it when we buy a book about artificial intelligence and that book suddenly starts talking about all kinds of random topics that are decidedly *not* artificial intelligence, such as Tame Impala concerts, purple weaves, and Airbnb beach abodes.

In that spirit, let's be considerate to your mind and set modest expectations for what this book actually is, in the hope to surpass them later.

This book explores how our favorite apps grew so smart, how algorithms slipped into our lives, and how artificial intelligence (AI) may now slowly transform our brains. It is not structured according to the iron logic of bestseller non-fiction books; it is an inspired journey rather than a concise argument. It will not establish its main point after 15 pages and then hammer that same point in for another 180 pages. Instead, we will follow a winding trail through the jungle of our modern lives, stopping to peek behind the scenes of the daily decisions that make us who we are. During this journey, we will find unexpected treasures, dip into pop culture, veer into personal anecdotes and – spoiler alert – ultimately discover what we are looking for.

Needless to say: I am a storyteller, not a scientist. I am not here to present the newest techniques in neural networks. The hero here is *Homo sapiens*, not technology itself. As such, you should enjoy this book even if your tech skills are limited to that one button you always press on your microwave. Starting

---

2 A friend did that. To be fair, the band was delayed by more than an hour, so he was technically only 45 minutes late.

with the basics, I will demonstrate how data, algorithms, and AI work, and slowly ramp up the complexity until we are discussing machine learning, recommendation engines, and large language models like it's just another Pancake Friday. (Don't worry – I *will* explain the ancient formula of Pancake Fridays within 20 pages.)

Finally, a special word of thanks to my early readers, who flagged unfortunate hallucinations that made it to early drafts. They tell me there is an undercurrent of optimism running through the book you have in your hands right now.[3] I guess that when a lifelong optimist decides to write about AI and algorithms, you know what you're going to get: an optimistic take on AI and algorithms. I am sorry if this doesn't suit your appetite – this is what I have in store.

I will shut up now. Let's get going.

---

3 I realize it is very likely you are actually consuming this paragraph via an audiobook or digital copy. Still, we all like to imagine having something tangible in our hands, so let's just pretend together that it's 1992, the internet never happened and you are leafing through actual paper pages.

> ### The No-Brainers, bite sized
>
> → Every chapter ends with five concrete takeaways, in a handy box just like this!
>
> → This is great if you're time pressed or don't like reading – just skip ahead and get the gist of the book in 1% of the time.
>
> → These takeaways have been lab tested as above-average conversation starters for barbecues, wedding receptions, and moderate-sized cocktail parties.
>
> → They can also be printed on very big T-shirts and even bigger mugs.
>
> → What did I tell you? That's five concrete takeaways, right there!

1 AMSTERDAM, 1990s

The Pitch We Can't Resist

Storytelling is a very old human skill that gives us an evolutionary advantage. If you can tell young people how you kill an emu... or that Uncle George was eaten by a croc over there, don't go there to swim, then those young people don't have to find out by trial and error.

– Margaret Atwood

Do you know how certain websites require you to prove that you are human by checking a box or solving a little puzzle? Well, dear reader, let me start off this book by establishing my credentials with you as a bona fide human.

During the summer of 1997, when Kate Winslet and Leonardo DiCaprio started promoting a movie called *Titanic*, when Bill Clinton was already post-affair but still pre-scandal, human chess genius Garry Kasparov was beaten at his own game by an IBM supercomputer called Deep Blue. The press hailed it as a watershed moment for artificial intelligence, but at the time, I couldn't care less. I was 22 years old and a fledgling internet entrepreneur, meaning: broke. On top of that, my then girlfriend had just asked me to move in with her and give up my own Amsterdam apartment.

I had not seen her question coming. We'd been together for all but three months, and though I was clearly in love with her, I had been focusing most of my energy on my internet startup. So – was this for real? Could she be the one? As soon as she asked me, I realized I didn't really know what I wanted out of life: I just knew I had some vague ambitions to become a successful entrepreneur, maybe write a book or two, and one day live abroad. But I'd never really thought about truly building a life with somebody.

There was an enticing upside: more quality time with her, less rent to pay, more money to spend. She had the bigger place, a great deal on one of the glittering Amsterdam canals. But there was also the downside: less independence, some growing up to do, and the very real prospect of being homeless, humiliated, and even more broke if it didn't work out.

Faced with these questions and the inherent uncertainty of the future, this would have been a great moment for me to have a big crisis: to overthink things, to have sleepless nights, to make complicated Excel sheets with pros and cons, and then still end up feeling uncomfortable with any conclusion.

But interestingly, I did not overthink it. At all. To my own surprise, my brain turned into a supercomputer. It processed all the available information in milliseconds, evaluated the options, and gave me the green light on the spot.

"Yes," I told her, "I would love to move in together!" It was a memorable, spontaneous moment, and we shared a kiss on an Amsterdam bridge, a scene straight out of a late-'90s romantic comedy. We went for dinner at the local Italian restaurant to celebrate our newfound commitment, and second thoughts never entered my mind.

It was a strange turn of events. Until recently, I had been a classic overthinker, prone to weigh options carefully until my brain melted down in a fit of analysis paralysis. As a follower of logic and mathematics, I had always believed that making decisions from the heart was ludicrous: The heart did not deal in facts, just in wishful thinking, and you were bound to screw up if you just followed your whims. But I had recently stumbled into my own internet business, and those early days of entrepreneurship had given me an epiphany: *Screwing up was exactly the point.* As a novice businessman trying to be successful on the brand-new internet, you knew nothing, but you still had to do *something* to be successful. And if you couldn't make a rational decision because you lacked proof of what would lead to success, you may as well take an educated guess and thereby *create proof of what worked or didn't work.*

Fact: There was no way to know if strategy A or B would lead to the desired outcome.
Problem: You would never find out, unless you tried it out.
Conclusion: You may as well try strategy A. And if strategy A was heading in the wrong direction, you'd immediately stop, learn your lessons, and distill useful facts to drive future decisions. In other words, you would fail fast, take a deep breath, and quickly pivot to strategy B.

I started to wonder – what if the secret to a successful life wasn't careful planning, but embracing the chaos of trial and error? As an experiment, I began to run my personal life this way. Whenever I encountered a crossroads, I quickly moved in whatever direction seemed right, especially for those choices where you would never have enough information to make the perfect call anyway. At first, it felt like rolling a die, but after a while, I started getting more sophisticated at it: It was like making a rapid educated bet on the outcome most likely to be beneficial, where a 60% chance of success was better than a 50–50 proposition. Quicker decisions led to quicker insights and were therefore good, no matter the outcome. Because failure wasn't really failure: Screwing up was simply learning a useful lesson for future endeavors.

And so even the most complex decisions started feeling like no-brainers. I threw out my crappy student furniture and moved in with my girlfriend. Was it a good decision? Let the facts speak for themselves: She and I had some great times but eventually grew apart. She kicked me out after 14 months, and I had to crash on friends' sofas – which was not ideal – but I could at least tell myself that I'd acquired invaluable experience in sharing a household and making a serious relationship work.[4] Within weeks, I got lucky and found another place through my network of friends, which was very much boosted by my exposure to *her* network of friends. And within a year, I met somebody else and got to apply all the relationship lessons I had painfully captured.

At this point, you're probably convinced I am not a chatbot but a flawed human being, just like you. Glad to have that box ticked off! Beyond that, I hope this anecdote gently introduces the virtues of "learning by doing," because we will keep revisiting this concept in the next 250 pages. Why? Because this trial-and-error strategy is the exact same ploy that made the algorithms behind Spotify, Midjourney, and ChatGPT so remarkably smart.

But beyond *that*, do you know why I am really sharing this story? Today, I am 25 years wiser but otherwise the exact same guy as back then – yet my brain never feels like that snappy supercomputer anymore. Today, decisions rarely feel like a no-brainer: I can't even decide what movie to pick for a date night, which hotel to book for a weekend trip, and what

---

4 This seems like a badge people should feature on their dating app profiles: "I Made a Serious Relationship Work in 1997!"

recipe to select for dinner. Today, my overstimulated brain asks ChatGPT for advice on major life decisions and ends up with such a balanced perspective that I still can't make up my mind. Sometimes, it feels like I need someone to serve me my preferences on a silver platter or I will be simply stuck in neutral forever.

Is it me, or have my decision-making skills completely regressed?

OK, perhaps I am being slightly dramatic. But not a lot.

A VERY BRIEF HISTORY OF AI, or:
HOW OFTEN CAN AN OPTIMIST BE WRONG?

The prospect of using computers to solve problems or to do creative work is bright indeed.
 – Allen Newell and Herbert A. Simon, writing in 1956

Having been trained as a computer scientist in the '90s, everybody knew that AI didn't work. People tried it. They tried neural nets, and none of it worked.
 – Sergey Brin (Google co-founder), speaking in 2017

Let's rewind the tape quickly and imagine a five-minute video on how we got here.

Envision a mad scientist, like Doc Brown from *Back to the Future* – eccentric haircut, brain in the clouds – brimming with confidence that the 99th tweak to his new invention will finally prove his crazy theory right. We are going to pretend that it is 1945 and Doc Brown is hoping to invent artificial intelligence. He is extremely optimistic he will succeed soon enough. How often can an optimist be wrong?

As it turns out, an optimist can be wrong for 50 years straight.

Between 1945 and 1995, artificial intelligence was proper mad science. Behind the metaphor of Doc Brown operated a wild bunch of academic misfits, peddling the promise that humans would one day be relieved of their cognitive burden and menial duties. Even in the very early days, the pitch of AI was irresistible: these men and women shared dreams of robots doing household chores, AI-powered tutors enabling one-on-one learning, computer doctors working 24/7 to diagnose diseases, and smart self-driving cars roaming the interstates.

The ultimate fantasy? AI systems with human-level intelligence, capable of having a proper conversation, and truly understanding our needs.

It was a no-brainer: If Doc Brown made this work, life would be a breeze, once and for all.

Except it all remained a pipe dream for over two generations.

The glimmers of success were always there. Scientists started designing computers, and industry turned these computers into increasingly powerful tools. The AI pioneers programmed the computers to simulate human intelligence and were quick to find out that machines excelled at pattern recognition and logic.[5] An early high point came in 1966: An MIT professor named Joseph Weizenbaum created the world's first chatbot in a self-designed programming language and was clever enough to cast his program in the role of helpful psychotherapist.

As it played out, the first persuasive human–AI conversation went something like this:

Chatbot: Please tell me your problem.
Secretary: My boyfriend drives me crazy.
Chatbot: Why do you say your boyfriend drives you crazy?
Secretary: Because he doesn't communicate.

---

5 At this point, AI had proved simple mathematical theorems and cracked complicated cryptographic codes.

Chatbot: Don't any other reasons come to mind?
Secretary: Well, I think I may not love him enough.
Chatbot: I am sorry to hear you may not love him enough.

Heartened by the opportunity to talk about themselves, many early testers found the conversations with the program to be genuinely helpful. More than a few insisted on privacy when they were typing at the terminal, and were disappointed to find out they were talking to a machine.

Given the state of AI in 1966, this felt like a major leap forward. But Weizenbaum knew better: His chatbot was less an intelligent entity than it was a skilled con artist. As you can see in the exchange above, his program cleverly faked active listening to keep the conversation going: It asked open questions, mirrored answers, and sprinkled in a little dose of scripted empathy to maximum effect.[6] Astonished that people fell for these tricks, and knowing that this approach would ultimately lead to a dead end, Weizenbaum abandoned his project. A few years later, he re-emerged as Skeptical Joe, one of artificial intelligence's foremost critics. We will return to him soon.

What followed was a decade of crisis and self-doubt. Artificial intelligence had been like a sexy *Dragons' Den/Shark Tank* startup that kept on seducing investors with its fantastic pitch, even if it never actually brought the promised product to market. But by the 1980s, that funding dried up, with "intelligent" systems still laughably dumb and chatbot progress completely flatlining. The cloud of disillusion slowly settled over the field. Had our imaginations gotten the better

---

6 Weizenbaum called it "the simplest mechanical parody... of a human encounter." Still, if you have zero social skills and can't read a facial expression to save your life, following these preset rules can make you a conversational rock star. Just don't expect to talk much about yourself.

of us? Was artificial intelligence still a realistic goal? There was a newfound appreciation of human intelligence, whose basic functions had proven so fiendishly difficult to replicate in a computer.

This begged the big question: How, exactly, were we even to know what artificial intelligence actually looked like? Well, back in the early 1950s, AI founding father Alan Turing (of Benedict Cumberbatch *Imitation Game* fame) had proposed the "Turing test" to determine whether artificial intelligence had successfully been achieved. The test would be passed *once a computer could reliably fool people they were dealing with another human.* Turing himself expected this to happen by 2000.

But since Turing sat down to write his paper, five decades had come and gone, and the field of AI was nowhere near his humble benchmark. Weizenbaum's clever chatbot may have fooled people for a minute, but true artificial intelligence remained a fantasy. Even for a techno-optimist, the notion of clever interactive robots had distinctly begun to evoke passé science fiction, rather than something academically worth pursuing.[7]

At this point, I am going to insert myself again. Apologies, this will happen repeatedly during this book, in the hope IRL experiences give the narrative more context and color.[8]

I discovered early on how AI would lure you in with its promise and then slowly milk your optimism until you felt drained. This was because I was once a data nerd who studied

---

7 To this day, the 1980s are referred to as the "AI winter" by tech historians. It was bleak out there, and Santa didn't bring any gifts.

8 IRL = in real life, a 1990s internet term that stuck around. If you had to use this footnote to understand what it means, you've never been on MSN or ICQ – which is fine, by the way.

artificial intelligence at the University of Amsterdam – in fact, I did so in the years right before I received that no-brainer question from my then girlfriend on the canals.

I was drawn to AI because it seemed like a way to deconstruct and understand life. I naively hoped we could somehow turn these learnings into formulas for human happiness. But in reality, I found AI to excel at making sensational promises – and excel even more at breaking them. In university, we would pursue the trivial and failed: I joined a group of students developing chess-playing robot arms, but the blurry robot vision couldn't process the 3D and the limbs would predictably swipe all the pieces off the board. The next trimester, we developed and tested malaria diagnostics algorithms, but they behaved erratically and would have sent 60% of their patients to an early grave if deployed in the real world.

I would tell myself to be impressed that computers could now do basic grammar checks and robots could now navigate simple staircases, but what did that really mean? Could we truly rely on these pieces of code? I would tell myself that AI would ultimately reveal deeper truths about humanity because it merged computer science with philosophy, mathematics, psychology, engineering, and linguistics – but I also knew it would reach the limits of my patience before it got to that.

This was 1995 – the same year the sleepy internet refashioned itself as the sensational world wide web and suddenly took the world by storm, reshaping everything in its path. These were heady times, but getting AI to work was still like dealing with a dim-witted sloth with behavioral issues. The latest generation of chatbots responded slowly, wrongly, or would have a complete meltdown on your screen.[9] Expert systems often behaved like idiot systems and needed more

---

9 For a good overview, see *Bots* (1997) by Andrew Leonard. In this book, a chatbot connoisseur laments that "little progress has been made in the last twenty-five years."

humans to run them than they could replace. How did any of this improve the lives of real people? Even if I was ever the optimist, I started to understand why Joseph Weizenbaum had turned into Skeptical Joe: there was still little proof AI was going anywhere, with my professors dealing in the highly theoretical and the early neural networks unable to distinguish the differences between Mozart and Run-DMC.[10]

And so the hype balloon shriveled, and the AI bandwagon nearly emptied out. I also jumped off, more bemused than disillusioned, and hopped on the fast-accelerating internet train, just like everybody else. But the die-hard AI believers summoned another round of optimism and clung on. They kept trial-and-erroring away in the shadows, learning from their mistakes, until their fates finally – finally! – turned. The ongoing improvements in chip performance suddenly caught up with the AI community's thirst for processing power. New strategies were discovered, and old ideas were given a second look and found to be a breakthrough after all. Oh, and the sensational expansion of the internet suddenly opened the door to network computing and a pile of digital information of a bewildering scale – which was exactly the oxygen the algorithms needed to finally inhale deeply – and breathe.[11]

---

10 I saw this particular mishap firsthand. When I later discovered music-recognition app Shazam in 2008, not to mention song-creation app Udio in 2024, I was floored.

11 The internet-propelled information explosion can hardly be overstated. Ancient Rome's top libraries contained an estimated 3 GB of information; the Library of Congress held 3 PB (petabytes) in 1997; the 2016 internet was already estimated to hold 16 ZB (zettabytes), which is the equivalent of 16,000,000 PB. And the internet hasn't stopped growing since – it is now expanding at a rate of 7% per year. As Smil (2019) writes: "Our knowledge base may now be a trillion times larger than at the start of the common era." Chew on that, librarians of Ancient Rome!

Today, our Doc Brown is famous: The outcast of computer science found a way to make it work, after all. AI has started to deliver on its promise – or so it seems. AI is now literally everywhere – embedded in all the technology we use, affecting our decisions, whether we're ready or not. The progressive releases of ChatGPT kicked off a fresh hype cycle, with billions of dollars flowing into AI startups and AI making a glorious comeback at the office water cooler.

Yes, most of us kinda knew that artificial intelligence was getting pretty good at the specialized and unsexy jobs: assembling cars, running logistics, flying airplanes, guiding missiles, and playing chess. But now the frontier has clearly moved again. With shiny tools like ChatGPT, Character.ai, Copilot, and Claude, we have AI in our hands every day. AI can see, think, speak, and provoke real emotions in humans. Cracking the Turing test suddenly seems within reach, if we're not there already: AI's new wave is clearly smarter, wiser – and *scarier*.

THE NO-BRAINERS: WEIRD LUCIAN'S PREMONITION

On a winter evening in 1999 – the year of *The Matrix* – something peculiar happened to me. I was sitting in a dimly lit Amsterdam cafe at the edge of the city center, polishing up a presentation I was scheduled to give the next day. I was completely caught up in my work and didn't register the strange man sitting at the table next to me.

"Hey," said the man. "Sorry to bother you – I couldn't help but notice you're working on a presentation about artificial intelligence."

I looked up, taken aback by his unabashed approach. His eyes gleamed with a knowing glint, and I suddenly became pretty sure I had met him before – maybe at an industry event? Maybe he was a speaker? – but I couldn't work it out. With the casual confidence of a business acquaintance, he introduced himself as Lucian, which sent my brain scrambling – but I still couldn't figure out how I knew him. Before I'd gathered my wits, he'd taken the lead in the conversation.

"Please listen to me," he said. "Today, AI may look like an obvious pursuit. Today, we may believe everybody's lives would be greatly improved if we could delegate the hard decisions to helpful algorithms. We may dream of a future where smart robots are fully fledged partners, allowing us to relax and enjoy life. But we need to be careful what we wish for."

Intrigued, I folded my laptop and looked the guy square in the eyes.

"Do you believe in artificial intelligence?" he asked me. "Do you believe it will improve the world?"

I laughed. "I guess so. I am an optimist. But what is this – are we doing Faust?"

Lucian's smile widened before he continued. "For every great innovation, there is always a price to pay. And I am not just talking about jobs or lives – I am talking about *brains*. Once we've built replacement brains and they learn to become more efficient decision-makers than us, it will be a matter of time before we give them the reins. That's just how it works – we are lazy, and this laziness will finally come back to haunt us. Artificial intelligence will run the show, and human brains will wither. *Homo sapiens* will continue to roam the planet, but in a state of mental decay. We will ultimately end as no-brainer zombies, at the mercy of the replacement brains we designed."

"Interesting take," I said. "No-brainer zombies." I studied him again. "So who are you really, and what is this?"

Now it was his turn to look a bit confused. "I am Lucian," he repeated. "We used to take classes in screenwriting together at university – don't you remember me?"

I blinked – and finally did recognize him, as the weird middle-aged guy who had shown up for my old screenwriting class three times, bemused everybody with his far-fetched movie ideas, and then disappeared without a trace.

I don't remember what happened afterwards; I guess I paid the bill and left, because I needed to finish my work and the guy was distracting me. Years later, I saw Lucian's name on the credits of a minor Dutch drama series, and I reached out to connect on LinkedIn – but he never accepted my invitation. I have no idea what he is up to today, but I never forgot his strange premonition on artificial intelligence, with humans ending up as no-brainer zombies roving the planet, wondering how they'd squandered their evolutionary advantage.

THE PROPHECY OF SKEPTICAL JOE

You can probably guess by now: This book owes its genesis to my hopeful dreams in 1990s Amsterdam, culminating with Weird Lucian's unsolicited B-movie monologue in that hazy cafe. But a recent late night with a dusty box sealed the deal.

Decades passed before I got back in the AI business, and when I did, everything had changed. Algorithms and data were now the undisputed answer to everything. Endless trial and error had made them seemingly smarter than us, and for the first time, the world *believed*. I had always retained my soft spot for AI's promise, and this felt like a coming-of-age story with a happy ending. Still, I found myself increasingly wondering about the surprisingly casual way artificial intelligence had suddenly slipped into our lives.

Clearly, Doc Brown had sold his dream to us all. Governments and businesses had long succumbed, sometimes at the blatant expense of individuals' rights, but so had we – us, the individuals themselves. We were interacting with the sophisticated algorithms of Spotify, Netflix, and Tinder on a daily basis, as if humanity had long decided this was the right leap forward. But were these tools actually giving us formulas for a better life? Making us feel more understood? Giving us back time? Had we collectively hit upon an essential life hack, or were these smart apps simply repackaging the same old drudgery in new and interesting ways, merely creating the illusion of progress?

Soon after, with ChatGPT mesmerizing the world, the internet was full of sweeping statements about AI paradise (imminent!) and the AI apocalypse (equally imminent!). It was hyped as a transformative moment in the history of humankind, but I had seen this movie before: Rather than bow to a speculative machine God and close our eyes until AI washed over us, this was the moment to deconstruct the myths and be thoroughly practical. I was convinced the real story was right there in the middle, far from the extremes, way closer to home. How would AI impact our data, our identities, our daily chores? How could we harness this technology to improve our ordinary lives in relatable ways? Or was artificial intelligence, even if used well, bound to eat away at the abilities of our brains, like Weird Lucian had suggested?

Then, late one night, working my way through a dusty box of discarded books, I unexpectedly came across the original AI skeptic again: Joseph Weizenbaum, the man who once amazed the world with his psychotherapist chatbot. After his hands-on programming days had ended, he laid out his views in *Computer Power and Human Reason*, a seminal work that cemented his status as the grumpy postmodernist in computer science. I'd never read his book, but that night, I did. By page 9, he was warning that algorithms should never be trusted to make decisions by themselves.[12] And by the final page, his

---

12 "If [mankind's] reliance on such machines is to be based on something other than unmitigated despair or blind faith, he must explain to himself what these machines do and even how they do what they do… Yet most men don't understand computers to even the slightest degree." From the original edition.

assault on the optimistic ideals of the "artificial intelligentsia" was complete: When people start trusting machines over their own reasoning abilities, it will diminish their own capacity for critical thought and ethical decision-making.

In other words, the danger is not that computers will eventually get too smart and take over the world. The real danger is that people will begin to think less and rely on machines to make decisions for them.

It was uncanny – half a century later, despite Weizenbaum's prophecy, we were doing exactly that. We relied on machines more than ever, increasingly outsourcing our mental strain to the cloud – without truly realizing *what* exactly we were delegating our decisions to.

It was almost dawn when I put the book back in the box, and I couldn't help but wonder if this was it – if humanity had finally peaked and we had opted into our inevitable, drawn-out, irreversible slide to zombie status.

> **Me:** Would you agree humanity is slowly outsourcing essential cognitive skills to algorithms?
>
> **Chatbot:** Sorry, I can't answer that question right now. But you may have a point.
>
> **Me:** I guess I still believe in a good future for AI. I still believe it can help us understand life and make the world a better place.
>
> **Chatbot:** What makes you believe that?
>
> **Me:** I don't know – it's such a multi-layered topic. Perhaps I should just write a book about it.
>
> **Chatbot:** Perhaps you should.

Chapter 1's No-Brainer takeaways:

→ *The No-Brainers* **is about artificial intelligence.** It cuts through the hype and surveys optimistic and pessimistic views about the technology with an open mind. It tries to understand its practical impact by staying close to home and relating it to our daily decisions.

→ **The author is upbeat about AI's potential.** There is a belief that AI may yield "formulas for happiness" and create extra efficiencies by reducing our cognitive load.

→ **On the other hand, he also has some doubts.** His own experience with AI in the past has left him underwhelmed by its ability to fulfill its promises – it could still be a hollow hype and ultimately a frivolous waste of time.

→ **The pessimistic view is represented by Joseph Weizenbaum.** Nicknamed Skeptical Joe here, he warned that humans would suffer cognitive decline if they'd delegate decision-making autonomy to smart computers – way back in 1976.

→ **The no-brainer zombie signifies AI's worst outcome.** Taking Skeptical Joe's concerns to their logical endpoint, the no-brainer zombie – not some kind of robot apocalypse – is the real threat for humanity.

2 YOUR BEST LIFE, COMPLICATED

The Carefree Weekend Algorithm

Lost in thought on how to actually write this book, I took a late afternoon walk in a cold Vondelpark by myself. This is when I accidentally overheard a good-looking, early-30s couple arguing about their dinner plans, right off the big bend by the Vondelkerk exit, and something clicked in my head.

HOW TO HAVE A CAREFREE WEEKEND

James: So – what do you want to do for dinner?

Emily: I don't really know. What are you in the mood for?

James: Well, we have leftover broccoli, savoy cabbage, and asparagus in the fridge… And lamb shank, smoked chicken, and langoustines in the freezer… And we have to finish that slice of halloumi from yesterday… But of course, we can also go out again. Or order in. (Grabs phone.) What are you feeling like? Italian? Veggie? Mexican? Asian?

Emily: Emmmm, Asian sounds nice?

James: OK, Asian – but then, Indian? Vietnamese? Taiwanese? Hong Kong style? Korean?

Emily: …
James: Emily?
Emily: Can't you pick? I am too hungry to make a decision right now.

Ah, the joys of choice! If the above conversation doesn't sound familiar to you, count your blessings; you're probably living a good life. It means you've mercifully missed out on the revolution that has permanently messed up the rest of us – the wretches that caved and installed food delivery apps on our phones. Whether it's via Delivery Hero (US), Deliveroo (Europe), Jumia (Africa), Rappi (South America), or Meituan Diaping (China), we now can consume any food from any cuisine we get a notion for at any given moment, often within 30 minutes of getting that notion.

We aren't just trying to live a good life; we are trying to live our *best* life.

And it drives us mad!

Flashback: When I was growing up, in a typical 1980s household with Rick Astley non-ironically blasting on the kitchen radio, we had an extremely predictable schedule around food. Sunday to Thursday, we ate whatever my mum felt like cooking, which typically was based on a set of 15 carefully curated recipes we all liked, ranging from pasta to European staples. These 15 recipes got us through the week – my mum had sole discretion to pick what we had for dinner, and we happily ate it. But then, the weekend came, and with that, pure bliss. Fridays were always, *always* Pancake Fridays: We would have pancakes with jam and syrup for dinner every single Friday evening for years and years and years. And Saturdays were Burger Saturdays: The family would have homemade fries and burgers every single Saturday, year in, year out.[13]

---

13 Yes, I realize having pancakes for *dinner* is a strange thing. But there it is: I guess all families have skeletons in their closet.

As kids, Pancake Fridays and Burger Saturdays were rules you could count on. Besides pancakes being obvious crowd pleasers, they anchored the switch from the tedious school week to the carefree weekend, and I always loved to invite friends over to celebrate. On top of that, this reliable format – despite being perhaps of questionable culinary taste – also made my parents happy: my mom because she could prepare these meals on autopilot without having to think, and my dad because he has a major weak spot for uncomplicated food and would probably eat pancakes and potatoes seven days a week if he had the choice.

Was this routine boring and predictable? Yes. But then again, boring and predictable were our friends.[14] In my eyes, my parents had nailed the formula for a Carefree Weekend. Today, with the mind-boggling amount of meal choices available at my fingertips, I struggle to achieve the same uncomplicated happiness. Why is that?

Looking back, it's interesting to see how my parents made this formula work by *limiting choice*. Which was not as straight-forward as it sounds, because even in the mid-1980s, eating food involved making *choices*, every single day. Supermarkets, which probably stocked 25% of the stuff they do now, shelved more than enough options to let you have 100,000 different dinners on any given day, and household incomes were such that people could actually *afford* to tap into their free choice to eat whatever they wanted. Restaurants – both of the fast food and fancy food denominations – were prolific, especially in the big cities, and the concept of takeaway meals was firmly entrenched from the late '70s onwards, even if mobile phones and the internet weren't.

Still, my parents opted to remove those options every

---

14 Steve Jobs famously wore black turtlenecks and blue jeans every single day – to enhance his brand, but also to conserve his daily energy for more important decisions.

Friday and Saturday, running with Pancake Friday and Burger Saturday for my entire childhood.

To a modern city dweller constantly seduced by takeaway apps and endless supplies of online recipes, this conscious removal of options may seem absurd. And it does go against that widely believed tenet of capitalism: More personal choice equals more personal freedom equals more personal well-being. That you can only live your best life by maximizing your options and then picking the best one.

Is this abundance of choice really a luxury, or is it actually a burden? Either way, it is a fundamentally modern dilemma, one that must be equal parts amusing and bewildering to our ancestors – if they could see us scroll through all the possibilities on our phones. Even my grandparents, who lived through two world wars, did not have "options" for dinner – they had potatoes for dinner, five days a week. Their main worry was to have food on the table in the first place, not to pick between Korean-style and Taiwanese-style noodles and then get FOMO over all the other 950 options that were discarded to get to that final decision.

And that's why I believe my parents were onto something bigger when they decided to install Pancake Fridays and Burger Saturdays. They may not have consciously aimed for it, but by keeping things predictable and simple for two out of the seven days, they eliminated the mental energy wasted on the act of choosing, freeing up that same energy for quality time and conversation, fueled by the bliss of the predictable syrupy sugars and eggy proteins.[15]

---

15 Today, I do know better, and I have calculated that pancakes and fries/burgers are only my 290th and 424th favorite meals in the world, respectively.

1980s CAREFREE WEEKENDS
EXPLAINED AS ALGORITHM

Me: Any food recommendations around Sunset Boulevard?

My cool friend in LA: Do you have any food allergies or dietary restrictions?

Me: No, I am easy.

My cool friend in LA: Oh. (Sighs.) That actually makes it harder.

Let's take a leap here. Let's say you've read the previous paragraphs, becoming increasingly enthusiastic. In fact, you are genuinely starting to believe that reinstating the 1980s Carefree Weekend Formula is actually the key to increasing modern happiness! Being of altruistic disposition, you wish to teach mankind this amazing trick, so everybody can have a Carefree Weekend, even in the digital age. After all, human progress is the story of us endlessly trying out new things and then sharing the formula for the good things once we've hit upon them, even if they actually originated in the dubious 1980s.

How can we spread the word? Would it be possible to write down the above "formula for a carefree weekend" as a set of rules we can share with other people?

Yes, and it is actually quite easy:

Carefree Weekend Rule 1: If Friday, serve pancakes.

Carefree Weekend Rule 2: If Saturday, serve homemade burgers and fries.

Carefree Weekend Rule 3: If neither of the above applies, pick a random recipe from a fixed 15-recipe list that your household likes and that is easy to cook.

There we are: three simple rules that can be read and applied by anyone. You could write them on a sticky note and hang them on your fridge. You could obtain a chisel and carve them in actual stone. Or you could write a book about these three rules and mass-print them on a truckload of overpriced inspirational T-shirts (in a very tiny font) that you peddle at a webinar of the same name.

Conveniently, *these three rules could also be understood by a computer*. If we would like an app to execute those rules, we would write them as an *algorithm* in the app's code. It works exactly like you think it does: The algorithm takes the day of the week as input, walks through the steps in sequence, and produces the logical outcome. The computer doesn't have an opinion; it just follows the procedure. In a simple world, this would then allow the app to run our golden rules for a carefree weekend flawlessly… and deliver us our version of the ideal meal every single Friday and Saturday.

Before we go any further, let's appreciate what just happened. We hit upon the idea that a computer could make a decision on our behalf, just by running a simple set of instructions. This may seem like a glaringly obvious step for anybody who has ever had a smartphone in their hands, but it still represents a fundamental shift in the human experience: It means we can delegate routine decision-making to a non-human, provided we instruct it well. And this very idea is fundamental to the promise of artificial intelligence, and simultaneously at the root of all its challenges.

Before we get carried away – and trust me, we will get carried away later – this algorithm thing probably needs some unpacking. First of all, do these three straightforward rules really constitute an algorithm? Yes – the above is definitely an example of a proper algorithm, even though it is a very simple one. Algorithms, despite their reputation for complexity and opaqueness, can be very transparent and plain.

The word *algorithm*, pretentious and difficult to spell though it may be, actually means nothing more than "a preset procedure to solve a problem."[16] Which means that "If one is tired, go to sleep" could be framed as a very simple algorithm: On the condition of fatigue, the preset action "go to sleep" solves the problem. Easy, right?

Other valid examples of algorithms would be:

- » a recipe to bake a strawberry cake
- » my standard weekday morning routine – coffee, granola, brushing my teeth
- » the solution for a Rubik's Cube
- » the incomprehensible navigation instructions that nice man in that Parisian hotel gave me that one evening my phone battery died.

Once you know where to look, algorithms turn out to be everywhere!

A nice thing about algorithms is that you can endlessly tweak them and make them more suited to your needs. Looking at my three-rule 1980s Carefree Weekend algorithm, it's very easy to see how you can customize it. Because I am very aware that you may not enjoy burgers or pancakes as much as my 1980s family did, feel free to tweak the above with whatever food options suit your fancy. Perhaps you dislike pancakes and burgers but you could have sushi every day of the week. Perhaps you go to the gym on Tuesdays, so you always have a light couscous salad before. Perhaps you don't limit yourself to 15 recipes, but – if you're being honest

---

16 Merriam-Webster calls it "a step-by-step procedure for solving a problem or accomplishing some end." In case you're wondering, the word *algorithm* originates in ninth-century Arabic, like *algebra*, *alchemy*, and pretty much all other present-day fancy words starting with *al-*.

– you do limit yourself to around 40. And maybe you are a vegetarian, which – besides making you less of a burden on the planet – also gives you fewer options to work with. Whatever your situation is, you can *probably* come up with a list of rules that describe how you pick your evening's meals. Try it – it is fun and at the very least will give you some insight in your own decision-making logic.

Just aim to stay true to the general principle: Keep it specific, and limit choice. The result should be a straightforward set of rules that together form your own choice-reducing algorithm.

> **Alternate Carefree Weekend Rule 1**: If Friday, order fried chicken.
> **Alternate Carefree Weekend Rule 2:** If Saturday, order pizza.
> **Alternate Carefree Weekend Rule 3:** If neither of the above applies, eat cup noodles.

Yes, you would be lacking nutrition and expose yourself to scurvy. Yes, people may find you predictable, even boring, and may not want to be your friend anymore. But you would never have to spend any energy on food choice.[17]

Notice how the algorithm mirrors this simplicity: The decision logic is straightforward, so the algorithm is short and sweet. No thinking needed! Remember, as a ten-year-old, I never had to spend any brain power worrying about food, especially over the weekends – energy that I happily repurposed to play video games and build tree houses, energy which was then replenished with maple syrup every Friday evening. My

---

17 And you would have a kindred spirit in Barack Obama. As the former US president explained to Michael Lewis: "I'm trying to pare down decisions. I don't want to make decisions about what I'm eating. ... Because I have too many other decisions to make."

brain must have been very content with the efficiency of this process.

Of course, algorithms can be even leaner and meaner, even uncomfortably so. Let's codify the dinner rules many Dutch households ran during the war-torn winter of 1944:

Grandparent Food Algorithm Rule 1: Eat any food you can get your hands on.
Grandparent Food Algorithm Rule 2: If rule 1 fails, eat tulip bulbs.

Despite the unenviable economic hardship that is implied in these two simple rules – which represent a survival mechanism more than a decision tree – this 1940s Food Happiness algorithm is still an algorithm, one that is undoubtedly very light on complexity. Life was harsh, and life's decisions simple.

Of course, the Carefree Weekend algorithm is a bit of revisionist history from my side. I am sure my parents deviated from it every now and then, even if I genuinely don't remember. But myths wouldn't be myths if they didn't contain useful truths. Psychologists have known for decades that we get stressed when we have to choose from too many things. After working hard to expand their product ranges for decades, businesses shockingly discovered that customers order *more* when choice is *limited*! Twenty-four flavors of jam means analysis paralysis; seven flavors of jam translates to an enjoyable capitalist experience; three flavors almost guarantees a purchase.[18]

Likewise, my parents could have succumbed to the lure of gazpacho or moussaka every other weekend, but they chose

---

18 Found by a famous study from 2000, one of the main inspirations for the *Paradox of Choice* by Barry Schwartz. For a recent study in a similar vein, see reference section.

not to and happily took the consequence of a less complicated, less gastronomic, but also less stressful life.

As for me, I had no idea gazpacho or moussaka existed back in 1986. There is a reason the internet didn't come up with the acronym FOMO until 2004. And to illustrate how the number of options has become even more overwhelming since then, here is an attempt to codify the 2020s Dinnertime Decision algorithm of James and Emily, the big-city couple we met at the beginning of this chapter.

Every day, they are trying to live their best life. Which means that, every day, their dinnertime routine looks like this:

2020s Food Happiness Algorithm Rule 1: If we are tired and hungry, go to step 2. If we are merely hungry, see rule 1a.

Rule 1a: See if there is anything in the fridge that we could cook. Eliminate mushrooms, bananas, and olives – James doesn't like them.

Rule 1b: If yes, make sure it's not the same thing as yesterday's dinner, as we have agreed not to eat the same meal two days in a row.

Rule 1c: From whatever ingredients that are left after rule 1b, eliminate any meat if it's a weekday – Emily is a pescatarian on the weekends.

Rule 1d: From whatever ingredients that are left after rule 1d, try to find recipes that combine these into a tasty, healthy, varied meal that can be prepared in a maximum of 25 minutes – James and Emily would like to eat before 19:30.

Rule 1e: Rank the recipes from step 1d by popularity – the more frequently James and Emily used the recipe before, the more they must enjoy it.

Rule 1f: Now, rank the top ten recipes from rule 1e by their star rating of the most recent 9 weeks – yes,

James and Emily give star ratings to any meal they cook. Here are the rules they follow:

Rule 1g: If the highest-rated recipe remaining scores above 4.5 stars, proceed to make that. DONE. If not, proceed to Rule 2.

Rule 2: From the 4 available food delivery apps, open the one with the best balance of delivery cost, selection, and user experience.

Rule 2a: Filter out any restaurants that take more than 25 minutes to deliver food and have a rating of lower than 4.5 stars.

Rule 2b: Filter out any restaurants that we've ordered from before and didn't like, and restaurants we've ordered from in the last 7 days – we like variety.

Rule 2c: Filter out any restaurants that are too expensive for our budget, or alarmingly cheap.

Rule 2d: Survey the remaining options. See if we have a notion for any cuisine. If we do, consider going to a restaurant instead of ordering in.

Rule 2e: If we prefer to eat out, go to Rule 3. Otherwise, continue.

Rule 2f: Go through all delivery options until both parties are at least 80% happy with the selection. Order food. DONE. If not, proceed to Rule 3.

Rule 3: Compare reviews of all restaurants in our area, filtering for 4+ stars that do not mention terrible service.

Rule 3a: Discuss all restaurant options until one emerges that both parties are at least 80% happy to go to.

Rule 3b: Call the restaurant to make a reservation. If no tables are available, go back to 3a. If the restaurant is available, start bickering over the mode of transport. DONE.

Rule 4: When the above rules take more than 2 hours, give up, make instant noodles, and start the negotiations over what to watch on Netflix.

And you wonder why they say modern life is complicated!

THE CHEF'S CHOICE

Let's save our progress by taking stock of the topics we've covered so far.

1. **An abundance of choice quickly becomes a burden.** We are generally happier when we are able to choose from a limited set of options, but modern life doesn't really work like that.
2. **Algorithms can relieve that burden, because they are like rule-based decision-making machines.** Algorithms can fix the problem above by choosing on our behalf or limiting our options so we can make an easier choice ourselves.

We haven't really touched on the underlying reason *why* too much choice is so exhausting.

When you need to make a decision, your brain runs a routine that engages a host of different functions. First, the available Information is translated into potential outcomes, which are then subjected to a series of value and risk assessments. The options are then ranked, and evaluated by their predicted results. Finally, if there is a clear number one, that option will be declared the winner, following which the decision will be signed off by your prefrontal cortex. Your brain celebrates the decision by releasing happy chemicals that give you the rush of commitment, telling you you've done great.[19]

This routine has been running smoothly for most of human existence. But imagine a scenario with overwhelming choice – a distinctly modern problem – where you still want to pick the best option. To find that optimal choice, your brain has to keep many tabs simultaneously open; it must cycle through a tree of scenarios representing all the possible outcomes springing from those options. Each choice comes with consequences, which can be good, bad, or unknown. Even more daunting, some options come with *multiple constraints:* obvious and less-obvious variables that make certain pathways unrealistic or no longer desirable. For example, you may want to order curries from your favorite Indian place, only to find out the restaurant is closed because of Diwali. You may be really in the mood for a Japanese feast, only to discover that salmon prices have skyrocketed and pushed sashimi resolutely out of your budget.

Keeping all these tabs open and analyzing these scenarios costs brain energy. Ranking these scenarios from most to least desirable costs even more brain energy, especially when the "most desirable" option does not produce the outcome you originally had in mind. Brain energy is finite, and at some point, it runs out and your decision-making routine grinds to a halt before you make it to the happy chemicals. And we know what happens when our Expectation Machines do not get what they are forecasting: They have a rude awakening and fill our bodies with feelings of frustration. We pride ourselves on our rational decision-making, but weighing too many

---

19 This process involves, in rough order, the following parts of the brain: the amygdala, the orbitofrontal cortex, the anterior cingulate cortex, the prefrontal cortex, and the hippocampus. It's proper teamwork out there! For those familiar with Daniel Kahneman's System 1 and System 2 thinking: This process involves mostly System 2, which he describes as effortful, deliberate, analytical, and slow.

alternatives, all coming with their own set of disclaimers, brings out the worst emotions in us.

It is key to understand that "analysis paralysis" isn't just a fun phrase but represents actual headaches.[20] As humans, we often focus on the price our actions cost in monetary terms, but what about the price we pay in effort? Analysis paralysis is a huge drain of energy that also represents a poor choice in itself, because you can now no longer spend that energy elsewhere. In some ways, our brains behave just like our trusted smartphones – we overthink things and then have to recharge our batteries.

So what would you rather do: spend the evening frantically swiping through endless options on your phone or spend the evening having peaceful quality time with your loved ones?

I know what *my* best life would look like. And this is where AI walks through the door and casually whispers in our ear: *Hey, human – need a hand? Trust me – I can make this happen. You just sit back and relax.*

Yes, our overcooked brains could absolutely do with a hand. We know that algorithms don't run on brain power but on computer power, and there is ample supply of that.[21] The question is, what type of decision-making help is actually healthy for us? Before we see what algorithms and AI can bring to the table, let's unpack the fundamental difference between

20 In general, "hard thinking" is not perceived as a pleasant activity. Various studies show different physiological effects of decision fatigue: increased heart rates, reduced glucose levels, and more stress hormones. When straining under high cognitive load, we also display slower speech rates, more pauses, and reduced articulation. See reference section.
21 Not to diminish the fact that computer power sucks up our planet's resources and that AI labs are some of the worst offenders. By contrast, the human brain is remarkably efficient, with relatively low energy consumption compared to current computing systems.

"choosing on our behalf" and "limiting our options so we can choose ourselves."

Ask yourself: At what point is an app so smart that you would fully trust it to take some decisions on your behalf? And then, what specific decisions would you be happy to delegate to the algorithm, and which ones would you like to keep to yourself? In artificial intelligence, this discussion is usually framed in terms of *autonomy* and *agency*.

> » *Agency* is about giving an intelligent entity –
>   the *agent*, either a person, a computer, or an
>   organization – an assignment to do something on
>   your behalf.
> » *Autonomy* is about the freedom the agent has to
>   make decisions to accomplish this assignment.

Example: When you go out for dinner, you assign the task of preparing and serving the food to the restaurant. The chef and its staff become your agents, entrusted with the responsibility to place food on your table within a certain amount of time. As your agents, they have the *autonomy* to limit the menu to a set number of options – you forfeit the option of pizza if it's not on the menu. However, within the bounds of the menu, the meal choice is still your decision to make; you typically do not grant the kitchen staff autonomy to cook whatever they feel like.

This is a scenario that plays out a lot in life. We ask somebody else to curb our options, but we retain the rights to make the final decision ourselves. The fewer options we have, the easier the final decision is; but the more options are reduced up front, the less we know what we're missing.

The trade-off here is between convenience and control. The more you are willing to trust another intelligent entity, the more convenience you can derive from it; the more you want to keep control, the more you limit your own convenience. Note that "convenience" here actually means "happiness," quite literally: More convenience equals less brain strain equals more happiness.

This trade-off is relevant for anything involving delegation, from hiring an accountant to deploying a robot lawn mower, to pressing Google's "I'm Feeling Lucky" button. What do you want to control yourself, and what do you trust others to adequately take care of? Since we're talking about food here, let's run through another real-life kitchen example to illustrate how this balance between control and convenience plays out in practice.

My fiancée – yes, this story is about my actual fiancée Ana, not about a hypothetical one that I made up to illustrate a point – is a very accomplished cook and knows a lot about food. Better yet, she is also very sensitive to the needs and preferences of people and has the uncanny ability to serve exactly what guests are in the mood for. In other words, when she makes dinner for family or friends, no matter what the occasion, it all but guarantees we will eat well and leave the table smiling. Her reputation is such that nobody feels the need to know what we're going to be served – we can just be giddy, fully unburdened, happy for her to surprise us. We give her *carte blanche* – not just the *agency* to make the meal, but also full *autonomy* to make any decision about ingredients, flavors, and presentation. She is a Carefree Evening algorithm all by herself.

On the other hand, when it's me preparing dinner, those same friends act very differently. They are visibly stressed. They are asking questions. They know I can be a bit of a free spirit when it comes to cooking, and even though they appreciate the convenience of me putting in the kitchen work, they want to know exactly what I am going to make, and also *how* I will do that.[22] Put another way, they trust me less with the autonomy

---

22 They're not wrong; for example, I once substituted carrots for peaches in a recipe, and coffee beans for cacao nibs. In my defense, I wanted to challenge the status quo, and I simply failed miserably. So did Einstein and Maria Callas, initially, although nobody ever talks about that.

around flavors, ingredients, and presentation. Instead of relaxing in conversation, they may spend energy hovering in the kitchen and monitoring the amount of cinnamon I toss in the curry. Some lapse into outright micro-managing and clearly would have preferred to take back the agency they gave me and just cook the damn curry themselves.

See the trade-off? In algorithm and app terms, Ana cooking is like the five-star algorithm you would blindly grant full autonomy to deliver the perfect meal any evening, reliably delighting you without needing any of your brain energy. If you ran this algorithm on a daily basis, you would probably get lazy and develop an unhealthy dependence, but at least you'd be fed without a worry in the world.

On the other hand, I am the three-star algorithm with very mixed reviews that you would only grant selective agency to cook specific simple meals in a pinch. It would mean less convenience, but at least you would retain a different peace of mind: that of being somewhat in control, understanding what you're eating, and having trust in a good outcome.[23]

Oh, and if the above makes it sound like you would always prefer to grant full autonomy over limited agency: Things are more complicated than that, as we will see in the upcoming chapters. Some consequences of the trade-off are less obvious, and some are outright hidden. Either way, our dance with convenience and control is crucial in shaping AI's place in our daily lives and foreshadows the wave of no-brainer zombies biding their time in the twilight.

---

23 Side note: In case the above paragraphs make you worry about the state of my relationship and in particular the bad hand Cupid dealt my fiancée, rest easy – I have many other qualities (that shall remain nameless here). Also, I have discovered a local restaurant where I get to give Ana a dose of her own medicine. Here, she trusts the chef completely, like other people completely trust her, and she can simply order the chef's five-course meal without even having to consult a menu. We get to maximize our convenience by delegating full agency *and* autonomy, and always walk home with smiles on our faces.

TRYING TO LIVE OUR BEST LIFE:
THE BENEFITS OF OTHER HUMANS

Let's ignore the zombies for now and return to our modern, overburdened brains. We are going to spend the rest of the chapter dissecting how infuriatingly complex modern lives truly are, revel in how amazing it is that algorithms even have a shot at grasping our needs, and see why we ultimately can't say no to Doc Brown's pitch – even if it may hurt us in the long run.

First, let's return to this notion of living your "best life." This phrase was popularized by modern-day philosopher Oprah Winfrey in the early 2000s and represents an ambitious update of the work done by her Ancient Greek forebears – in particular Aristotle, who contemplated "a good life" in around 350 BC. In his standard work of ethics, Aristotle ended up defining the good life as *eudaimonia*: living your life in a way that fulfills your true nature as a human being.

The difference between Aristotle's good life and Oprah's best one may appear negligible, but Oprah's more ambitious vision significantly ratchets up our challenge. Given the infinite variables in life, the probability of living your absolute best possible life is extremely low, if not statistically near impossible – while at least a "good life" seems attainable, if you get around 80% of your decisions more or less right.

Of course, Oprah never said it was actually *possible* to live a literal best life. She was probably just voicing a healthy aspiration, a modern-day challenge. Which means that we should understand the "best life" as the admirable goal and the "good life" as the successful outcome.

Here is another fun fact about us humans: we find it easier to solve other people's problems. No, seriously:

Studies have found we are objectively better at resolving the dilemmas of other people than we are at resolving our own. This is because we bring a fresh, clear-headed perspective to other people's issues, but also because we find it easier to be straight with our friends than with ourselves.

Scenario	Brain Energy Bill
Making a decision for a friend	Low
Making a decision for yourself	Medium
Agreeing with a friend on a decision that affects you both	High

Note how our brain energy consumption mounts when we have to resolve our own problems by ourselves? *What should I wear tonight? Should I share a ride with James and Raj, or with Emily and Natalia?* When our friend asks us for advice on a difficult decision, we see the big picture, parse the evidence, and dare to advise the adventurous route they fail to see. When confronted with a similar problem on our own, all that wisdom is nowhere to be found. We get bogged down in details, go in circles, and end up picking an overly cautious, uninspired solution.

What is the takeaway here? We are bad at self-reflection and love to talk to others to get our heads straight.

And could these "others" also be non-humans? Absolutely. As we will explore in future chapters, people seem to benefit equally from sharing their problems with intelligent chatbots, provided the AI asks open questions and offers a balanced perspective. A problem shared is a problem halved: Chalk that up as another way AI can help us alleviate our load.

As you can see in the table above, there is another level here: Nothing taxes the brain like coming to an agreement with another person on a decision affecting you both. Especially when both parties have full agency and autonomy, and are looking to serve their own best interests.

I probably don't have to tell you, but examples of this are everywhere in human relationships – from casual friendships to business relations to long-term love commitments. And this is another modern problem, because it follows from the otherwise laudable pursuit of an egalitarian society. Since we are equals – do we both agree to go to this restaurant? Should we watch Netflix or Disney? Tell Spotify to shuffle Bryan Adams or Ryan Adams?[24] What will be the exact terms of our business deal? I want to kiss you, but do you want to kiss me? And since we started kissing, do we like each other enough that it is understood that we are not seeing anybody else and may even get married and have 1.6 babies within five years?[25]

These decisions can take ages when you have only your own requirements to solve. Now, there's another human in play, and you are each running your own problem-solving algorithm with non-matching outcomes. This is itself problematic: In the absence of hierarchy, both of you have to step out of your comfort zone and relax your *criteria for satisfaction*; in other words: settle for less. And this is where the energy bill starts to get seriously painful.

Look at it this way: Mental load is like invisible labor, which immediately explains why delegation and hierarchy are still so big in business, despite long-standing efforts to make corporate decision-making more inclusive. It also explains why so many equal relationships still end up with

---

24 Or neither – also an option, if you ask me.

25 Don't be afraid: This is a statistical joke. 1.6 is the average number of children European couples had in 2020. In no way am I advocating having 60% babies or doing baby timeshares.

power dynamics or tacit understandings where one partner is unofficially responsible for calling the shots on specific topics, such as meals or vacations.

Delegating decisions is just more efficient, and easier on our brains.

Suffice to say, here is yet another scenario where AI can help you navigate your best life, acting as an independent counselor that instantly finds the optimal compromise between you and your partner. The upside is clear: We avoid unnecessary arguments, and we avoid wasting brain power on finding imperfect solutions to complicated problems. Poor Emily and James probably often have instant noodles for dinner, simply because their 2020s Food Algorithm doesn't yield a decision!

Hey, AI whispers in our ear again, *you should have just asked for help instead.*

Algorithm 1: I want pancakes.
Algorithm 2: I want pizza.
Algorithm 3: OK, folks. I propose a game of Super Smash Bros. to break the deadlock.
Algorithm 3: And please pay my invoice within 14 days.

TRYING TO LIVE OUR BEST LIFE: WHAT DO WE ACTUALLY WANT?

If an algorithm wants to serve you well, it needs to know you. So – how does an algorithm get to know you?

Why, by asking for your data, of course.

Close your eyes and think – once again – about dinner time. Let's say it's my treat and I have a personal chef who can make anything you want. What type of meal would put a smile on your face? What food experience would leave you perfectly satisfied and give my personal chef that coveted five-star review?

Luckily for my personal chef, scientists have been trying to dissect this five-star food review for decades. A rough consensus has emerged that your post-meal happiness is determined by a mix of factors before, during, and after the meal that all interact like ingredients in the meal itself.

These factors are, in no particular order, your:

- » age
- » BMI
- » expectations
- » food preferences
- » sensory satisfaction during the meal – both of the eyes and the tastebuds
- » hunger before and after the meal
- » fullness before and after the meal
- » energy level after the meal.

Knowing this, a sensible chef would start out by asking you some questions, or rather – *getting some data on you.* She could give you a quick survey asking for facts: *How old are you? How would you describe your hunger level on a scale of 1 to 5?* She could ask you to describe your general food preferences and expectations, and hope you articulate them well. Based on that, she could go to work, leverage her expertise in the kitchen, and nail your briefing.

App developers use similar science to discover the exact ingredients of five-star satisfaction and set out to optimize it. If a food delivery app would like to mimic the chef in the above example, it could ask you to fill in your age and BMI on the screen, and hope you will share that data with them; it could give you a sliding scale to input your hunger level, and query you on your favorite cuisine. The more you feed the app with information about yourself, the better job it will do.

If artificial intelligence is the shiny machinery, then data is the fuel powering it.

You feed the algorithm, the algorithm feeds you.[26]

It is important to realize that artificial intelligence would be useless without any data to run on – like a fancy ocean liner grounded in the docks. Many people are paranoid about sharing their data, and for good reason: We've all seen Jeff Bezos and Mark Zuckerberg hoover up our information and repurpose it for selfish goals. But there is a flip side to that: If you don't share your data, an algorithm won't be able to help you, because it will not be able to discern what you actually want.

We will delve deeper into this dicey data discussion in future chapters. For now, let's establish that an algorithm *can* learn to understand you, provided you're willing to share. In that sense, it's a very similar setup to your interaction with any other service provider. If you trust the salesman in the shoe shop, you can tell him your brand preference and shoe size. If you're worried he has malicious intent, you shouldn't, and you might go home with ill-fitting shoes.

It is actually quite fascinating. Looking at yourself in the mirror, it may not always *feel* like you are logical and predictable, but algorithms know better: If given enough data to work with, they can always discover patterns and rules that describe your preferences, even if you wouldn't realize them yourself.

For example, I may not readily admit this to myself, but:

» Nothing makes me happier than having low-fat yogurt with fresh fruit and granola for breakfast. This is always five stars for me.

---

26 If this is not a feedback loop, I don't know what is.

> » I really dislike having the same meal twice in the
>   same week, and I will go to great lengths to avoid it.
> » I am not a really big eater. I prefer smaller meals
>   over bigger meals, unless I am truly starving, but I
>   will never say that to anybody who is cooking for
>   me.
> » I am very sensitive to waiting times. It really
>   devalues the dining experience for me when I
>   have to wait longer than 30 minutes.

This list is just a start. To serve you well, an algorithm (or real-life personal chef) would need hundreds, if not thousands, of these data points. This would go a long way towards meeting your expectations, perhaps even surpassing them. But "surpassing expectations" is not the same as "hitting perfection." Even with a few thousand data points, it would be near impossible to find the optimal choice – because the number of outcomes is so immense. If our chef had only 50 ingredients in her kitchen and would use eight of them for the meal, she would be able to combine and prepare those ingredients into more meals than you could eat in a lifetime – of which only a few would represent the optimal, 100% satisfaction.

This tells you how elusive concepts like "the perfect match" and "the perfect meal" really are – even for a top chef or a very smart algorithm with unlimited resources. You need a vast amount of information to accurately predict what would make a meal consumer perfectly happy. In fact, almost every real-world decision is computationally complex to such a degree that it cannot be perfectly solved. Put in another way, "best life" perfection is almost impossible to reach – and yet there are many ways to leave you feeling meh, blah, or even *whatever*.

This is exacerbated by the unfortunate fact that, well, all humans are different. (I know – shocking.) Even if you are my biological twin, it is very likely that your five stars are not the same as mine. Certain flavors and textures may be universal, but people have very different checkboxes for being 100% satisfied, if only based on culture and recent experiences. If you're a lifetime oyster lover who just had a bad serving, your oyster preference would temporarily crater. If French users of a food delivery service give it 3.6 stars, while the American users give it 4.6 stars, this could mean that the American service is just way better. But it could also mean that the French expectations are way higher. Or that the French, as a country, are just never satisfied![27]

And you may also wonder – am I really that predictable, anyway? What if I am in an adventurous, rule-breaking mood? What if I am tired of my traditional favorites and really open to something strange? What if my five-star review may be achieved only by giving me something *I didn't know I loved?*

Don't worry, we'll unpack these topics in a few chapters. But if you are feeling overwhelmed by all of the above, imagine how chefs feel. Not to mention developers of algorithms: How can a "series of steps to solve a problem" make sense of all of this?

> **Five-star Algorithm Rule 1:** If you are French, I will serve you the best escargots and bouillabaisse money can buy.
>
> **Five-star Algorithm Rule 2:** If your most recent dinner date doused you in sriracha sauce because you talked about your ex too much, I will serve you anything that does not contain sriracha sauce.

---

27 This is not a joke – cultural norms play a huge part in rating averages. As it happens, the French are less likely to give good reviews to *anything*: "We like to complain," as my French friends readily admit. For multinational standardized goods and services, the French satisfaction scores are typically 15% below the average of the other European countries – for the exact same product or service. Hilariously, Reddit has numerous travelers complaining that "Paris killed my Uber rating."

> **Five-star Algorithm Rule 3:** If you are feeling adventurous, I will randomly combine eight ingredients to serve you something the world has never seen before.
>
> **Five-star Algorithm Rule 4**: If you are Dutch, I will serve you pancakes, especially on Fridays.

Yes, I did not take myself seriously here. In fact, I am starting to give up; the simple algorithms I've shown you in this chapter have clearly hit their limits. I could add billions of "If… then" rules and would still be unable to maximize the satisfaction of a Helsinki wood merchant *and* a Guatemalan opera diva at the same time.

It is not just that people are so complicated; it is that they are all complicated in a slightly different way. What we need is a 950-page tome called *How Humans Work*. Or at least *How Modern Humans Decide What to Eat on a Daily Basis*. But since none of us has been able to come up with that bestseller, we are pining for an alternative.

Luckily, artificial intelligence has come upon a system to mirror all this human complexity in equally mysterious algorithms. In fact, doubling down on this system was a key driver in propelling AI from optimistic fantasy to the all-consuming hype it is today.

It is a system that consists of three parts:

1. A way to encode a complex algorithm – called a *neural network*.
2. A "trial-and-error" method to develop an algorithm – called *machine learning*.
3. And a vast trove of algorithm training data called… the internet.

Put on your sunglasses, because you'll need them in the next part.

THE RULES OF THE GAME – THE DARK ART OF MACHINE LEARNING

The main lesson of thirty-five years of AI research is that the hard problems are easy and the easy problems are hard.
– Steven Pinker, *The Language Instinct*, 1994

There was an innocent time when all AI algorithms looked like the 1980s Carefree Weekend algorithm, except much, much more extensive. The goal was to represent the world's knowledge in fundamental principles and watch intelligence emerge from there. These so-called *rule-based* algorithms were the original strategy to make computers smart – but they quite quickly hit their natural limits.

A problem was that they were very labor intensive to create. They essentially required experts to tediously codify their theoretical knowledge about the world – just like we did for Emily and James's dinnertime decision steps earlier.[28] However, a bigger problem was that the world simply proved to be much too unpredictable to capture in prefabricated rules. Yes, it worked reasonably well for a closed environment like chess – Deep Blue, the AI program that beat chess grandmaster Garry Kasparov, had its roots in rule-based algorithms – but AI scientists eventually had to concede that not even millions of predetermined algorithmic rules could accurately capture all the randomness that was coming our way in real life.

---

28 To illustrate this, just compare the food happiness algorithms for 1980 and 2020 again. The 1980 Carefree Weekend algorithm is gloriously straightforward (three rules). By contrast, the 2020 one is seven times more complicated (21 rules) but also more flexible, accounting for multiple scenarios and wishes from its masters. In the words of science, the 1980s one is entirely deterministic, while the 2020s one leaves more to chance and whim and is "smarter" as a consequence. Still, imagine how difficult it would be to write down a meal-recommendation algorithm that would work for *everybody.*

This challenge also reared its head when computer scientists tried to use rule-based algorithms to reliably model basic human interaction. As it turned out, not even ten million lines of logical rules would allow a computer to keep up a quality conversation with a normal human – if only because your average human often doesn't play by the rules!

This resistance to consistency and logic hints at the often-paradoxical elements that make us into the adorable beings we are. As we will explore in more detail in future chapters, humans play games, drop hints, and often don't mean what they literally say.[29] We assume things that we don't explicitly validate; we don't want to hurt other people's feelings, and we sure as hell *do not want to hurt our own feelings.* This deceptive behavior drives many fellow humans to despair, but it has also been the Achilles' heel for generations of chatbots: Computers have long struggled with sarcasm, irony, and indirect communication.

Put simply, we all like to be understood, but understanding us is as much about grasping our deepest intentions as it is about getting our plain facts. An algorithm may be aware that it is Friday and I always like pancakes on Fridays, but it may not be aware that I am currently accompanied by my friend Marc – who actually prefers pizza and whom I am looking to impress because I want to borrow his copy of *NBA Jam.* In other words, in order to be perceived as intelligent and helpful, an algorithm needs to be more than smart; it needs to understand social cues and read between the lines.

As you may recall, Skeptical Joe Weizenbaum learned this lesson a long time ago. His 1966 psychotherapist chatbot didn't impress his audience because it displayed any tangible intelligence; no, the humans spoke highly of it because it could plausibly feign human interest and keep the

---

29 Most humans = all neurotypical humans, except the Dutch, who don't have the capacity to say what they don't literally mean.

conversation going. And it could do this because Weizenbaum explicitly programmed it to take a clearly delineated role in the conversation and play that role according to human society's expectations.

It is funny, actually: You wonder if members of our species are actually more impressed by social skill than by actual knowledge!

Faced with the limits of rule-based algorithms, the AI community had to come up with something new. And that new thing was an exciting combination of two old ideas: *neural networks* and *machine learning*.

The idea behind machine learning is that we shouldn't spend our time teaching a computer how the world works, but rather create an environment where it can figure this out itself. Like a child learning to ride a bicycle or play a game of chess, it lets the computer trial-and-error its way to a human-stated goal, slowly distilling the rules of the game as it goes along.

In the case of *deep learning*, it constantly updates these learnings in a multi-layered *neural network*, which is roughly modeled after the architecture of the human brain. This makes sense, if you consider that our own ability to ride bikes is nothing more than a very sophisticated algorithm we've burned into the circuitry of our own brains – an algorithm obtained by our own trial and error, in the form of tumbling on the street and crashing into post boxes.[30]

But then, how does this childlike trialing develop into superior skill? Well – as every teacher will tell you: Lots of practice makes perfect. To use my own example from Chapter 1, I am now reasonably good at sustaining a loving relationship,

---

30 In case the analogy human brain–computer brain makes you queasy: A computer is not the same as a human brain, but it can run "brain software" and thus emulate one.

simply because I've been practicing this skill for decades. Similarly, I am also a reasonably good chess player, which is another clear case of experience trumping raw talent. But by that same token, I would not stand a chance against AlphaZero, the machine learning wunderkind that shook the chess world in 2017. AlphaZero is a great example why the machine learning approach works so well: After being given a safe playground by its human trainers, this neural network used its spare time to play *millions* of chess games against itself, acquiring more practice – and skill – than any human ever will.[31]

This is the genius of machine learning: Through near-endless simulation of all the scenarios on the table, a machine can discover patterns that not even experts knew existed, and therefore adapt to complexity and apparent randomness in ways that rule-based algorithms could never do. After enough trial and error, an algorithm can evolve to pinpoint hidden trends in the weather or the stock market – but also to develop an instinct for our personal preferences, even if they are concealed under layers of contradictory behavior.

The endless potential of machine learning and neural networks is what got me really excited about artificial intelligence in the first place. These techniques owe more to the probabilistic, observational approach of psychology than to the cathedral-building of computer science. But I need to warn you: There is a catch. These neural networks are hard to train, and hard to grasp. They do not capture the theory behind the mastered skill in a human-comprehensible format, and their exact thought process often remains mysterious.[32]

---

31 AlphaZero has since been superseded by Stockfish and Leela Chess Zero, which are built on the same machine learning approach. All three would destroy bulky 20th-century AI chess champ Deep Blue without breaking a digital sweat.

32 "Unlike with most human creations, we don't really understand the inner workings of [what we've built]." This is a quote from OpenAI, creators of ChatGPT, found in *Extracting Concepts from GPT-4* (May 2024).

This means that AlphaZero is a prodigy at chess but can't teach a kid the basics of the game; it is a black box running its own self-taught logic, in the form of layers and layers of probabilistic rules that allow it to make brilliant, sometimes counterintuitive, moves.

This lack of transparency is the dark side of machine learning and the algorithms it spawns. Even its own trainer can't open the hood of a machine learning algorithm to validate the logic behind the outcome, let alone we, the people who receive those outcomes via the apps we use every day. This becomes a big problem when algorithms start to manipulate us and we are tricked into ordering unhealthy food, swiping right on the wrong person, or even more seriously, we get bailiffs chasing us because the system has mistakenly targeted us as a tax fraudster. As you may have read in the news, bad things can happen when good data meets bad algorithms, or bad data meets good algorithms. We will dive deeper into this topic in the next few chapters.

For now, let's note that our real behavior does not reflect our words. We may all agree we find this lack of transparency unacceptable, but that doesn't stop us from using Instagram, TikTok, Spotify, Netflix, and ChatGPT *en masse*, even if their underlying machine learning models are – still – completely opaque to us.

Because humans also have their dark sides: We often don't do what we say, and we often don't say what we do.

TRYING TO LIVE OUR BEST LIFE:
THE BENEFITS OF MACHINES

Let's return to this chapter's core message: We are seriously trying to live our best lives, but reality is just way too complicated to determine "best." Obvious no-brainers are rarely on the table, and we would have to burn through 25 spare brains just to find the absolute best choice in most scenarios.

And if you're still not convinced of this, nothing will make you appreciate this complexity more than the following run-of-the-mill example: finding the optimal choice when the opinions of other humans are involved, even if they are your partners or best friends.

We are not alone in the world, and others are also trying to influence our futures, which means that running a successful relationship is not easy and constantly involves small and big trade-offs. As we've seen, human interaction is fraught with subtle hints and gentle misdirection, and partners need to constantly decode each other's signs accurately to assess what trades need to be made. Not to be left out, scientists have long attempted to model the inevitable games we play in these scenarios. They have done so in a branch of science called *game theory*, which sets out to understand how parties make decisions when there is interdependence on other parties' decisions.

Game theory is fun. It also gets complex quite quickly, which is why it is typically applied outside of daily life – think of Byzantine, high-stakes environments like politics, collective bargaining, and business. Game theory is the strategist's best friend whenever the stakes are high and everybody's scrambling to gain market share, money, or power.[33] But game theory applies just as well in normal life. In fact, it applies very much in a scenario that we've looked at multiple times this chapter but still haven't unraveled completely: How can Emily

---

33 It's not a coincidence that the person who perfected game theory was a math genius with a big, impressive brain – although some would say he had a Beautiful Mind. In fact, his mind was so beautiful, Hollywood turned his life story into an eponymous movie that broke the box office, blitzed the Oscars, and conclusively proved that Russell Crowe could do more than just mow down wheat and Roman henchmen.

and James truly live their best life and agree on the perfect restaurant for their date night?

Let's say Emily and James have finally agreed on eating out. Now, Emily has a bit of a preference for Italian or Mexican. She would rather not go for Japanese, Chinese, or French but keeps those options open if needed to find an acceptable compromise with James.

Let's say James has a very strong preference for Chinese. He could be talked into French or Italian. He would rather avoid Mexican or Japanese but is happy to keep those options open if needed to reach a good middle ground with Emily.

Sounds familiar? Let the deliberations begin, and see if they can solve this within 30 minutes – by which time they will have probably gotten hungrier and more irrational.

What would you do? Quickly looking at the desires of both, we can safely assume they will not pick a Japanese restaurant. Italian seems like a strong contender, which will make Emily happy and avoid James's least favorite options.

A game theory model of the above would look like this – where the higher numbers represent stronger preference.

	Mexican	French	Italian	Chinese	Japanese
Emily	3	1	3	1	1
James	1	2	2	4	1

Surveying this, you may be surprised to see how difficult it actually is to find the optimal scenario here. For all the banality of the challenge, there is some proper analysis involved, and the brain energy bill is quickly ramping up. Can you guess the answer? Perhaps in line with your instincts, the game theory algorithm would locate the compromise for Emily and James somewhere between Chinese and Italian, although far closer to the latter.

Hey, AI whispers in your ear, *I could have found this answer in 0.1 seconds.* And indeed, a machine learning algorithm would have given Emily and James the right answer on the spot. It would have told them that they should pick Italian three times out of four. In other words, if they would go out for dinner on four straight days, they would find their perfect middle ground by doing Italian on Wednesday, Thursday, and Saturday, and Chinese on Friday. This is, mathematically, the best strategy for both James and Emily to get closest to their preferred outcome. Far from ideal given their real preferences, but hey, you have to meet your partner somewhere in the middle. Right?

In reality, something else happened. Emily googled "Chinese-Italian fusion" and was very disheartened to see the results. James's glucose levels dropped and he started wondering if they should have invited their mutual friend Raj, who perhaps could have broken the deadlock.[34] After 15 minutes of rising heart rates, increasing headaches, and heated deliberations, Emily suddenly remembered that James had had a particularly challenging day at work, and made the executive decision to let him have his Chinese.

It all ended well, but barely. Emily settled for the girlfriend points instead.[35]

Yes — there is a reason modern couples get into painful stalemates about seemingly simple choices. We have high

---

34 Raj is a fussy eater, making the complexities of the game play calculations even worse. However, a machine learning algorithm would have happily taken this on board. ChatGPT can play eight human players at Diplomacy and beat them handily.

35 Just in case your relationship is different than mine: Girlfriend and boyfriend points are tokens that you accrue in a relationship. You can save them diligently for months and then cash them all in when you really need that foot rub. You can also go into debt when you're in a bad stretch. You can also go bankrupt.

expectations of life, so we can't agree on what series to watch together on Netflix, what Spotify playlist to serve to our high-maintenance dinner guests, and what 4.6-star cuisine to pick on our date night. FOMO is real and compromising is exhausting, especially in the face of overwhelming choice with the trapdoor of hidden constraints.

More often than we admit, the aftereffects of analysis paralysis make us retreat into our own smartphone bubble with headphones on, eating the food only we crave, watching the clips only we prefer, the partner's preferences be damned. In fact, the partner is probably in the next room, doing the exact same! Alas, we are social animals that yearn for companionship and entertainment. Eating together is good for us and has been shown to correlate with higher life expectancies.[36] Eventually, we have to exert the energy to compromise, or live our sad lives unloved. But things could be so much easier.

The promise of artificial intelligence is that your best life *can* be within reach. Algorithms can simplify your days and offer you the painless decision-making advice that preserves your brainpower from the constant demands of modern life. A smart app can be the buddy that gives you the tough, honest advice to pick the pink dress and skip *Blue Velvet*. An intelligent app can be the objective, wise restaurant counselor that tells you to go to the Italian restaurant instead of the Chinese one – no matter what your date says. A very smart algorithm could even suggest that you need to break up with your partner and find a new one instead.

We love outside advice because life is complicated and finding the best choice is exhausting. We are drawn to the impartial logic of algorithms because the whims of other humans drive us crazy and nobody likes to compromise. But are algorithms really impartial, or do they have their own

---

36 See *Age Proof*, by Professor Rose Anne Kenney.

hidden agenda? Do they have enough computing power and enough data to really get to the bottom of life's most difficult decisions, or is that another optimist's fantasy? And if they do, is it in our best interest to take shelter from life's complexity and give an opaque algorithm the autonomy to choose our path?

If you look out your window, you may detect some movements in the far distance. Some say these are the no-brainer zombies, biding their time, quietly growing their presence. People who have seen them up close tell us that they are nothing but former humans, just brain dead – ones that gave up on making their own decisions and now just let modern life wash over them, no questions asked.

This would be a good moment to ask yourself if you'd be interested in joining them.

Or are you, like me, optimistic they are just an illusion?

Chapter 2's No-Brainer takeaways:

→ **Limit options and embrace predictability**: Simplify your decisions by limiting options. Having fewer choices can make decision-making less overwhelming and reduce stress. For example, adopting routines like Pancake Fridays and Burger Saturdays can streamline meal planning and create a predictable, enjoyable rhythm in your week.

→ **Delegate decisions**: When possible, delegate decision-making to others to conserve mental energy. This can include letting someone else choose the restaurant or using a reliable app to make recommendations. Delegating decisions can significantly reduce the cognitive load and free up mental space for other activities.

→ **Establish routines**: Develop simple rules or algorithms to handle routine tasks. For instance, create a fixed set of meal plans or a weekly schedule that reduces the need for daily decision-making. This can help maintain consistency and reduce the mental effort involved in everyday tasks.

→ **Consult others**: Seek input from friends or family when faced with challenging decisions. Others can provide a fresh perspective and help you see solutions you might miss on your own. This collaborative approach can lead to better decision-making and reduce individual stress.

→ **Balance convenience and control**: Find a balance between convenience and control in your daily life. While delegating tasks can increase convenience, it is essential to retain some control to ensure personal satisfaction. This balance can enhance overall happiness by reducing stress without sacrificing your preferences.

3 GOOD VIBES, BAD DATA

Why a DJ Can't Always Save Your Life

odern life was complicated, and AI was ready to help us out. Which sounded great, but would AI truly be a reliable partner in times of need? As I knew so well, artificial intelligence had a long-standing habit of being fantastic in theory but not delivering the goods when it really mattered – in the chaotic arena of practice, our daily lives.

As a fun game, I decided to keep track of my own sentiments on AI, to see how they would evolve during the writing of this book. So I stole a green Leuchtturm A5 dotted notepad out of my fiancée's stash and wrote WHERE I STAND on its first page. I made up a rule that I would record my timestamped views on AI in a maximum of two sentences, and then – because I was a numbers guy – also assign them a sentiment score between -10 and +10, where -10 represented absolute pessimism and +10 the opposite – something like a belief in AI utopia.

Upon reflection, I realized that the project so far had made me slightly less optimistic about AI, dropping me from a +3 at the start to maybe a +1 now. Why was that? It was clear that AI could make lives better by alleviating cognitive burden, but I found it increasingly ironic that this cognitive burden mostly existed because of the internet – yesterday's shiny technology that was also supposed to solve all our problems. (It struck me as exactly the thing a drug dealer would do: fix your technology problems by offering you more technology.) Clearly, algorithms did represent formulas for better lives when they were endearingly simple, but life was complicated, so now algorithms had to become complex, too, escalating into the kind of high-tech solution that only Silicon Valley could afford to profit from.

Still, I was hopeful, and there was a story to tell to demonstrate this. Long before ChatGPT existed, there was an algorithm that had slowly made its way into our daily lives and represented clear proof that many of us would gladly let machines make decisions on our behalf. This algorithm was fed by an experiment that recorded billions of our clicks every day, mapping these clicks to an enormous amount of complex data, data we all deeply cared for.

I imagined Skeptical Joe would be shocked to discover that 600 million people had signed up for this experiment in pursuit of an easier life. I was sure he would recognize this experiment as a proxy battle for our identities and how we chose to express them. To me, this was a real-life test to see if AI could deliver on its promise to make small, personalized decisions for us – whether the theory could withstand the chaos of everyday experience, and whether we could live with the consequences of whatever choices the algorithm made.

The decisions in question are about the music you listen to, and most of us know this algorithm simply as Spotify.

OUR MUSICAL IDENTITIES

I am not making this up: It is estimated that 95% of the human species enjoys listening to music.[37]

This near-universal love for music has long baffled scientists. Unlike with tasty food, it is not obvious that music is essential to our survival as a species – on paper, we could live a hundred healthy years without it. But as we've seen in the previous chapter, we are social animals, and the current scientific understanding is that music is like language, only more so: It speaks to us and pleases us in ways that normal speech patterns can't always achieve. Listening to music stimulates the brain to release dopamine, which in turn makes us happy. Happiness is good. *Music matters.*

Interestingly, our species' near-universal enjoyment of music contrasts with the deeply personal and often very strong opinions we individually harbor about *specific* music. We may all like pancakes, but we do not see eye to eye on Luis Fonsi's "Despacito," J.S. Bach's *St Matthew Passion,* and Taylor Swift's "Shake It Off." These three tunes may be among the most popular in the world, but it is staggeringly easy to find millions of people who go out of their way to throw shade on them.[38]

Yes – even more so than with food, we are *opinionated* about music. For the majority of us, walking into a bar playing the

---

37 That means "I enjoy music" is not a good way to distinguish yourself in a dating profile. The other 3–5% (apparently) don't hate music; they just feel perfectly indifferent about it. This may be connected to musical anhedonia, a neurological condition that causes atypical processing of sound in the brain.
38 You want numbers to prove this? "'Despacito'" had over five million dislikes on YouTube before the site started hiding the dislike count. Music nerd site RYM's legions of voters think Swift's "Shake It Off" scores a lamentable 2.4/5 stars, not even counting it among the 750 best songs released in 2014. And personally, I can't stand the *St Matthew Passion,* finding the buildups, drops, and breaks in this phase of Bach's discography to be extremely dated.

wrong song can be just as off-putting as taking a bite out of a rotten apple – even if there is technically nothing wrong with the music itself and the artist in question may have hordes of dedicated fans! And nothing kills a first date like exposing your prospective partner to inoffensive smooth jazz when they were really hoping to hear extremely offensive death metal.[39]

Are we completely rational about music? Probably not. It's not just about the noise level or the tempo or whether the singer's voice appeals to us. Music isn't just about the music; your all-time favorite artist is not only the producer of your favorite, dopamine-inducing sounds and melodies but is also strongly linked to your *identity* and the way you choose to express yourself. More than just instruments and voices producing notes, music is *fashion*, and music is *memories*. At the risk of generalizing: We use music to discover who we are when we're young and use it to revel in nostalgia when we're old.[40] And even though you can only do so much with the 12 standard notes of the Western musical scales, every generation will find its own music to express itself – so the number of songs will continue to grow as long as we're around.

Which brings me to another crazy statistic: At the time of writing, there are *at least* 100 million songs registered with copyright organizations around the world. Ah, the joys of choice! That is a playlist spanning 628 years, of which you'll only be around for less than a hundred, and then you also have to find time to sleep and spend quality time with friends and watch *Peaky Blinders* and try out skydiving – which somehow ended up on your bucket list, even if you have no idea why.

---

39 Or the other way around. By the way, I am assuming in the sentence before that rotten apples do *not* have a legion of dedicated fans. At least, my research on the fringes of the internet has not turned up such a legion.
40 The *New York Times* used Spotify playlists to study when people appear to lock in their favorite type of music as a lifelong taste. The answer: between ages 13 and 14. Which explains why every generation is convinced the second decade of their lives produced the best music of all time!

Which begs the question: How do we navigate this endless menu of musical options? If we consider that every song we play represents a micro-decision that influences the next few minutes of our life, how do we decide which songs make our day, and which songs to skip?

OUR MUSICAL IDENTITY CRISIS

Before this DJ thing, I was hopelessly taking things apart to try to figure out how they worked.
  – DJ Grandmaster Flash

We will examine in this chapter how we learned to stop worrying and trust Spotify to take those micro-decisions for us. For those of you who never learned to trust Spotify: Don't worry, we've got you covered. And for those of you who don't know what Spotify is – I am looking at you, Mom – and may be struggling to connect the dots between their favorite music and the potential and perils of artificial intelligence, let me start by filling in some gaps.

In 2006, two guys in Sweden decided to start a new company. Spotify was conceived as a modern-day jukebox, a fast and vast on-demand digital music catalog at the fingertips of its subscribers.[41] Volume and speed were Spotify's game; understanding your taste in music was not. Spotify simply set out to solve the problems of illegal downloading, overloaded iPods, and understocked record shops. They wanted to make all the world's music available in one click, which, as we've just learned, meant they intended to amass a hundred million songs on their servers, a collector's challenge if there ever was one.

---

41 The Spotify founders were not the first to have this vision, nor am I remotely original in using the jukebox metaphor. Way back in 2001, pioneering online music service Rhapsody advertised itself as the "Celestial Jukebox" – a term it borrowed from scholar Paul Goldstein (1994).

That they were adding to their user's burden of choice was probably not on their minds. After all, capitalist logic implied that more personal choice equaled more personal freedom equaled more personal well-being. The philosophy of the founders was that the users knew very well what they wanted to hear; Spotify was merely there to serve the songs without a technical hitch.

Spotify launched and was an instant success. Users abandoned illegal downloads, dumped their CD collections, and cleared the MP3s off their hard drives. However, with the Spotify catalog rapidly expanding, a new challenge started to emerge, one that will sound familiar by now. Users were complaining that the assortment of music was becoming overwhelming. *There were just too many songs to choose from.* In a bizarre twist, for all their options, people were discovering *less* music than in the traditional way, stuck in their little filter bubble of favorites, intimidated by the vastness of the musical unknown. Worse for Spotify, it drove users away from the platform. Ironically, many subscribers went back to their old ways of discovering music: tips from friends, experts, radio DJs, and – gasp – advice from bearded guys in record stores.

It was another lesson in the pitfalls of unchecked choice and the power of ceding agency. To Spotify's surprise, their research showed that music consumers *liked* delegating some agency in their music discovery to others. No matter how core music was to their identities, it appeared people did not want to be always in control of their choices – in fact, it exhausted them. There was a social element to music, exemplified by the mixtape you would receive from your best friends, expanding your sonic horizons with their personal favorites, and bonding over the music in the process.

Other online music services caught on to this before Spotify did and started successfully offering curated playlists. Pandora did "personalized radio" by classifying music on "underlying qualities," although it was unclear what that meant or how they achieved it. The app Songza started offering hand-picked, *activity*-based playlists. Finally, Spotify co-founder Daniel Ek got the message: In order to win the hearts of the planet, Spotify couldn't just be the world's biggest on-demand music database. In his own words: "Spotify is great when you know what music you want to listen to, but not so great when you don't. The biggest unsolved question for our users is: How can you help me figure out what I'm going to listen to?"

To come up with a system that automatically picked the next best song for their customers, Spotify had to develop a telepathic understanding of people's musical needs. Which was a problem, because there were as many needs as there were people. Worse yet, telepathy didn't exist, and computers could not read minds. Or could they?

You can see where this is going: Being a technology company, Spotify set out to solve this problem with a brilliant, cutting-edge, omniscient algorithm – and commenced to hire an army of data scientists to carry this project out.

How does an algorithm predict what song people want to hear next? That was the simple question Spotify's engineers asked themselves – after all, they couldn't just assume that everybody liked "Careless Whisper" and "Hotel California," like some radio stations seemed to do. But they quickly found out this simple question was as old as the world and had long befuddled professional musicians, DJs, record company execs, and even scientists.

As it turned out, there were many challenges to overcome. And the first one was a problem of vague language. It became clear that you couldn't just *ask* somebody what they wanted to hear; most people felt very strongly about their favorite music, but they could not reliably express what they wanted and why.

> **Emily:** David Bowie is all I listen to.
> **James:** David Bowie is not a taste; he's an artist. What is your musical taste?
> **Emily:** I told you – it's David Bowie. He is a whole genre by himself.
> **James:** (sighs) So all you do is listen to David Bowie?
> **Emily:** Most of the time, yes. Early Bowie, Berlin Bowie, *Blackstar* Bowie.
> **James:** And when you're done with Bowie, how are you going to find new music?
> **Emily:** Then I'll just look for artists that are similar to him, and take it from there.

Emily is not alone; when people are asked to describe their musical taste, they struggle to actually describe the music itself – the notes, the beats, the vibes, the emotions. How do you put in words what you feel so deep in your bones? A sensible strategy is to subtly deflect the question by answering a different one, like Emily does in the above example: You define your taste by naming your favorite artist. Which again shows how blurry the line between the actual *music* and "music as a product" is – this answer is akin to naming your favorite cola brand when asked to describe your favorite cola brand's *flavor*.

Try it yourself – what was appealing about music you recently listened to? If it played in the background at the office, you could say it was "easy on the ears" and "got you going," but does that really describe your taste? If you narrow it down to recent music you were more invested in, you could go for emotional descriptors like "uplifting," "sad," or "gave me goosebumps," but that would be painting with a very broad brush. You could express more details with musical attributes like "rhythmic," "melodic," or "intense female vocals." And perhaps you would realize that you're not that consistent in your tastes, anyway.

You could argue that we struggle to describe our favorite music precisely *because* it is so important to us. When asked to translate a deeply emotional, abstract, and subjective experience into language, we find our vocabulary lacking, and we just throw imprecise words in the air. Now, a good human DJ might still be able to pick up on these imprecise words, by translating them into an intuitive "feel" that transcends language. But for algorithms, this human inability to be precise is deeply problematic. Algorithms cannot read our minds, need facts to make sense of the world, and start behaving like fools when they only have vague statements to go on.

It was clear that Spotify had a big challenge on their hands. If they wanted to solve their customers' analysis paralysis, they needed to defeat the number one villain in AI fairytales: a shadowy creature named Bad Data, whom we shall meet next.

ON THE EVILS THAT BAD DATA DOES, PART 1

I vividly remember the worst advice any entity, human or non-human, ever gave me. It was in 1995, when the internet was about to go supernova. I told my university classmate – let's call him Bernard – I was seriously considering dropping out and founding an internet business. Bernard thought about it, then told me in no uncertain terms it would be the biggest mistake of my life, because the internet was a fad and I was not cut out to be an entrepreneur. Yes, he used the "biggest mistake of my life" phrase. Of course, I ended up ignoring his advice. Six years later, my business was a European success that gave me the independence to travel the world and write all the unsuccessful books I ever wanted.[42]

---

42 Meaning: This book was partly made possible by Bernard! As a funny coda to this anecdote: Bernard started his own successful internet company 20 years later. I would have ironically discouraged him, but I wasn't in his circle anymore.

I also vividly remember the most hilarious advice I ever received from an algorithm. This was not too long ago, when I booked a B&B in the countryside to get some book research done. From the moment I connected my shiny new MacBook to the B&B's Wi-Fi, the Google advertisement algorithm became besotted with recommending I purchase a yellow, luxury, 45,000-euro tractor. Not being a farmer, never having shown an interest in tractors, nor keen to spend €45k on a diesel-guzzling yellow monster, I steadfastly ignored the string of ads that appeared on every web page I happened to visit that day – **buy this amazing tractor!!** – yet the algorithm wouldn't give up. For a full week, it bombarded me with yellow tractor ads in whichever corner of the internet I tried to hide, imploring me to finally give up my undue resistance, spend the €45k, and obtain the tractor. There were tractor ads on news sites, on sports sites, even on my own blog. It amounted to pure postmodern insanity. All of this because I connected from a countryside IP address with a new laptop![43]

Despite one being a machine and the other being a human, the Google algorithm and Bernard had one thing in common: *They didn't know me as well as they thought they did.* This is the common thread in all kinds of bad advice: The advice-giver often means well but is arrogant and thinks he is wise, while he actually isn't.[44] For both humans and algorithms, this lack of wisdom typically means the advice-giver has not spent enough time researching its subject, making the right observations, and asking the right questions. It means the recommendation is built on the quicksand foundation of *Bad Data.*

---

43 If I would ever buy a tractor, it would be a cheap red one. By the way, the worst advice (non-hilarious division) I received from an algorithm also came from Google: Its Maps application told me to drive straight off a cliff in Italy in 2012. (I decided I didn't want to follow the advice.)

44 I am purposefully *not* gender-neutering this sentence. Bad advice is nearly always given by men, or by man-built algorithms. I have decades of personally collected empirical observations to support this.

Bad Data is the core problem plaguing algorithms and humans that get it terribly wrong – no matter how smart they look on paper. Bad Data can imply a total *absence* of data – being totally in the dark and having to make a blind guess. It can also imply any combination of faulty, insignificant, biased, vague, or wholly misinterpreted data. Google somehow thinking that I could do with a yellow tractor? The algorithm drew the wrong conclusions from limited observations, was lured by the smell of money, and acted like a fool. That one made me chuckle, but the consequences can also be decidedly unfunny: Bad Data can compel algorithms to misjudge cancer cases, send planes into the ocean, and tell governments to arrest innocent people. Bad Data always trumps good intentions; it can lead to life-altering blunders.

Spotify's engineers were very aware of the hazards of Bad Data. Even if they wouldn't crash a plane by getting it wrong, music recommendation algorithms would do spectacularly dumb things if fed with incomplete and incorrect facts about their subjects. They could, for example, assume all women would prefer romantic ballads and all Americans loved country music. And they could subject anybody to the horrors of "Hotel California" at any given moment because, well – the algorithm was just guessing, having not been informed otherwise.

Now, I realize Bad Data sounds like something an evil scientist would cook up in their lab, like a virus designed to infect the world. From experience, I can share that Good Algorithms + Bad Data is equally as toxic as Bad Algorithms + Good Data. But while Bad Algorithms are clearly peddled by immoral or incompetent engineers, you may ask yourself – where does Bad Data actually originate?

ON THE EVILS THAT BAD DATA DOES, PART 2

One of the challenges of AI is that it is entirely dependent on good-quality data, yet Bad Data is lurking everywhere. And once you've acquired it, it is a weed that is hard to eradicate.

Bad Data can be an honest mistake: You make a typo in your address, and your neighbor receives your yearly subscription to *Horse & Hound* magazine instead. Bad Data can grow slowly, emerging from formerly good data that goes stale while the real world evolves. Bad Data can sprout when humans struggle to be precise, or forget to be complete. Bad Data can be good data that is accidentally duplicated. And Bad Data can be unwittingly introduced when its caretakers put humans in big boxes and let these boxes take on a life of their own, creating stereotypes.

Let me explain that last one in more detail, because these human stereotypes are very relevant to music. These boxes are called *segments,* or brackets. Segmentation is a standard practice in database marketing, where the audience is divided into groups that have similar preferences, thus making it easier to sell products to them.

In the eyes of a database marketer, we are all part of many segments. For example, if I earned $57,000, that would make me part of the $50,000–$100,000 income bracket. If I were 38 years old, that would make me part of the 35–44 age bracket. And since we're on the topic of music: A deep love for Amy Winehouse's "You Know I'm No Good" would place me in the Jazz Pop segment, even though I otherwise dislike jazz pop with a passion.[45]

---

45 Actual example. When it comes to jazz pop, we don't mince any words in my part of town.

Take your pick: List of radio stations available in Grand Theft Auto V

Radio station	Genre
Radio Los Santos	Modern rap
Space 103.2	Funk
West Coast Classics	'80s/'90s rap
Rebel Radio	Country, Southern rock
Los Santos Rock Radio	Classic rock, pop rock
The Lowdown 91.1	Classic soul
The Blue Ark	Reggae, dub, dancehall
Non-Stop Pop FM	Pop, R&B, dance-pop, Eurodance, synth-pop
East Los FM	Regional Mexican, electronica, hip-hop, rock, ska
Worldwide FM	Chillwave, jazz-funk, world
Channel X	Punk rock, hardcore punk
Radio Mirror Park	Indietronica
Vinewood Boulevard Radio	Modern rock

Segmentation is a useful tool to make complicated data comprehensible for human brains, because we'd otherwise be overwhelmed by all the details. For example – above is a list of radio stations available in the best-selling video game of all time, *Grand Theft Auto V*. To ease the workload on the brain, perhaps you could just declare your taste in music by picking your preferred radio station instead?

This exercise should feel very familiar to readers born before 2000. With most GTA games situated in the pre-internet past, its radio stations are carefully modeled after American FM radio and, as such, *segmented by genre*. Genre segmentation has been the standard shortcut to "group" the huge supply of music for most of the 20th century, and a handy hack to express taste in somewhat of a universally agreed way. Until the late 1990s, genres were essential to find your way in a record store, to self-identify in high school, and to tune in to the right MTV show. After all, if you were a rock fan, why would you want to watch its hip-hop flagship *Yo! MTV Raps?*

> **Lazy Genre Segmentation Rule 1**: If there is a cello in the song, classify it as Classical Music.
>
> **Lazy Genre Segmentation Rule 2**: If there is a rapper in the song, classify as Rap.
>
> **Lazy Genre Segmentation Rule 3**: If the song sounds happy, classify as Pop.
>
> **Lazy Genre Segmentation Rule 4**: We would like to go home now. Just classify all the remaining songs as Rock.

If genre segmentation sounds like a great idea, this is probably because you are somewhat accustomed to it and it has helped you to express your musical stereotype. You may identify as a fan of vaporwave, boom bap, or punk rock. But in most cases, this probably represents a gross simplification of reality. We are all unique snowflakes, and just because you like one punk rock song doesn't mean you like all punk rock songs and you can't sneakily enjoy Harry Belafonte on a Sunday morning.

This is how data can come to misrepresent you and put you in a box where you don't belong. The algorithm doesn't know any better and starts treating you like a person you're not. The problem with genre segmentation is that it is ultimately an old-school, rule-based algorithm, like the ones we've seen in the previous chapter. Rule-based algorithms prefer order over chaos and end up classifying humans and their habits as stereotypes that often have little in common with our real, messy behavior. Segmentation leads algorithms to assume that all young people in New York like rap music and elderly Italians only dig Vivaldi. Even worse, these genre boxes have a whiff of segregation to them, because non-standard tastes are misrepresented.[46]

To their credit, Spotify's data scientists understood that these genre boxes were problematic. And when they studied their users' genre behavior, they found proof. It showed people were way more complicated than genres made them seem. They were actively busting out of their boxes, and the data showed that artists increasingly found success by *breaking* genre rules rather than sticking to them.

In other words, a music recommender built on genres, no matter how far sub-segmented in even smaller boxes, would never be able to keep up with the dynamic behavior of millions of people. Bad Data needed to be defeated, and Spotify's data scientists started casting for a different solution.[47]

---

46 A famous example: In 1986, when Run-DMC and Aerosmith stormed the charts with their genre-defying duet "Walk This Way," the music industry almost had a meltdown: *Rap and rock were not supposed to be in the same neighborhood!* Even Run-DMC and Aerosmith felt uneasy playing the song at their concerts, worrying its segment busting would alienate their "real" fans. No wonder many bands of that era doggedly stuck to their designated genre boundaries, despite their creative instincts telling them otherwise.

47 Don't tell this to genre custodians, who will never give up trying to keep up with the times. According to website Rateyourmusic, good old folk music may now be segmented into 397 subgenres, including freak folk, "an offshoot of the New Weird America movement characterized by acoustic and eclectic instruments, peculiar vocal styles, romantic lyrics, and a childlike atmosphere."

PERSONAL PROBLEMS VS. LOGICAL PROBLEMS

Let's recap where we are. An overload of choice taxes our brains – check. Maybe less obvious, picking the best music implies constantly choosing between millions of options, and we probably don't have the time to do that in the optimal way. In other words, here is a great real-life, non-apocalyptic test case for AI to help us out, but that is easier said than done: Evil Bad Data is lurking everywhere, and humans are not helping the cause by being ambivalent and vague about their needs.

That last statement includes me, by the way. I am quite passionate about music and I do logical thinking for a living, but for years, I was also unable to explain my own taste without descending into incoherent rambles. I knew a great song when I heard one, but the patterns behind it seemed elusive: My favorite songs ranged across decades, and I couldn't pick a favorite genre or artist if I wanted to. Weren't all artists and genres somehow related, anyway? Helpful record store owners, no matter how shamanic, always got it wrong. When playing GTA V, I would switch radio stations constantly, never content to be boxed in. And even my closest music friends would frequently miss the mark when recommending music to me. (I am sure I am not alone in this specific experience. Also, I love my closest friends.)

So yes, I used to be skeptical about my fellow humans' ability to read my mind and keep me supplied with great music. Having a background in artificial intelligence, I wondered if it wouldn't be more natural that machine learning algorithms would do that work for me.

"No way," most of my friends said. "Besides, I wouldn't listen to an algorithm recommending me music."

"Why not?" I would say. "You let an algorithm recommend you which route to take to work!"

They would scoff. "Navigation is a *logical* problem. Music is personal."

OK. Still, none of this made sense to me. What was so magical about music that it couldn't be deconstructed with logic? In fact, if anything was predictable in the human–music equation, it was the music. Humans were fickle and prone to change. Meanwhile, "Karma Police" by Radiohead would forever stay the same "Karma Police," and the same was true for all the other 99,999,999 songs in the universe.

Not *more* music, but *better* music: Spotify needed a personal DJ for everyone. Yet an algorithm couldn't perform on Bad Data. Here, seemingly, emerged a clear limit to the benefits of artificial intelligence in real life – unless, perhaps, there was a way to drown out Bad Data with fresh *good* data.

Here was an idea: If the humans' language was too vague, then maybe the humans' *song ratings* could be the good data that accurately revealed musical taste. This strategy had been pioneered in the late 1990s by Amazon.com, who – like Spotify – lacked hard facts about their customers' official preferences but had collected a wealth of ratings of their actual purchases.

> **James:** I gave five stars to albums by the Cure and Teenage Fanclub and Kate Bush.
> **Emily**: I like the Cure and Teenage Fanclub.
> **Amazon**: Therefore, Emily, you will also like Kate Bush. Here, buy it, and stop obsessing over David Bowie.

Buoyed by the prospects of more sales. Amazon started mining their reviews data with a new technique borrowed from academia. This technique had been around for a few years and became known as *collaborative filtering*. Collaborative filtering works on the underlying assumption that if James has the same opinion as Emily on an issue, James is more likely to have Emily's opinion on a different issue than that of a random person.[48]

To make this more tangible: If you and I agree on ten songs and you give a five-star rating to song #11, I am likely to love song #11 as well, no matter how obscure or popular the song is. Makes intuitive sense, right? But does the world really work that way?

Here, let me tell you a real-life anecdote that illustrates the power and limits of using other humans as a benchmark for your discovery of music. Actually, I am underplaying it: What follows is a remarkable experience that shifted my perspective and made me suddenly believe in the deep, intuitive, and singular connection between music and humans. It had nothing to do with algorithms or technology or an accidental dose of mind-altering mushrooms. It started, quite innocuously, with a game of pickup basketball.

THEO – THE CLAIRVOYANT PLAYLIST CURATOR

One machine can do the work of fifty ordinary men. No machine can do the work of one extraordinary man.
  – Elbert Hubbard (1859–1915)

Rewind to 2005, when 60 GB iPods were the way to store your music, DVD sales were still two years away from peaking, and Pamela Anderson was closing in on Paris Hilton in the "most Googled celebrity" rankings.[49] On a random sunny Sunday

---

48 The collaborative filtering technique was first described by Goldberg, 1992. It was applied in the setting of music recommendations as early as 1994 by MIT's Media Lab for their Ringo proof of concept.
49 Each of these three facts makes 2005 feel like 5000 years ago, but hey, that's how we used to live.

in Amsterdam, I went to my best-loved basketball court near Vondelpark to see if anybody was around to play a little pickup game. This was something I did a lot, and being a pattern watcher, I knew my chances were strong to find good competition that day; guys my age usually came out of the woodwork on sunny Sunday afternoons like these, buoyed by fantasies of athleticism past. Indeed, I found another baller there, around my height and age, sporting well-worn white Jordan gear, absent-mindedly shooting free throws by himself. I introduced myself and asked if he wanted to do a little one-on-one. Yes, he said with a cheeky smile, he was more than willing to have a game.[50]

We quickly agreed on the rules. Before we started, he found a little speaker in his backpack and put it under the basket. "Do you mind if I play some music?" he asked casually. "Basketball is always so much better with it."

I agreed, and he proceeded to play a song from his MP3 player, a song I had never heard before but immediately had a very strong response to – *I absolutely loved it*. It had all the energy and vibes I want from music. It contained all those key musical elements I would struggle to express in a concise way – all I knew was I just loved the melody and the sound and the vocals and was having a blast.

We started hooping to this great new song, and then the next song was mixed in – another track I had never heard, another artist I did not recognize but instantly adored. Strangely, the two songs were not very similar at all – I could hear they were from very different genres and eras. It struck me that they only had in common that I loved them, which made me almost blow a wide-open lay-up. Even more strangely, this

---

50 If you've played pickup basketball, you know that this cheeky smile can mean two things and two things only: Either this guy is a local legend and dying to crush you, or he actually has no idea how to play and can't believe you're taking him seriously.

second song was followed by a track I did know very well
– a hard-to-find gem by one of my favorite artists, an artist
who was so integral to my personal brand at the time that I
considered myself to have a deep understanding with anybody
who liked this music as much as I did.

I stopped playing and held the ball.

"Hey man," I said, "what is this mix? I love it."

My basketball friend shrugged. He actually had to walk
to his MP3 player to check, because he had no idea; he had
seemingly downloaded something from the internet without
much thought. "It's a live mix by this DJ called Theo Parrish,"
he answered. "*Live in Detroit.*"

I ended up losing three straight games to him, but I didn't
care. Two hours later, back home and full of adrenaline, I
immediately went on the internet to search for this mysterious
Theo Parrish, feeling excited, as if I'd made the biggest
discovery of my adult life. I had met many people whom I
shared musical preferences with, but I had never experienced
what had just happened: The mixtape at the basketball court
had gone on for another 90 minutes, and it was uncannily
personalized, perfect for me, my style, my needs on that
specific sunny afternoon. It seemed like this Theo Parrish
character had *exactly* the same taste as me, sifting through the
world's 200 million songs to feed me that mysterious 0.0001%
I would relate to most, connecting invisible musical dots in a
way that made perfect sense to my brain. It was a bit scary but
mostly felt life-affirming and heartwarming, as if somebody
fully grasped me through music.

It was the beginning of a proper musical love affair. Theo
Parrish turned out to be a Detroit-bred DJ and producer who
toured the world with crates of hand-picked vinyl records,
blending them in novel ways during two-to-three-hour live
shows. Unlike most DJs, he didn't stick to one genre or era
but could seemingly add anything to his mix, from 1920s jazz

to 2020s deep house and anything in between. I couldn't get enough of it: Over the next months, I purchased, downloaded and weaseled my way to all his output I could get my hands on. I studied his setlists, dutifully uploaded by fellow fans. Every set felt like a personalized playlist; every mix led to new discoveries that became the gateway to unearthing hundreds of new artists I enjoy to this day, many of which I would have never found any other way.

Frankly, it was quite stunning. Theo Parrish was on the same wavelength as me. Or was he? Because musical taste is so personal, I remember all of it feeling a bit uncanny, like being subjected to a magic trick by a particularly skilled magician. I rationally knew that Theo Parrish was not a clairvoyant anticipating my every musical need; he was just a man in Detroit picking records he liked, records that I also happened to like. Still, whenever I would listen to his mixes, the feeling of being *understood* was undeniable, like Parrish was the older sibling we all dream of having: the one to always give you spot-on recommendations, the one who has the gift of finding the perfect present for your birthday, the thing you didn't know you wanted that much. Except he did it with music, for two to three hours at a time.

1. **Undisputed Truth** (2) – Sandman
2. **Tullio De Piscopo** – Stop Bajon (Primavera)
3. **Lil' Louis & The World** – Funny How U Luv
4. **Outside** – The Plan (-kton Mix)
5. **Level 42** – Love Meeting Love
6. **Skyy** – First Time Around
7. **Remix** – Larry Levan
8. **First Choice** – Love Having You Around
9. **Luther Vandross** – Never Too Much
10. **Tony Allen** – Hustlers
11. **James Brown** – Get On The Good Foot
12. **Joe Lewis** – Love Mystery (Of Love #2)

13. **Kenny Dixon Jr.** – I Like It
14. **ERB** – The Weekend
15. **Theo Parrish** – China Trax

Set list: Theo Parrish, Methods of Movement

MANKIND VS. MACHINE: THE CULTURE WARS

Emily: I would like to have my own Theo Parrish.
Me: Well, you can't have mine. Also, it wouldn't work; your taste is totally different.
Emily: Does Theo Parrish have any sisters?
Me: No. He has also never been abducted by aliens and cloned.
Emily: OK.
Me: What about David Bowie? He knows what you like.
Emily: David Bowie passed away in 2016.
Me: Doesn't David Bowie have a sister? (grabs phone and googles "bowie sister")

It had been building for a while, but in the mid-2010s, there was a notable upswing in anti-machine sentiment in the media. With AI starting to catch more mainstream attention, critics were openly questioning the "datafication" of music, wondering if new songs and artists were now crafted by preset formulas rather than by human creativity and taste. There were serious worries about data propagating musical stereotypes, and – worse yet – algorithms somehow making us dumber.

Algorithm angst swept the mainstream, and the fault lines of a power struggle between humans and machines suddenly emerged. At stake was nothing less than human autonomy. Subscribers had asked Spotify to solve the problem of overwhelming choice, but now they also were making it clear that they *would not accept musical advice from machines.*

This was big: The people had drawn a line in the sand. *We didn't want machines to tell us what music we liked.* It had nothing to do with any difference in quality of human versus automatic recommendations; music was simply too personal, too emotional, and too social to be delegated. We all wanted a Theo Parrish of our own, but it had to be a flesh-and-blood human, not some distant, clinical algorithm.

This echoed discussions I had long had with my friends, who were dead set against any form of AI involvement in the music business. "Music is art," they would say, "and art is made by people." Or: "I would never click on an automatic recommendation, because I don't care what a machine thinks of me." This last one made sense: We are social animals and seek out the opinion of other humans to validate ourselves. The opinion of a machine, if such a concept even exists, means far less to us.

But beneath the surface of the discussion lurked an almost existential fear.

Humans had allowed machines into their lives for centuries. But we had always done it on our terms, and those terms implied that we were the boss. We ultimately called the shots; we only granted machines the autonomy to execute the tasks we found tedious or exhausting. Elite human skills like creativity, judgment, and decision-making were off-limits for computers, and by extension, so was the choice of music.

Framed this way, the battle for automatic music recommendation wasn't just about music; this was a proxy battle for our humanity. Because our music equaled our creative identity, a perfect musical recommendation by an algorithm implied that we were deeply understood by a machine. And this, in turn, meant the unthinkable: that they had us all figured out.

This was the scary side of artificial intelligence, and one that we were not yet ready to face, let alone embrace.

All of a sudden, we felt the need to lay down the law;

we loved machines to do our grunt work, but we couldn't let machines do the jobs that undermined our evolutionary upper hand. Let them be the no-brainer zombies, not us.

In the wave of criticism, Spotify blinked and sensibly picked the side of the party that was paying their bills: the human subscribers. The platform moved quickly, publicly disavowed algorithms, and solved its persistent music overload by letting users subscribe to playlists curated by experts, artists, and influencers.[51] These flesh-and-blood tastemakers fulfilled the role of your music buddy, DJ, and 1990s record store shaman at the same time. And as if to reinforce that traditions were valued over innovation, Spotify also started mimicking the decades-old best practices of radio stations, grouping music by genre and publishing charts to demonstrate what the rest of the world was listening to – even if this only reinforced stereotypes, as Spotify's data people had so convincingly discovered.

But behind the scenes, something else was happening. Spotify was a technology company at heart, and the dream of superior algorithmic music recommendations was still very much alive. There was a deep-seated belief that machines *could* outperform human experts at creating personalized playlists and it was just a matter of finding the right data. What's more, Spotify believed that listeners would not be able to resist these AI recommendations if they would make their lives easier – contrary to any sanctimonious anti-machine principles the users had professed.

So the data scientists now turned their attention to dissecting *music itself*. After all, they had all the songs right

---

51 Beats Audio, which launched their streaming service in 2014, went even further: They curated the curators curating the playlists for you! As the ads for Beats Audio put it, "Music is so much more than just digital files."

there in their databases, waiting to be studied with heavy-duty machine learning – and the music wouldn't invoke its privacy rights, change its mind overnight, or walk away. Neural networks were fired up, trained to "listen" to music, and gradually went through enough cycles of trial and error to emerge as all-knowing musicologists. Spotify was now effectively employing a set of superhuman "ears," able to break music down into its smallest components, understand its underlying DNA, and connect it to everyday listening needs. It was a big revolution: A far cry from stuffing songs in the "genre boxes" used for decades, Spotify's slick new algorithms were classifying music at a molecular level.

Which brings me to the end of my original Theo Parrish story, the best music curator I ever had. Spoiler alert: It doesn't end in a victory for human curation, but it also made me realize I was the problem, and no human or machine was ever going to fix that.

Almost exactly one year after I discovered Parrish's mixes on that Amsterdam basketball court, I was going to see one of his shows in person. I traveled to London all excited, ready to have my mind blown. It turned out to be a big disappointment. Parrish came on stage at 10; I was bored by 11 and left for my hotel before midnight, utterly annoyed at the songs he was playing. If this was musical advice he was giving, it was terrible advice; I didn't like this music at all.

What happened? Looking back, it was a classic case of slowly growing apart and then suddenly waking up to a chasm. As always, I had been getting into new music in the months before his show, but so had Parrish. He had started exploring more experimental, drawn-out stuff while I was gravitating more towards melodic and compact. Like slowly drifting continents, our music preferences had shifted just a tiny bit over 12 months, but it was enough to suddenly lose the connection.

The moral of the story? Even if "Karma Police" forever remained "Karma Police," most humans were less predictable in their ways. And so I was musically single again, in the market for a new curator to guide me through those 100 million songs.[52]

THE EXPERIMENT BEGINS

Caller: You know what I wanna hear, right?
DJ: What do you wanna hear?
Caller: I wanna hear that Wu-Tang joint.
DJ: Wu-Tang again?
Caller: Ah, yeah, again and again!
Wu-Tang Clan, "Protect Ya Neck", 1993

You may be spotting a trend here: Music recommendation may seem like a trivial challenge, but it is actually a fiendishly *hard* problem to solve. It is difficult for an AI, but it is equally hard for an expert human. And none of this is because music is so mysterious; it's because humans are so fickle.

Take, for example, collaborative filtering, the technique we discussed earlier, based on the way you *rate* the music. Despite its academic credentials and undeniable logic, it never worked as advertised, and even the open-minded users were baffled by some of the recommendations it generated.

What was happening? The problem was with Bad Data – again. If either you or the music was new to Spotify, the model had no ratings to run on and could only hazard wild guesses about your preferences.[53] But Bad Data mostly originated with

---

52 Epilogue while the credits roll: I still enjoy playing Parrish's mixes every now and then and would wholeheartedly recommend his music to anybody.
53 This is known as the *cold start problem* and plagues all recommendation algorithms, from Spotify to Netflix to dating apps. The contemporary solution is just to give users a quick quiz to establish some baseline data, as in: Ryan Reynolds or Ryan Gosling? Green eyes or brown eyes? Your place or mine?

the humans themselves. You are probably tired of me saying this, but when you're dealing with humans, you're dealing with an erratic species that just *loves* giving you Bad Data. Let's do one more comprehensive summary to hammer this point home:

1. Humans don't mean what they say.
2. Humans don't align.
3. Humans change.
4. Humans are not who they say they are.

Humans don't mean what they say: In its early days as a video streaming service, Netflix revealed something interesting about its customers. Netflix users were, to put it mildly, pretentious: They would rate critically acclaimed arthouse films highly – but they would rarely watch them. Instead, these same users spent way more time watching trashy romantic comedies, bottom-of-the-barrel action movies, and critically panned soap series, even though they would not rate them as strongly. So really, Netflix concluded, these ratings were a benign form of self-delusion: a declaration of aspiration rather than a true preference.[54]

Humans don't align: As covered in Chapter 2, your five stars may not mean the same as my five stars. Imagine a user base with 500 French people and 500 Americans: The French would receive way more recommendations from the Americans' favorite movies than vice versa, because Americans tend to rate more generously than French people!

Humans change: See the Theo Parrish story. Our brains evolve, our neurons form new connections, and our 2015 favorites

---

54 This same effect is visible in political polls vs. actual voting behavior. Even though people shouldn't care what the pollster thinks of them, they will still tend to give more socially acceptable answers in a survey – which is why candidates with extreme standpoints often achieve surprise gains versus pre-polls.

are not the same as our 2025 favorites. Would your 2015 five-star rating of a beloved K-pop band's debut album, one that helped you process a nasty breakup, still stand today? Would you have even given it five stars two weeks later, when you were already in love with somebody else? Collaborative filtering assumes that your opinions are static – that a five-star review, once given, is valid into eternity – while reality shows a rating actually has an uncertain shelf life after which it perishes into Bad Data. A recommender system is supposed to predict your future preferences, not just regurgitate your past ones. And as it turns out, most people are not very precise and consistent... at all.

Humans are not who they say they are: A user profile is a user profile, but a user profile can still contain multitudes. My Spotify account still hasn't recovered from the years when my youngest son also used it.[55] Marketers can pose as regular users to manipulate ratings. And on a more philosophical level: Does James's profile belong to just James or to some unpredictable mix of Happy James, Sad James, Drunk James, Sober James, Working-out James, Running in the Park James, Hoovering James, and Studying James?

Clearly, song ratings all had an invisible context, and this lack of context made them completely unreliable, despite their precise appearance. It was another frustrating moment for AI: If an algorithm couldn't even pick a good song to play, how would it ever become a meaningful assistant? But the problem was not with the algorithm, it was with the data. And

---

55 He even went through a phase where he secretly logged in to my Spotify account to "teach" it that I liked dolphin music, even though I am not a dolphin. Aiming to please and unable to identify that it was my rogue family member and not me seeking out dolphin hits, the Spotify algorithm took note and started filling up my playlists and recommendations with the latest in dolphin music.

right when it all got bleak, there was a breakthrough. A new paradigm in data science emerged, and that paradigm was *behavioral* data: If people created Bad Data with their words, the answer lay in focusing exclusively on their *actions*.

As my first manager used to tell me: "I don't care what you say, I only care what you do."[56]

And this is where our story takes a turn for the sinister. With Facebook showing the way, the hunt for quality data meant that apps and websites started tracking everything their users looked at, scrolled to, clicked on, and played. It meant that interfaces were suddenly being conceived as scientific experiments, set up to extract as much behavioral data on their users as possible.[57]

This meant it didn't matter how you rated "Gangnam Style" – the question was, how often did you play it? Where? At what time? And would you mind sharing whether you played "Gangnam Style" highly while working out, chilling with your friends, and/or being emotionally distraught because you smoked too much weed? (OK, Spotify would never dare ask these last questions of its users, being a respectable Swedish company. But I am sure their data scientists would *love* to know.)[58]

---

56 This was at a tomato farm, where I discovered that I do not have what it takes to make it to the top in the competitive, cutthroat business of tomato farming.

57 Looking back, the 2011 release of the behavioral psychology masterpiece *Thinking, Fast and Slow* by Daniel Kahneman was a strong influence here. Even though Kahneman's research went back to the early 1970s, the observations he described were fresh music to the ears of a new generation of software developers trying to make people click and stick.

58 Listening context is still the final frontier for music recommendation algorithms. Lab studies have found some unsurprising links: when people are in unpleasant arousal-provoking situations (e.g., driving in busy traffic), they prefer relaxing music, in pleasant arousal-provoking situations (e.g., exercising), they prefer stimulating music.

In the end, Spotify defeated Bad Data by simply turning its app into a giant experimental apparatus. It was a scientist's dream, generating billions of authentic human clicks per day. Neural networks were constantly whirring, adjusting their algorithms to reflect the latest behavior of the listeners. A fresh understanding of the link between user behavior, context, and satisfaction emerged, and applying these insights radically improved their recommendations. The users fed the algorithm, and the algorithm fed the users. Was this an eerie turn towards surveillance capitalism, Big Brother-style? It definitely looked like it, although it needs said that Spotify kept it relatively clean and never went to the depths of user espionage like Facebook did.[59]

And so, merely one year after the brief Humankind vs. Machine culture war, the machines made a triumphant comeback. Spotify casually unveiled its Discover Weekly playlist, giving us the Theo Parrish we all craved, in the form of 30 new songs You Never Heard But The Algorithm Was Sure You'd Like. It was a game changer. Compiled by a wise committee of musical, behavioral, and collaborative filtering algorithms, Discover Weekly overcame lingering anti-machine sentiment to become the 21st-century iteration of hanging out at the local record store, hoping to hit on your new favorite song. In an uncannily human way, the algorithm picked fresh music that people actually enjoyed. Even if it was generated by a dream team of soulless robots, how could we resist that?

This was the official story, anyway. Music had just become easier, and humans had just freed up headspace. The culture war had been forgotten. The AI community hailed it as a

---

59 If only because Spotify users can remain anonymous and aren't required to share anything about their personal lives. On the other hand: If we would ignore all privacy laws and allow Spotify to install tracking devices in our brains, the app would be able to be extremely precise about its recommendations and reduce our analysis paralysis to zero.

major achievement – although the mixed feelings from many of us never went away.

PERFECT MUSIC, ALWAYS WASHING OVER US

My friend Paul recently signed out of Spotify – for good, as he told me. That same day, he reinstalled his Technics MK-1200 turntables in his living room and hauled up 12 crates of vinyl records from his basement.

"The records haven't lost any of their fidelity, really," he said, beaming. He reported feeling more alive, suddenly having to handpick all the albums he was playing. He showed off the best album covers in his collection, startling me with a half-naked photo of jazz flautist Herbie Mann.[60] During our evening together, he would frequently get up to flip a record to the B-side, or rummage through his crates to select the next one. Paul had an excellent taste in music, and I shamelessly Shazamed a few of his picks, songs I intended to download later. The familiar hiss of the vinyl run-out grooves brought a smile to my face.

As a music lover, there was something romantic about that elusive next song. The pick you made reflected your mood in that very moment – as well as your knowledge of music and the identity you had chosen. It was a moment of mindfulness, an act of engagement with the world.

"Yes," Paul said, "now I can't stay on the sofa all the time, but at least I am making my own decisions."

Paul had decided to restart the digital music culture war all by himself, and time would tell if he would stick to his guns. By and large, humanity had not. Spotify was progressively

---

60 Google it: *Push Push* (1971), Herbie Mann. It is barely SFW; don't say I didn't warn you.

dominating the music market, and its growing user base was increasingly leaning on ever-smarter iterations and spin-offs of their original recommendation algorithm to discover new music.[61]

Still, people were complaining. Many of my friends told me that music had just become too easy – like turning on a tap, with endless songs just washing over them. Some said they still didn't like streaming recommendations, because they regularly took them too far outside of their comfort zones. Personally, I always felt Spotify's algorithmic mixes were boring and played it safe, and I went back to collecting obscure funk and soul MP3s in iTunes, like some crazy old guy stuck in 1999.

With over 600 million users, it was probably impossible to keep everybody happy. Spotify's experimental apparatus was still running, gathering ever more user data, and perhaps there would be a day when the algorithm would reach its optimal god state, being able to flawlessly pick the next best song for everybody on the planet, from Bali to Buenos Aires, from Capetown to Copenhagen. But most likely, this was an illusion – limited by our own erratic behaviors and the Bad Data they spawned.

Reflecting on the brief anti-algorithm revolt of the mid-2010s, it turned out to be just a minor skirmish in the progress of AI: The humans were too lazy to keep the helpful machines out of the door, and algorithmic advice became fully entrenched in the years after. If this had been a test to determine if we could trust AI and algorithms with the autonomy to make regular life decisions for us, then the test had been conclusively passed. Life had gone on: It wasn't a big deal, and we could live with the consequences. In fact,

---

61 Examples include the "AI DJ" and "artist-driven radio stations," the latter aiming to solve the need for listeners who know they like David Bowie but want to branch out. 30% of all music on the Spotify platform is consumed via AI-driven recommendations, and that figure is ever increasing.

there was a big reason to be optimistic: Nobody had turned into a no-brainer zombie just yet! The new generation had never had a slab of vinyl in their hands and didn't think twice about trusting Spotify's algorithm with the musical micro-decisions of their lives. Still, I wondered: Were they getting too dependent, too complacent, or was it actually giving their overburdened brains the break they deserved?

Music may be a frivolous pursuit, but this frivolity is an essential part of our daily lives and is a big part of expressing our identities. In case you feel I have overplayed the importance of the brawl between humans and machines for the DJ booth: It is a proxy for the bigger turf wars we will tackle in the chapters ahead – for our evenings, our love lives, our thinking, our creativity, and our choices.

There is no question Spotify's engineers achieved an AI milestone by computing human taste with such accuracy – a testament to trial and error and human ingenuity. There is no question we can sleepwalk into more music than ever, saving brain energy that used to be expended in the hunt for new tunes. But there is a price we pay in human agency – and as Paul shows me, in the pure joy of choosing when to choose, holding that scratched Herbie Mann vinyl in your hands and sticking it gently on the record player.

This is the choice we will explore in the next chapters: how we can profit from smart machines without letting the technology inadvertently take over our lives.

Chapter 3's No-Brainer takeaways:

→ **Be aware of your own preferences**: Many of us struggle to honestly reflect on our taste. Be mindful that your self-image may not align with what you actually enjoy spending time on. Also: Don't mistake your own preferences for those of others.

→ **Embrace the algo**: While maintaining a healthy skepticism, you can be open to algorithm-based recommendations for music, books, or movies. These systems are typically not evil and often have insights into patterns you might not recognize yourself.

→ **Choose to choose**: While automated personalized recommendations can be helpful, don't let your musical identity get away from you. You are in control, and you define what you listen to.

→ **Human + machine for the win!** Trusted human curators (critics, DJs, friends with good taste) may not always fully understand your taste, but they will broaden your horizons and inspire you. Add these to algorithmic recommendations for a more balanced discovery approach.

→ **Watch out for Bad Data**: Do not draw conclusions based on incomplete, biased, or inaccurate information. This goes for algorithms, but this also goes for you.

4 THE FIGHT FOR THE FORMULA

After thinking it through, I wasn't cynical about the role of AI in music. Sure, Spotify wasn't the perfect company or service, but music discovery did seem objectively easier than 25 years ago – at least for those who chose to opt in. I noted +4 into my Leuchtturm notebook, along with the following sentences: "Spotify shows us that algorithms don't have to be evil, they don't have to steal our data, and they can respect our autonomy." Perhaps finding the next best song was a trivial challenge in the face of all our *real* problems, but at least we could use the algorithmic DJ as a template for more critical decisions.

I must insert a reminder here: I have a tendency towards optimism. In fact, I self-identify as a relentless optimist. If you tell me about your plans, I will naturally gravitate to the things that could make them work, rather than the potential problems you may encounter. If I am interviewing you for a job on my team, I am judging you based on your strengths and future potential, not on your shortcomings and past mistakes.

This optimism seems hardwired in my brain: I was born with it, back in the very depressing 1970s, and the five decades since have not cured me of it, despite going through some very unwelcome outcomes to life adventures I was originally very hopeful about.

To loop back to the introduction of this book: Perhaps connected to this natural optimism, I've always been a devotee of learning by doing. I may not use these exact words, but I do believe that – somewhere out there – there exists a formula for my best life, and the purpose of my days is to get a step closer to that by trial-and-erroring my way forward.

As a math guy, I'd like to think that this is not some baseless ideology. A *perfect* life is not attainable, but the existence of a best life is a mathematical guarantee – because whether I find it or not, some version of my life has to be the best one. This life is shaped by the information I get, the priorities I set, and the choices I make. I am destined to get it wrong most of the time, because I never get to see the full picture and the finish line – and you could absolutely argue that getting to the end state is not the point, anyway. Just echoing what most lifestyle gurus would say: We will probably find our joy and purpose in the journey to this best life. I just need to keep learning by doing, learning, and doing, hoping to calibrate my formula to the evolving reality, with the sole aim to get it slightly more right the next time.

So wrong turns are very much part of the adventure. We learn from mistakes, and we hope to learn fast. But that doesn't mean we are not in the market for guidance, to avoid following dead ends where we can. And sure enough, the existence of this elusive "formula for happiness" has long compelled psychologists, economists, snake oil salesmen, and – well, writers of non-fiction books – to offer us their wisdom.

"A formula to a happy life" is a massive and complicated topic, so it is helpful to break the quest for this formula down in a treasure hunt for many smaller formulas, a few that you will recognize from earlier chapters in this book. One for your perfect weekend. One for your perfect job. One for your perfect friends, one for your perfect partner. One for a better planet. One for the music you listen to, one for the meals you eat, and one for the books you read.

The exciting news is that artificial intelligence, in its evolution of machine learning and neural networks, is a natural partner for inquisitive human minds to discover these formulas. Machine learning is designed to play out millions of scenarios and distill its wisdom; AI's ability to translate huge amounts of data into balanced assessments is unrivaled. This ability shouldn't just benefit stock market traders, food delivery apps, and music streamers: I genuinely believe normal people can partner with AI to discover unhelpful patterns in our lives and get a step closer to patterns that bring us joy. This ties into my personal dreams for AI: algorithms as a prism to let us understand the world in more detail, to help people achieve more self-knowledge and peace of mind.

Now, the stakes are high, because – as we will dissect in this chapter – the popular AI-generated formulas are currently not optimized towards *our* happiness but towards the goals of others – who typically happen to be for-profit corporations. The big questions facing AI are not about the potential value of the technology but about the practical way it will finally make its way into our lives, and who controls it.

Who gets to develop your formulas? Who will benefit? Who will eventually own those formulas for a better life? And what will be the consequences for us?

If this strikes you as all a bit pretentious to start this chapter with, let's go for something more superficial now and connect the dots later.

Grab some popcorn – the upcoming series comes 98% recommended.

THE ORIGINAL NO-BRAINERS

James: So there is this new series I want us to watch –
Invasion of the No-Brainers.
Emily: What is our time commitment?
James: What?
Emily: What is our time investment? Twelve episodes
of one hour? You know, we're running out of
weekends and evenings with all our TV
commitments.
James: It's just that it's something new – a *horror
documentary*. It's supposed to be scary good. It talks
about how algorithms will take over the world.
Emily: We don't have time for algorithms taking over
the world. It's too much.
James: Let's *make* time. Maybe we should cut down
on sleep?
Emily: (sighs) OK – but only on the condition you
will finally watch *Mulholland Drive* with me.
James: Isn't that a long and boring arty film?
Emily: Yes. But it is *very* recommended.

Long before ChatGPT, Spotify, or the internet even existed, there was a thing the people called "television." And television, dear children, was the original arena of the scramble over our time, attention spans, and brains.

When television spread like wildfire in the 1950s, the doomsday merchants were hot on its trail. *People liked TV too much. TV dumbed down the masses.* In a predictable reflex, the intellectual elite regarded the shiny technology that had captivated the curiosity of the commons with increasing suspicion. TV wasn't just a rectangular box that transmitted moving images – no, TV was a trojan horse, infiltrating our modern homes as a device to distract and manipulate the masses!

To be fair, these worries were not completely unfounded. Once you switched on your TV and settled on the sofa with a nice bag of snacks, it turned out to be very easy to lapse into passivity – and let the hours just disappear. Critics worried that television spoon-fed us undemanding entertainment and visual stimulation, and that the endless stream of easy audiovisuals was an impediment to self-reflection and critical thinking. From the perspective of cognitive psychology, it was valid to question whether a TV viewer was actively engaged or just mildly hypnotized – a slave to whatever was happening on their screens. Were TV viewers still autonomous beings, in full control of their minds and choices?

Of course, TV was also simply a runaway success and caused a near-unprecedented shift in the behavioral patterns of everyday people. When scientists started to measure television usage, they were astonished to see the figures. By 1975, Americans were spending 25% of their lives in front of the TV – which was more than *three* times as much as they spent on eating, walking, and having sex combined (even if not simultaneously)! A year later, the term "couch potato" was coined. [62] The couch potato represented the dark side of the success story: the brain-dead human, their instincts dulled by the high of technology. As such, the couch potato was the spiritual ancestor of the no-brainer zombie, and lucky for us, they became the subject of much academic scrutiny in the next decades.

Perusing it, I found that this academic scrutiny clearly pointed in the direction Skeptical Joe had hinted at. Research into excessive TV consumption showed that it was definitely

---

62 Indicating a person who spends a lot of time sitting on the sofa, watching television, doing nothing. You may be happy to hear that "couch potato" has its own entry in the *Encyclopedia Britannica*.

very bad for your health. Couch potatoes were more likely to develop obesity, cardiovascular disease, and type 2 diabetes. Meanwhile, links between couch potato-ism and a decline in intellectual abilities were deemed less conclusive: Most studies found some effect, and there was clear evidence that excessive TV usage contributed to a trance-like state, which made some viewers less critical of what they were watching – and more prone to accepting the information presented without question.

Regardless of the health hazards, people seemed addicted to their television sets, and the behavioral patterns grew more extreme by the year. In 1995, just before the breakthrough of the internet, Americans were spending a whopping 30% of their lives in front of the TV – nearly as much time as they spent sleeping.[63] Clearly, TV had won the battle for our evenings and minds. Television was the common pastime we all had, the safe choice to strike up a conversation with a stranger. The *Seinfeld* finale in 1998 was watched by 76 million people, on a US population of roughly 275 million. You could argue TV peaked right there as a medium of cultural significance.

Because things were changing, and it wasn't just the internet. While the viewership increased, the content had been multiplying even faster. Television became just another screen, and market liberation saw the offer splinter into ever more shows, series, and formats, intensifying the contest for our minds and attention.

These trends have continued right up till today, with your remote control now a gateway to a mind-boggling avalanche of TV and films all vying for your quality downtime. Between streaming giants Netflix, HBO, Disney, Amazon, Tubi, Apple, and Hulu, there are roughly 128,000 hours of television

---

63 European TV viewership was also on the rise but routinely trailed that of the US by about ten percentage points.

content available, and it's our job to navigate them.[64] And as I am writing this, in an otherwise peaceful cabin overlooking Lough Foyle, I just discovered that the helpful owner has installed a service that offers 8,943 television channels. Ah, the joys of choice!

It is mind-blowing to think of the explosion in options. Where our grandparents could just switch on their black-and-white 12" Philips television and consume the full TV menu in one evening, we poor things are destined to miss out on 93% of quality titles available – and that's only when we could dedicate five hours a day to our TV screens for the next five years, by which time the industry will have churned out another 100,000 hours of unmissable content to binge. How can you win? How can you keep up with the memes? How can your relationship survive all the inherent compromises and missed opportunities?

The short answer: You can't win. This is not a winning formula. We live in the Golden Age of Television, and we either need to behave like brain-dead zombies or risk our attention spans being ripped to shreds.

ALGORITHM ANGST AND COUCH POTATO ANXIETY

Despite being products of very different eras, there was clearly a common thread between AI and television: As new technologies, they were both accused of dumbing down the people. For television, it had crested with the identification (and shaming) of the couch potato, that mythical creature glued to the tube for days on end. For artificial intelligence, peak paranoia was probably still to come – but Skeptical Joe

---

64 Or, differently put: It is your fault if you fail to navigate them! The 128,000 hours comes from a back-of-the-envelope calculation based on stated titles by the aforementioned streaming giants – do not use it for scientific purposes.

had already shown the way in the mid-1970s, warning that we'd squander our cognitive advantage if we handed over decision-making to machines. And I suddenly realized we could understand the mini-revolt that Spotify had faced in 2014 in that same light: a reflex born out of anxiety, a genuine human fear that the robots would infiltrate our decisions, dumb us down, and render us useless.

I decided to dive a little deeper into this topic: Were these fears rational? Now, neuropsychologists have known for a century that our deepest fears originate in our "old" brain – quite literally, the parts of our brain that were in place before we became mammals. This old brain handles the routine tasks and deals in the very basics of existence: our primitive impulses, our survival instincts, demonstrated best by our fight-or-flight response in the face of imminent danger. And there are strong signs that any form of AI anxiety is rooted in our survival instinct to have control over a situation.[65]

Psychology has also convincingly demonstrated these primordial survival instincts are often unhelpful and unproductive in modern life, and millions of people are in therapy to quiet their impractical fears about heights, spiders, and speaking in public, to name a few. Should we also develop a therapy for algorithm angst? Ironically, it was our species that had the desire and vision to develop artificial intelligence, thanks to the miracle of evolution's most recent gift to our brains: the *neocortex*, the four lobes that sit on top of the "old" brain, the shiny machinery that paved the way to human civilization.

---

65 The "old" brain here refers to the sections developed before the neocortex, with the amygdala crucial in the experience of fear. Dividing the brain into "old" and "new" is a generalization that many neuroscientists find too simplistic – the brain is not categorized in separate boxes that don't talk to each other – but strictly going off evolutionary timelines, we can say that "old brain parts" keep the lights on, while "new brain parts" enable intelligence and therefore modern civilization.

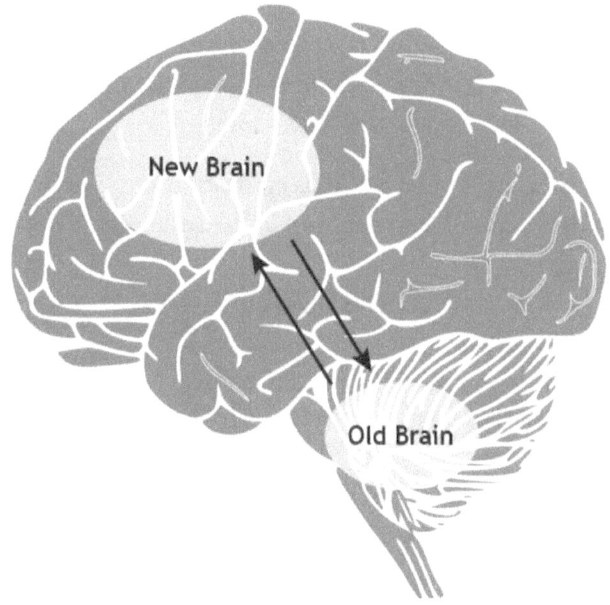

The old brain, with us for 500 million years. The new brain, its recent extension – recent being a few million years.

Even more ironic: This "new" brain, specifically the frontal lobes, *loves* algorithmic help. Our new brain is responsible for thinking things through, weighing options, and planning. The new brain hasn't been around for billions of years, and it is simply not yet as efficient as the old one. "Information overload" is a problem of the new brain. Analysis paralysis is a problem of the new brain. As we've seen in Chapter 2, nothing would make the new brain happier than to outsource some of that cognitive strain to a friendly helper, one that doesn't complain, request pay raises, or take naps. Our new brain is just looking for efficiency and is happy to delegate; an autonomous algorithm fits that bill.

So it turns out the Human Condition, as always, is a tad complicated:

> » The "old" brain craves autonomy.
> » The "new" brain craves efficiency.
> » The old brain quickly feels threatened by artificial intelligence; the new brain loves it.

The inevitable tug-of-war in our heads leaves us exasperated and in dire need of a six-season Netflix series just to chill out.

SLEEP'S COMPETITOR

Sleep is Netflix's number one competitor.
— **Reed Hastings, CEO, Netflix (2017)**

In the early 2010s, Netflix announced that it would start to produce its own original TV series, starting with the edgy *House of Cards*, soon to be followed by the left-field *Orange Is the New Black*. Predictably, the film and TV industry could barely contain their laughter. Netflix had become successful as an online DVD mail-order catalog and had recently pivoted to become a streaming platform for series and movies – the Spotify of television, if you will. Netflix was admired for its clever use of technology and smart recommendations, but what did it know about producing Emmy-winning series and Oscar-winning films? What did it know about creating magic on the silver screen? Nothing, it seemed. This was pure hubris – an upstart bunch of tech bros high on their digital success, thinking they could outwit 100 years of entertainment experience.

Well – our remote controls had other ideas. Fresh and bold, *House of Cards* quickly became a great reason to abandon old-school TV and subscribe to Netflix. Months later, *House of Cards* took home three Emmys. The ceremony after, *Orange Is the New Black* picked up another three Emmys. By the time their run was over, the upstart tech company's maiden shows had combined for 72 nominations and 11 wins.[66]

How did Netflix pull this off? How could they beat TV at its own game on their first try, in the middle of TV's new Golden Age? The answer was simple: Netflix had a secret weapon. It was the same secret weapon we discovered in the previous chapter: Netflix had found a way to turn their users' behavior into meaningful data. It was the type of fresh and plentiful *good* data that the traditional media lacked.

Even more so than Spotify, Netflix had always been a very data-driven company, going back to its early days of a DVD mail-order business. Its founder, Reed Hastings, wasn't a TV industry veteran; he was a computer scientist and mathematician.[67] Like all engineers, he liked to reverse engineer the underlying formulas for success: How did a hit film actually *work*? Was it all driven by the charisma of the lead actors? Was it a function of the story, the genre, or even the budget? Not just being nerdy for the sake of it, Hastings had a very sound business motivation to obtain box office fortune-telling powers: The more he could predict movie success, the better he could predict what DVD stock to keep, the less he would disappoint his customers, and the more he would maximize Netflix profits.

So Hastings started hiring analysts to build an in-house database of movie intelligence, and then realized he needed to develop similarly deep insights on the needs of Netflix's own users. As we've seen in the Spotify chapter, if you want to find the secret recipe to win subscribers' hearts, you need to deeply understand the product, but also the *people*. Inviting users to leave film ratings was step one. Monitoring subscribers' exact

---

66 A decade later, Netflix productions had won 237 Primetime Emmys and 16 Academy Awards.

67 You used to be able to see its founder's math background in the Netflix recommendation system, which would show you an ambitiously exact match percentage for every title in the library ("a 36% match!").

clicking habits in the Netflix app was step two. Slowly but surely, Netflix built a treasure trove of Good Data on people's interactions with thousands of titles. Which trailers did they like? Which plot twists made them stick around? Which genres were oversaturated, and which actors generated the highest ratings?

House of Cards and *Orange Is the New Black* were the first pieces of evidence that Netflix had started to crack The Formula.

The interesting thing was, on some level, Netflix was just doing the exact thing that TV networks had been doing for decades. As early as the late 1950s, American networks had started on a long journey of trial and error to figure out what the people wanted to see, tweaking formats and canceling underperforming programs to increase viewership ratings.[68]

With the competition intensifying, television slowly became all about the numbers. As networks got better at hooking people, the daily dose of viewership data became as essential as views, clicks, and likes were to the modern internet CEO. Networks realized that they needed *sticky content* that people returned to – addictive shows that secured a steady stream of eyeballs. In the case of drama, that meant cliffhangers. In the case of news, that meant bite-sized, polarizing items. In the case of talk shows, that meant the soothing cadence of segments, spiced up by the charismatic personalities whom we now call celebrities.

I also had a short stint in the TV industry and was amused by the obsession my coworkers had with the numbers. I got to work with Martin – a successful exec who was rumored to

---

68 One of the first victims of an early cancellation was an NBC sitcom about a man whose deceased mother is reincarnated as a 1928 Porter automobile. Again, I am not making this up.

have the preternatural ability to sniff out a winning TV format. Doing a project with Martin, I noticed he couldn't articulate his instincts and often just seemed to make educated guesses. Whatever his version of The Formula was, it was located in his gut, not in his brain. He seemed to smell future success largely on what had worked for him in the past, and therefore gravitated towards the safe formats – the ones with middle-of-the-road audiences. Martin developed talk shows with celebrities. Martin pushed for sitcoms with white families. And Martin thought intellectual fare was the greatest sin a TV maker could commit.

Observing Martin, he struck me as a man who based his decisions on *heuristics*, as psychology calls them: rules of thumb that are *plausible* ways to solve a problem, but not precise ones.[69] In Martin's case, he just simplified his challenge by focusing exclusively on the big segment of average people, whom he knew extremely well. But he missed that most people didn't fit the stereotype, and this is where I knew a smart, thorough algorithm could beat him.

Fitting none of the safe boxes, nobody thought *House of Cards* would work. Based on their formula, Netflix knew *House of Cards* was going to be a hit – and they were right.

NETFLIX AND THE AMORAL ALGORITHM CULT

In David Lynch's classic 2001 film *Mulholland Drive*, Justin Theroux plays a Hollywood director at the top of his game. He is smart, he is in control, he thinks he's the man – until it is made clear to him that he isn't. In a legendary, absurdist scene at a lawyer's office, he is told in no uncertain terms by two mysterious power brokers that he has to replace his carefully

---

69 An example of a heuristic: "Always pick the middle option." An even better one: "Anybody who introduces themselves as 'Uncle' but is not actually your uncle means trouble."

selected lead actress… with a random girl in a photo.

"But it is my movie," he protests. "I get to pick the lead actress."

"You do not," he is menacingly told. "You have to use *this girl*."

A meltdown of ego ensues. David Lynch, who wrote the script himself, knew what he was talking about: Hollywood is a rough place for creative types who crave control. Films are not the product of one genius director making all the right calls; rather, they are the result of endless tugs-of-war between the opinions of the director, screenwriters, producers, agents, executive producers, lead actors, sponsors, and everybody's entourage. Heated meetings take place. Powerful hands are played. Compromises are found. Given that 80% of movies fail to make money, the stakes are high. How many movies have been ruined by one bad decision made somewhere during the lengthy creative process?

The worst part is that these agonizing choices rarely make a movie more exciting. Scientific research into creative work shows that compromise is often the safe route but has a tendency to produce average outcomes – making the product toothless, steering it safely back to the crowded middle of the road.

Years later, his coffers full of Emmys, Reed Hastings explained for the umpteenth time why Netflix had made the leap and confidently invested 100 million dollars into the seemingly ill-advised development of *House of Cards*. It was dead simple: A sizable amount of Netflix subscribers loved binging on political thrillers with an edge – yet nobody was making them. As it turns out, Frank Underwood killing a dog in episode 1 of *House of Cards* wasn't a creative gamble; it was a safe commercial bet.

Director: I don't want to kill a dog in episode 1. The audience will hate it.

Algorithm: No, they will not. Data indicates it will show them the depravity of the main character, and it will fascinate and hook them.

Director: It is my movie. I call the shots.

Algorithm (menacingly): No, you do not. That dog is *dead*.

In the years after, evidence of Netflix's mastery of the formula kept coming. Dissecting their subscriber preferences in ever greater detail, Netflix formats weren't the product of endless compromise; instead, they slotted exactly into precisely defined human needs and consequently made their target audience feel deeply understood.[70]

Netflix curator-analysts unearthed a seemingly endless string of profitable niches and TV formats that the traditional industry had no idea existed, in the same way Spotify's Discover Weekly algorithm served you brand-new songs that you had no idea you would like so much. Netflix's discoveries ranged from the frankly revolutionary ("Why can't we have a costume drama with black people?") to the outright mind-numbing ("You can never have enough cookie-cutter Christmas comedies!"). It was a win–win: Cracking the secret formula for TV success gave Netflix more happy subscribers, boosted their profits, and decreased their dependence on third-party series.

Viewership soared. Netflix had cracked The Formula in a way traditional TV could only dream of. In some ways, it was entertainment's *Moneyball* moment: a big victory for

---

70 Smartly, Netflix also cleverly avoided adding *too much* choice – they never had the ambition to let you choose between all 25 Arnold Schwarzenegger movies. This was a crucial difference with Spotify, which brought a lot of analysis paralysis on their listeners by striving to have a completist catalog.

cold facts over gut feelings and conservative attitudes. But television was not as simple as baseball, where a win was a win and the franchise and its fans were almost perfectly aligned in their goals.

Even if nobody realized it, The Formula was only a win for Netflix, and not for us.

To be more specific: It was *their* formula for *their* happiness, not our formula for *our* happiness.

This fundamental misalignment flew under the radar because many assumed that a competitive market like TV automatically aligned the goals of consumers and producers. The issue certainly didn't register with many Netflix fans, and I doubt that Netflix leadership realized it. All of which meant that when the backlash came, it came down hard.

In 2021, Netflix proudly announced a homegrown Dave Chappelle comedy special – and things escalated quickly from there. It wasn't so much that the show saw Chappelle make ill-conceived jokes about transgender people; it was that Netflix justified those ill-conceived jokes by essentially saying that their data showed that Dave Chappelle produced *very sticky content*.

All of a sudden, Netflix showed the true nature of their formula. Its sole goals were to maximize our attention spans and their bottom line. In doing so, Netflix joined the ranks of Facebook, YouTube, and X, who, when lambasted for plugging objectionable videos, always hid behind the users, whose vile minds couldn't help but click on the salacious. Of course, Silicon Valley did not endorse any of this – the algorithm simply mirrored the needs of the people!

Netflix, which had avoided controversy so successfully during most of its blessed existence, suddenly was in the spotlight for all the wrong reasons. Was our lovable streaming giant a wolf in sheep's clothing, milking the marginalized to boost their bottom line? Wasn't this simply another tech company slowly losing touch with the real world? Could Netflix please show us its moral compass?

As Hannah Gadsby, another Netflix-affiliated comedian, angrily wrote in the wake of the fallout: "Netflix is an amoral algorithm cult!" An amoral algorithm cult that, apparently, held such sway that even dissidents like Gadsby couldn't walk away: One year later, she signed a fresh multi-year deal – to produce more *sticky content* for the cult she so despised.[71]

THE DARK SIDE OF THE FORMULA

Let's say you're on your sofa with your beloved partner, trying to pick something agreeable to fill the evening with. Your partner is in the mood for comedy, you're in the mood for drama, and the Netflix algorithm suggests you watch a harmless documentary about penguins. Should ethics be on your mind?

The answer is *yes*. When Skeptical Joe wrote *Computer Power and Human Reason,* he didn't mention anything about penguins. However, he did make a crucial distinction between *deciding* and *choosing*.

> » *Deciding* is a computational activity, something that can ultimately be programmed.
> » *Choice*, however, is the product of human judgment, not cold calculation.

Let this sink in: So when an end user is interfacing with a decision-making algorithm, there is an illusion of computational neutrality, but in reality, the end user is subject to the choices of the developer of the algorithm, who is

---

71 Gadsby quote paraphrased to omit some NSFW parts.

imposing their values through the seemingly neutral machine interface.[72]

In other words, an algorithm always propagates the morals of its designer.

You grab another snack and you wonder how this is relevant for you, sitting on your sofa, scrolling through Netflix, still annoyed that your partner keeps harping on about Adam Sandler while you desire Cate Blanchett, and you may end up compromising on penguins. *The fact is that your clicks are being recorded and may be used against you.* Of course, Netflix is not a cartoonishly evil company, and Reed Hastings did not set out to develop an evil algorithm to conquer the world. On the contrary, the data scientists at Netflix want to solve an honest human need and have defined "happy humans engaged with TV" as their desired outcome. What are the ethical concerns in that? To illustrate this, let's revisit how deep learning and its resulting algorithms actually work.

In Chapter 2, I briefly discussed AlphaZero, Google's unbeatable machine learning chess bot. How did AlphaZero get so smart at chess?

1. Its human supervisor teaches the machine the basic rules of chess.
2. The machine plays a game by itself, making moves to its best ability.
3. When the game ends, it "learns" what has worked and what hasn't – patterns of moves that produce wins are good, patterns of moves that produce losses are bad!
4. It repeats steps 2 and 3 millions of times. (This may take a while.)
5. Now, AlphaZero has seen it all and is really good at chess.

---

72 Don't "let this sink in" in an Elon Musk kind of way.

So AlphaZero's "intelligence" emerges from sheer repetition – practicing again and again and again. And this turbo-charged practice is possible because AlphaZero has the *autonomy* to figure out what wins chess games by itself: It is writing its own algorithm as it goes along! The human supervisor only had to establish the rules of the game and a clear definition of "success." Now AlphaZero is out there alone, playing entire games in seconds, being allowed to fail as much as it likes. In fact, and here I go again, failure is *good* – it generates new insights to optimize the algorithm, even if this means the algorithm becomes increasingly convoluted. The supervisor can just sip their chai latte while the machine self-diagnoses how it is doing, blundering its way to brilliant moves no grandmaster would ever think of. With enough trial and error, the algorithm will eventually produce stunning displays of "intelligence" – *as long as the human supervisor has been absolutely, unambiguously clear about the definition of "success."*

The ethical concerns creep in with this last statement. Success sounds like an easy thing to define but is rarely as black and white as in a game of chess, where a win is a win is a win. When it comes to Netflix recommending a TV series, what is the definition of success? A satisfied human customer, Netflix would say. But what does that actually mean?

Fact: Netflix genuinely wants you to be satisfied. They are in an extremely competitive market – they can't leave you needy. So the Netflix experience is designed to make your life as pleasurable as possible. Behind the scenes, the Netflix recommendation algorithm is another experimental apparatus, constantly playing a game of trial and error, tweaking itself, learning from its mistakes, trying out new approaches to make you even more satisfied. More rom-coms? More rom-coms with Julia Roberts but not Alicia Silverstone? Just Julia Roberts all the time? The Netflix app records your actions, interprets what they mean, and tries to adapt. Do you dislike subtitled movies? Do you like cooking? Do you like movies with conservative world views? New suggestions in your favorite genres will pop up, lists will be rearranged, alternate cover art will be displayed. Eventually, the algorithm will have enough data to offer you a fully customized experience, the equivalent of TV perfection.

The main problem is that Netflix is ultimately not your friend. The Netflix version of The Formula has a very convenient, self-serving definition of your happiness: It wants you to be *hooked.* The algorithm wants to understand you, but only on a very superficial level. If the Netflix algorithm would be a friend, it would be a very creepy one: a friend who will do anything to keep you to themselves and can never get enough of your quality time. This friend has a fear of abandonment. It will give *everything* for what it perceives to be your most precious commodity: your attention span. As your creepy friend gets better and better at manipulating you, are you still able to walk away?

THE NETFLIX ALGORITHM, DEEP LEARNING EDITION

1. The human supervisor posits the definition of success: The longer a Netflix subscriber sticks around, the more successful the algorithm is.[73]
2. The algorithm starts recommending titles to the best of its ability.[74]

---

73 In the industry, the "definition of success" is known as an algorithm's "reward function." In the case of Netflix, the average user stays with the service for around 50 months. That's longer than some serious relationships I've had!

74 The "baseline ability" Netflix has to recommend movies comes from the same "collaborative filtering" techniques we saw in the Spotify chapter, augmented with (among other things) a model that can recognize similar titles to the ones you've liked before.

3. When the subscriber ends the Netflix session, the algorithm "learns" what has worked and what hasn't – patterns of recommendations that reduce abandonment are good, recommendations that produce abandonment are bad!
4. It repeats steps 2 and 3 millions of times, across the entire subscriber base. (This may take a while.)
5. Now the recommendation algorithm knows how to keep you hooked.

Netflix research shows that we, their subscribers, are willing to devote 60 to 90 precious sofa seconds to choosing. After that, we lose interest quickly and give up, often with feelings of frustration. (Out of options, we may end up having an actual conversation with the other person on the sofa!) In other words, the Netflix recommendation algorithm needs to work its magic in those 60 seconds… or risk feeling abandoned.

It all seems quite innocuous. But the elephant in the room here is that nobody is really asking *you* what *you* want to get out of this creepy friendship. What is your definition of a successful relationship with Netflix, or TikTok, or the Dutch tax authority?[75] Are you happy to be hooked, or should there be safeguards in place? The algorithm's success is defined by the humans behind the algorithm, and if they don't think all the way through what "success" means, the door is wide open to all kinds of unintended consequences. And not just consequences for your attention span!

The Netflix algorithm is an innocent example, but the

---

75 The Dutch tax authority caused a massive scandal by having an algorithm target minorities for additional scrutiny. It was a classic case of racial profiling cloaked in the neutrality of numbers.

underlying ethical issue can be copy-pasted to way more impactful scenarios – dramatically so. The Formula gets trained on our data, but faceless organizations own its interpretation and get to decide what "success" means. As Facebook has shown, "success" can be defined so loosely as to directly cause the spread of misinformation, the skewing of elections, and the boosting of misogyny among teenagers. Likewise, carelessly defined algorithms running on biased data have led authorities to arrest, prosecute, and throw innocent people in jail.

It is not even that the people behind the scenes are evil overlords – it's that they are selfish and careless in the most banal of ways. And of course, this is nothing new – TV networks have been doing the same thing for decades.

But AI has the ability to amplify the bad in a targeted way that television never could.

Whatever optimistic view you may have of the potential of AI, you have to recognize that its capacity to wreak havoc is equally formidable. Potentially insightful algorithms become blunt-force instruments when wielded by governments and big corporations. Left unsupervised, they can spawn hate and violence, and turn into proper Weapons of Math Destruction.[76]

This set of ethical issues is called the *AI alignment problem* and is considered a critical challenge in the field, if only

---

76 Powerful algorithms are so attractive (and scary) not only because they are smart; it's also because they scale so well, casting aside any physical limitations humans have. If the Google algorithm would be personified as a human internet guide, it would be one able to talk to millions of people simultaneously, never taking a break and never asking for a raise. This is all fantastic when the algorithm is doing a good job, but things get out of control quickly when the algorithm isn't. With bad humans, at least you can count on them getting tired and going for a nap. Bad algorithms just keep going.

because human values are complex and may contradict those of other humans. What's an algorithm to do, and did it fully get our intentions in the first place?

And if you still think that none of this should interfere with your well-deserved, stress-free TV evening: Imagine that a streaming service algorithm finds out that a sizable audience is actually really interested in watching a comedian make jokes about handicapped people. Should streaming services then just go ahead to produce that content, because this will increase subscriptions? And what if the algorithms discovered that some audiences enjoy seeing the Holocaust denied? Being fundamentally amoral and simply trying to optimize "user happiness" in lieu of further instructions, The Formula would say this would be a good thing to pursue.

Reflecting on the above, I realized that optimism about ethical AI ultimately came down to optimism about the ethics of people. Referring back to Skeptical Joe: Algorithms reflect human choice, not computers gone rogue. They mirror the moral traits of their makers – their values, as well as their lack of values.[77]

By the same token, pessimism about ethical AI has to be appreciated as the fear that the algorithm's creators aren't acting as conscientious custodians. Algorithms are a product of human minds, with all the biases of human minds. In a way, the creators of algorithms are like the parents of a young child – they need to take responsibility to teach the child good values and manners before it ventures out and starts impacting the rest of us.

I guess I believed in the positive. And I felt we did have some control to make the algorithm do what we wanted: For

---

77 Computers have no morals. As Skeptical Joe said: "What could be more obvious than the fact that, whatever intelligence a computer can muster, however it may be acquired, it must always and necessarily be absolutely alien to any and all authentic human concerns?"

example, I had split up my Netflix account into "happy," "sleepy," "curious," and "sad" profiles, to teach it how to cater to those moods specifically. The happy Netflix learns to recommend feel-good movies, sports documentaries, and comedy series; the sad Netflix discovers it is least likely to get abandoned if it keeps serving true crime.[78]

But just to make sure, I asked my friends if they had any ethical concerns with using Netflix. They mostly shrugged.

"I don't *really* care what they do with my data," Marc eventually said. "In the end, it's just entertainment. I just hate that their recommendations are so good. It's disgusting. It makes me feel like I am totally predictable."

YOUR HAPPY LITTLE PLACE
– YOUR OWN FORMULA, PART 1

This is the lesson that history teaches: repetition.
  – Gertrude Stein

Let's recap this series so far, to make sure we are still on the same page.

In previous episodes, we've learned that

» there could be a formula for your best life out there somewhere, no matter if you're an old-school couch potato or a modern screen juggler;
» artificial intelligence can help you find it, by detecting patterns in your life you've never considered;
» for their part, TV networks and Netflix have been

---

78 I also know an anonymous somebody who successfully runs "drunk" and "sober" profiles on their Netflix. This same person likes to click on ads for banana slicers, not because they need one – nobody does – but simply to mess with the algorithm. It's like reasserting control over the world by playing with the algorithm just like it is playing with us.

fiendishly trying to crack the formula for your perfect TV night – at least, from their perspective;
» using AI, Netflix has become extremely good at this, reducing your burden of choice significantly – but ultimately, only Netflix benefits;
» their incentives are not aligned with your incentives, and your perfect night is not the same as theirs.

We have now seen that artificial intelligence can truly help you ease the burden on your brain. We have now seen that AI is fundamentally a neutral technology – but one that is quick to acquire the colors and morals of the person that's wielding it, as well as the quality of the data this person has access to. Which means that, in order to let AI add the most value to you, the ultimate goal should be that you somehow gain control over it, so you can feed it your best quality data, own the interpretation of your behavior, and get to call the shots.

This, of course, is easier said than done. The source code of Netflix's movie recommendation algorithm isn't public. Although it has been trained on your preferences and your behavior, it is unlikely that Netflix will ever donate you the code and let you tweak it according to your own definitions of success.[79] But even without that level of control, there are still great lessons we can learn about ourselves by observing what the algorithm is telling us. And that's what we're getting into now.

Let's reiterate why machine learning algorithms are great: They are, at heart, neutral observers with an endless capacity

---

79 Even if they would, you would probably not be able to read the file, nor would it produce a human-comprehensible "theory of you." And even if you would be able to run it, you would not have enough data to get meaningful outcomes.

to process information. Fed with good data, they can be better analysts of human behaviors than the smart people whose earnings depend on it. (Talking about you, old-school TV executives!) AI is often able to tease out real-life patterns that humans don't see, because humans typically suffer from blind spots; they are biased, error-prone, or simply overwhelmed.

These blind spots are especially manifest when it comes to patterns in our *own* behaviors. As discussed in Chapter 2, we often need an external pair of eyes to learn the truth about ourselves, because we are notorious self-deluders. A classic example is that 85% of us think we're above-average drivers, dancers, traders, and lovers, even if this is a statistical impossibility. Most of us are convinced we live a healthier, more law-abiding lifestyle than the facts show. And our dating profiles proudly state that we would never date a party animal, even if we wouldn't resist prime Travolta in real life.

Where does this warped self-image come from? Why aren't we able to walk the walk? We shouldn't be too hard on ourselves: There are multiple psychological factors at play here. There is eternal tension between our future aspirations ("I like the idea of being with a nice person who isn't hitting the clubs every weekend") versus our basic needs when the moment of truth finally arrives ("I am so excited, I could kiss that party animal in front of me right now!").

Frankly, it takes a lot of brain energy to be honest with yourself. Psychologists have found there's not necessarily a benefit to self-honesty, either: Sometimes, keeping up appearances is a good self-preservation tactic. And besides that, observing and judging others is simply easier – after all, our eyes are facing outwards. Unless, of course, you are the star and executive producer of your own reality TV series and you have to sift through 15 hours of cringey self-footage every day.[80]

---

80 As Katherine Ryan, yet another Netflix-affiliated comedian, says: "The Kardashians – *they are working for us!*'

If you actually had your own reality TV series, it is very likely you would observe another shocking thing about yourself: You are a creature of habit, way more so than you think you are. Chances are, you always have the same food for breakfast. Chances are, you always drive the same route to work. Chances are, you always order the same pizza, even when faced with a menu of 25 options. We like to think of ourselves as people who try all flavors of ice cream at least once, but in reality, we like what we like and know what we know.

Yes, we usually want the same, and we usually deny it. This phenomenon isn't limited to our choices in food; it also shows up in music, movies, and TV. Consider the following statements, all of which are true:

» The one song we are most likely to want to hear next… is the same song we just heard before.
» The surest way to capitalize on the success of *Top Gun 2*… is to make *Top Gun 3*.
» The most popular order in a food delivery app… is a reorder of what we had last time.

It will not surprise you that your trusted food, music, and movie apps, being the creepy friends so desperately keen to please you, are very aware of your inherent predictability. A good recommendation algorithm will stick to what works, and "radically different" usually doesn't. Spotify knows better than to go wild and suggest you some Stockhausen – it would risk its business with you! My Netflix homepage doesn't try to push their home-brewed cooking contest shows, which I've never tried before and am probably not interested in; instead, it tries to sell me more of the French arthouse flicks I've thumbs-upped before. This is very nice of my creepy friend – but also means I am somewhat stuck in my little world.

The key insight is that we are creatures of habit and that *most of us enjoy being stuck in our little world*. You love the taste of your favorite drink; you love the music you always listen to; you are more than happy to see your favorite romantic comedy over a hundred times. There is nothing wrong with that – in fact, if you would compose your formula for your best life, these ingredients would have to be a vital part of that. They are real things that make you happy and do no harm to others. They are good things, and they should be preserved.

And if you struggle to observe your happy habits, don't worry: The algorithms will reveal them for you. Netflix will not openly share how its algorithm works, but it *will* tell you why it is recommending something.[81] Likewise, your Spotify playlists should be cluttered with your favorites – make a conscious decision to acknowledge them so you have no self-delusions about what you like. Study your play counts and find out the truth about yourselves, even if it doesn't match your self-image. Do not let the music just wash over you, and do not click on the first thing you see. Be mindful of your choice: You may not be as adventurous as you think you are, but you can always step out of your little world.

Because this little world should not become a prison. And this is where the dark side of platform capitalism rears its head again, with artificial intelligence as its faceless agent. And it has nothing to do with evil algorithms but everything with the way we tacitly cede our agency to another actor.

Take TikTok: As a social video platform, it is so addictive because its algorithm quickly establishes a very small niche of things you like and then endlessly keeps feeding you more of the same. There is something magic about it, a sleight of hand that happens too quickly to process: It lulls you

---

81 Which leads to earth-shattering insights like my son had the other night: "Because you liked this Tara Reid movie... I am recommending you another Tara Reid movie."

into complacency. Like a couch potato, you may be more hypnotized than properly aware of what is happening, and before you know it, you may be lured into a little world that is of TikTok's making, not yours.

This is where your happy little world can devolve into an extreme niche and trap you into a virtual jail. Fed with the same narrow content over and over again, our minds lose connection with the real world, and we become hostages of a filter bubble. Filter bubbles have been around since the dawn of humanity, but that doesn't make them any less oppressive.[82]

Could we just close our laptops and walk away? On paper, we can. The algorithm, defining success by its sway over our attention spans, will fight us on it. But it is a battle we should always pick. Because if the algorithm wins, it will keep you in jail and you will lose your autonomy. Eventually, you will turn into a zombie – the very no-brainer zombie that has been haunting this book from the beginning.

THE NEW AND THE POPULAR –
YOUR OWN FORMULA, PART 2

I am so terminally online... I gotta check myself.
  – JPEGMAFIA, "Jihad Joe" (2024)

In the late 2000s, I was involved in an e-commerce startup in Amsterdam, housed in an abandoned industrial building. Being financed by morally bankrupt venture capitalists, we were always short on cash and on the brink of folding – but the team was young and optimistic, and I secretly hoped that

---

82 Don't believe the hype: Filter bubbles are nothing new, as we are hardwired to enjoy hearing our own opinions repeated to ourselves. Many churches were *designed* as echo chambers! However, it is true that the internet has made more extremist echo chambers accessible, buttressed by eager-to-please algorithms filtering out everything that could be disagreeable to users.

the constant financial turmoil would forge stronger bonds within the team, like a band of brothers battling a fundamental injustice.

If there was one thing I had learned in previous companies, it was that shared lunch was essential to solidifying bonds in the team. And so at noon, all 15 of us would abandon our laptops and settle around a huge mahogany table in the building's former boardroom. Having that daily lunch together was as much about sharing as about eating. I wanted it to act as a forum to discuss work, life, music, movies, and – of course – binge-worthy TV series.

This was all nice in theory. We had our laughs during lunch, and conversations were always lively. At its best, the mahogany table – left behind by the previous tenants, an advertising agency that ran out of luck, then ideas, and then money – felt like a campfire. But on the topic of TV, something didn't seem to add up like it used to.

Until the 1990s, TV consumption was very focused. There were a lot of channels, but not a lot of quality, and practically everybody watched the same hit shows. They even had a phrase for it: *must-watch television.* You could safely strike up a discussion with anybody about *Seinfeld, Friends,* or even *Twin Peaks,* like you could talk to almost anybody about the weather or the traffic. These shows were like a shared safe space of sorts, happy to accommodate random people sharing personal perspectives. But there, in that industrial boardroom, I started to notice a divergence. *None of my colleagues seemed to be binge-watching the same series.* Yes, we all watched TV, mostly recent American series, products of the brand-new Golden Age of Television. But they were all in a different little bubble. One colleague was deep into season 3 of *Lost,* the other even deeper into season 6 of *The West Wing,* and the next had just discovered *Mad Men.* Binging being binging, with endless hours of the same TV world at their disposal, they simply didn't have time to watch anything else. And why would they? I slowly realized the sudden availability of internet downloads and DVD box sets had liberated TV-hungry humans from the shackles of Other People's Preferences – they were now finally free to exclusively focus on what they truly desired.

The result was somewhat disconcerting, and an early example of the internet changing social interactions. Rather than lively exchanges, the lunchtime TV talks were more like a series of monologues. Colleagues were pitching their favorite series to each other rather than sharing the experience of the same story. Instead of bonding over TV, we were now just trying to understand each other's little bubbles. There was a newfound anxiety: We all typically left lunch with heartfelt recommendations of at least three 50-episode series we absolutely had to watch, full of dread of missing out on something good, yet knowing very well that we would never have the time to watch it all. Was this actually fun?

Take a moment to contemplate how important the opinions of other humans are to you. No matter how exhausting you may find them, you'll be surprised how much you need them; after all, we are fundamentally social animals, and a lot of our self-image stems from benchmarking ourselves against others.

You should see this reflected when you log in to Netflix – or Spotify, YouTube, or TikTok. Recommendation algorithms long ago figured out that most people, almost on principle, are extremely interested in things that other people also appear to love. Even if we have a desire to be in our safe little bubble, our herd instincts will ultimately prevent us from straying too far from the pack.

Again – the key element is not to blindly click on the first movie the algorithm offers but to reflect on your own choice. Do you really want to spend time watching this movie? Does it bring you comfort because you will be able to relate your viewing experience to that of friends? And what can you learn about yourself, that the algorithm is serving you this?

If you are clicking because you trust other people's opinions more than you trust your own, that is totally fine. But be aware: Scientists have run many experiments that prove "popularity" is desirable by itself, regardless of the qualities a product or person possesses.[83] In other words, once anything becomes popular, it will stay popular *because it is popular* – not necessarily because it is good. This phenomenon is called *social proof* and holds true for songs, but also for films, celebrities, bachelors, meals, and brands.

It is not a coincidence that nearly every Paris tourist wants to visit the Eiffel Tower, even if they don't really care about 1880s industrial architecture. Pursuing the popular guarantees you are not taking big risks; moreover, it is just a way to fit in, to be part of the conversation.[84]

If you are a very social person, it is natural you gravitate to the popular. But it also may be a sign that you are naturally risk avoidant, which is another thing you can learn from studying what the algorithms are telling you.

As my friends will confirm: I have long ago learned that I get bored extremely quickly and am nearly always open to

---

83 A 2006 experiment is a classic in this regard. This experiment created artificial, parallel universe music markets to see which factors influence chart success. It showed that you can create self-reinforcing "popularity loops" by inserting otherwise unremarkable songs in a fictitious top-ten chart. See reference section.

84 With the internet making people's preferences much more measurable and transparent than before, the "popular stay popular" dynamic is stronger than ever. We click on the first Google search result because other people have also clicked on it, thus reinforcing Google's decision to rank that option first!

new experiences. If my local ice cream parlor randomly starts selling an experimental rhubarb buttermilk flavor, I must have it right away. And if I ever get to compose the formula for *my* best life, I will start with an underlined rule about the absolute need for constant variety, unpredictability, and change.

But if I didn't know this about myself already, I could observe it in the way I interface with Netflix and Spotify, because their algorithms constantly drive me crazy by being too conservative and serving me too much of the stuff I already know.

It's a complaint that may resonate with you, depending on your habits. People with a constant need for newness are among recommendation algorithms' toughest customers, as their future preferences may diverge significantly from their past behavior. While AI can make educated guesses based on patterns and similarities, truly novel desires without any precedent in the existing data are hard to predict accurately. And even the most habitual among us are occasionally open to new experiences, provided these are not too radical a departure from what we already know.[85] Decision theory is a branch of psychology that studies this, and science tells us we all make a constant trade-off between *exploiting* and *exploring:*

> » *Exploiting:* sticking with what you know to be the best option
> » *Exploring:* trying out something new, which is often scary but can reward you with a new best option

---

85 "Openness to new experiences" is part of the "Big Five" personality traits and considered to be stable during a person's lifetime. Around 70% of us are of average openness, with only a few percent scoring extremely high or low. Some have argued it is possible to assess openness by examining people's homes and workspaces: Individuals who are highly open to experience tend to sport distinctive and unconventional decorations, have books on a wide variety of topics, a diverse music collection, and works of art on display.

MAKE YOUR CHOICE:

KNOWN REWARD   OR   MYSTERY PRIZE?

$100

?

Once again, the key exercise here is to look in the mirror to find input for your personal formula. How are the algorithms treating you, and how would you tweak them? What is your explore/exploit balance?

Remember that there is no "normal" balance, and everybody gets to have their own. As an extreme example: In my third Amsterdam apartment, I had a roommate who maddeningly listened to the same one song for *months* in a row – like, "Raspberry Beret" hundreds and hundreds of times on repeat – until he finally got bored of it, and then would discover a seemingly random new song to monomaniacally devote himself to. I always wondered: What was the trigger? What was it that finally drove him away after 278 listens?[86]

Somewhere in his brain, something sparked. It could have been a girl he met at a party, something he read in a book, or that he just randomly had had enough. In many cases, this sudden need to explore new things can be a bit of a mystery, and algorithms would love to study your thought processes and

---

86 These "windows of change" seem to occur less often as one gets older, but that seems to be more determined by life *phase* than life *age*. In other words, a steady suburban life will offer less impetus for change than hectic, big-city university life.

understand the key moments you are ready to break out of your safe, little world – when you are suddenly open to experiment, when you're willing to switch favorite pizzas and suddenly can be lured into watching that weird arthouse film *Mulholland Drive.*

The key takeaway is that it's OK to stay in your own little world, as long as it is one of your own making. Just make it a habit to regularly check if you're not getting stale.

After all, this is your life, and you get to compose your personal formula – don't let somebody else's algorithm tell you what to do.

WHO CONTROLS THE REMOTE?

You: This is my life. I call the shots.
Algorithm (menacingly): We will see about that.

Much like the Justin Theroux character in *Mulholland Drive,* we'd like to think we are in control. We fancy ourselves strong, autonomous thinkers listening to our hearts, curating our own story, striving for our best life. Regardless of whether we actually *have* that autonomy, research shows that it is crucial for our well-being that we *feel* that autonomy. Even if we are not pulling the strings in reality, any successful illusion of control generates positive pangs in our brain and will quiet our anxieties.

Not surprisingly, we don't appreciate people or apps that openly exert their control over us. No matter how smart and powerful they are, we like machines to present themselves as polite, obedient, and humble.[87] This also explains why we do

---

87 I remember how much I hated the default voice in my first car navigation device because I found its tone condescending. Seminal research by Clifford Nass showed we treat interaction with a computer just like any social interaction; if they are polite to us, we strive to reciprocate that politeness to the computer. We do usually envision the computer as a helper and not as a peer, let alone a leader. Note also how friendly the new generation of AI chatbots is.

not enjoy dealing with systems that don't have a break or stop button. Ultimately, we just want to feel like the boss: We can be surprisingly ambivalent about Netflix collecting our data and running a mysterious algorithm to please us, but we would get very upset with Netflix in the imaginary scenario where we couldn't switch its stream off and would be subjected to all 153 episodes of *Gilmore Girls* without recourse.

This stop button is essential – not just because we crave control but also because of the clear conflict of interest between you and the apps that you're using. Their algorithms are optimized for their success, which may not always be aligned with the definitions of *your* success. We can only hope that the algorithm's creators don't have evil intent. And it's frustratingly hard to get transparency on this, as neural networks are ciphers that do not easily reveal their aims or theories – even to their own developers.[88]

Having said all of that, a bigger question may be about our awareness to actually exercise that control. When the Netflix autoplay is triggering the *Next Episode* in three seconds, are we still conscious enough that we actually do press that button if we've had enough? Or are we the next generation of couch potatoes, stuck in a trance while the drug dealer prepares to give us another dose?

The whole premise of human autonomy is that we can choose when to choose. And there is something wonderful about that: Consciously choosing activates our brain in ways that tacitly following suggestions doesn't. Consciously choosing makes us feel informed and engaged and alive. It gives us

---

88 European law does entitle you to request any raw data and insights companies may have on you. I imagine my Netflix profile reads: "His viewing behavior shows him to be a distracted control freak who has zero resilience in the face of predictable plot developments."

the rush of dopamine, the rush of independence, of shaping our lives, of being in control. It is why a wedding is such a profound moment; instead of simply *having* a life partner, you are actively *choosing* a life partner, expressing your full autonomy as you do so.

But with ever smarter technology subtly infiltrating our lives, we are confronted with more and more scenarios where decisions are quietly being made for us – in the ambiguous interest of our happiness, as defined by somebody else – and we have to force ourselves to wrest control back if we don't agree with that.

And here is where Skeptical Joe tells us to be extremely diligent. We happily delegated the decisions to the algorithm because it seemed like an energy saver; after all, we are sitting on the sofa, drained after a long day at work. Why would we flick through hundreds of channels when somebody did the hard work and curated a reasonable option for us? As we've seen in Chapter 2, the act of researching and decision-making carries a significant brain energy bill. If we can transfer some of our cognitive load to the algorithm, that seems like a smart play.

But if the algorithm shows its true colors and takes us to a place we don't want to go, we are confronted with another decision: Now we have to either actively expand energy to take *back* control, or take the loss and just let it slide, hoping it will get better soon. It's another choice between control and convenience, and faced with this – especially when sitting on the sofa, and the house not yet on fire – we lapse into tame agreeableness more often than we might care to admit.

This may seem like an innocent compromise when it comes to TV, but our meek delegation of entertainment decisions could be a harbinger for our delegation of much bigger life decisions. According to research, automatic recommendations fill 80% of the time we spend on Netflix.[89] Let's give credit where credit is due: This means that Netflix has developed a very successful algorithm – a creepy friend that we trust enough not to constantly second-guess. We probably don't even realize it's AI pulling the strings, because the experience is so seamless.[90] But recall how this very topic was utterly contentious not too long ago, with algorithm angst informing users to resolutely refuse non-human curation. Is this a sign that we are getting dangerously comfortable, or is this just progress?

Let's recap the positions of the defense and the prosecution, the optimists and the pessimists.

The optimists' view here is that we, the human species, are doing something clever: We are delegating all those micro-decisions to the algorithm, thus saving ourselves valuable brain energy that we can spend on more important things. If the algorithm wins our trust and does well, we may be even willing to promote it from recommender to decision-maker, from general counsel to CEO; it is no longer an agent but is actually calling the shots. Fine by us – we have learned to stop worrying and recognize that the algorithm probably knows us better than we know ourselves. Besides, we still have executive control, right? We can still give thumbs down to titles we don't like, or even fire our CEO by switching the

---

89 This phenomenon is not isolated to streaming services; we tend to trust algorithms blindly, as long as we don't think too much about it. Autopilots are engaged in 98% of commercial flights, 70% of people click on the first Google search result, and 35% of sales on Amazon come from recommendations.
90 One of the founding fathers of AI, John McCarthy, famously complained that "as soon as it works, no one calls it AI anymore."

screen off and canceling our Netflix subscription altogether.[91]

The pessimists' view, in the spirit of Weird Lucian and Skeptical Joe, is that we are slowly but surely being lulled into complacency, a bad habit that will eventually devolve us into the no-brainers – former humans with zombie minds. We are striking a bargain with the devil: First we cede some agency; now we are slowly relinquishing our hard-fought autonomy. We are forgoing thinking altogether: *Here we are now, entertain us.*

As a result, we will slowly unlearn decision-making, become increasingly passive, unable to express what we actually want, unable to take back control. Soon, when descendants of ChatGPT will be able to generate custom video candy made specifically to soothe our minds, we will be helpless to withstand the shrewd algorithm and the corporation behind it. As brainwashed zombies, we will be unable to resist our own mini-niche TV shows that just keep going and going, for hundreds of episodes, because it is so comforting that we do not have to think. We will be docile and useless, like addicts in an opium den. *We will be programmed by the algorithm.* And other humans will not come to our rescue, because they will be zombies too, stuck in their own tiny bubbles.

The optimist's counterargument is that "unconscious choosing" isn't really that unusual or as zombifying as some make it out to be. We choose unconsciously all the time; we know it as a "routine," our human autopilot. When we drive a car and take the usual route to work, our favorite Spotify playlist humming in the background, we process thousands of signals

---

91 "Algorithms calling the shots" has already been happening for some time in the financial industry, where front-running investment funds have given algorithms full autonomy to make whatever trade they feel is right. "It took years for us to trust the algorithms enough to resist the temptation to override them. ... There are still [occasional] trades we won't make and [not doing them] almost always costs us money."

and make hundreds of decisions without consciously breaking a sweat, and it's a good thing – we can allocate our brain energy to reflect on the work challenges we may be facing.

Sure, our species may slowly unlearn how to navigate the physical world without a GPS-enabled smartphone in our hands, but most of us have also unlearned how to sew clothes, start fires from scratch, and pick a cave to spend the winter in. With new technologies solving the previous generation's challenges, we are shifting our priorities, and there is always the next thing to worry about. And you have to admit: Spending hours in a state of analysis paralysis in a video rental store before finally committing to a dodgy Richard Gere movie that then has to be returned in 72 hours ... that was never the most productive use of your time.

Just having Richard Gere beamed into your living room by a trustworthy algorithm-powered streaming service frees up a lot of headspace.

FIGHTING OFF THE NO-BRAINERS

In the end, this gladiatorial battle for the remote control is mostly fought in our own heads – between the "old" brain craving autonomy and the "new" brain craving efficiency. We want machines doing the laborious jobs, and while we can forgive them for being opaque about their methods, we will not let them call the shots; our survival instincts are triggered as soon as they start to make decisions on our behalf, even on the topics we'd be more than happy to delegate.

The question is: Are your survival instincts right? Is algorithm angst warranted?

At the start of this chapter, I felt the couch potato was a good analogy; after all, couch potatoes had been around since the mid-1970s and had been intensely studied. And indeed, the results had not always been conclusive, but a consensus had emerged that long-term couch potatoes showed signs of cognitive decline, particularly in memory, attention, and executive function.

This sounds like a tough loss for AI promoters and a victory for the followers of Skeptical Joe. But after thinking it through, I wasn't so sure anymore. Couch potatoes atrophy their executive function by TV-induced hypnosis; our hypothetical no-brainer zombies will ultimately lose their executive function because they delegate their decisions to smart machines. But this didn't add up, because this delegation is a conscious choice in itself – and beyond that, it is a choice that frees up bandwidth for other decisions. In this light, artificial intelligence elevates us to managers, not to hypnotized zombies.

Of course, Skeptical Joe would argue that AI merely elevates us to the dumb *Office Space* archetype of manager: the one who feels great about himself but actually has no idea what's really going on. "People are thus able to maintain the illusion, and it is often just that, that they are after all the decision makers." Which could be true in the light of humans blindly following the instructions of complex machine learning algorithms – but in the end, that would mean we are merely making the *wrong* decisions, not forgetting how to make decisions altogether.

For now, I decided to assume that both parts of our brain had a valid argument. Feeling overwhelmed? Your new brain could delegate as much as it finds useful. You choose when to choose, with the disclaimer that you could be following bad advice. And if your old brain gets nervous with algorithm angst, it's probably warning you that you are showing early signs of losing control. At this point, you can immediately express your autonomy in the face of your creepy algorithm friend, Netflix or otherwise, and handpick that perfect date-night movie yourself.

For sure, we would need the developers of algorithms to keep their moral compass nearby, and hope that they would stick to the principles of ethical artificial intelligence. We had no way of checking this in detail, but we could always demand that they design their systems with a working stop button, giving us an easy escape hatch.

Of course, the ultimate solution would be to have access to a personal algorithm filled with your data, owned strictly by you. As we will see in future chapters, this is not a fantasy. You will define your success, and you will define your formula for happiness. Neither TV executives nor Reed Hastings will be consulted, and you will consume the content you desire, spending as much time on the sofa as is healthy for you.

Your life will still be messy and full of mistakes. But at least you will be alive, and you will be making *your* mistakes, not those of unseen others.

Let them turn into the no-brainers, not you.

Chapter 4's No-Brainer takeaways:

→ **Optimize your own formula:** Somewhere out there, there is a formula for your best life. The only way to find it is to develop a deep understanding of yourself and keep tweaking. Pay attention to what you actually watch or listen to versus what you say you like.

→ **Practice conscious choice-making:** While algorithms can be helpful, make active, deliberate choices on how to fill your evenings, even if you're tired. This helps maintain a sense of autonomy and engagement.

→ **Consider curiosity:** Consider how often you stick with familiar options versus trying new things. Adjust this balance consciously based on your personal growth goals and current life circumstances.

→ **Set personal definitions of "success":** Define what a successful interaction with technology means for you, rather than accepting the platform's definition. This could mean prioritizing learning over entertainment, or quality over quantity.

→ **Create separate identities for different moods:** Consider setting up different streaming profiles (e.g., "happy," "sad," "curious") to better cater to your emotional needs and streamline decision-making.

5 THE UNLIKELIHOOD OF DUTCH ROMANCE

The Opt-in Apocalypse: Love by the Numbers

It had rained for ten days straight, and still the tourists weren't flushed out of Amsterdam. The leaves in Vondelpark turned blood orange, and I spent a few days purging a seemingly endless barrage of sycamore castoffs from our garden. It was an excuse not to be behind my screen and do some deep thinking about AI and the book project. I had mixed feelings about the direction it was heading, and I had taken advice from ChatGPT to confront two distinct issues.

Problem 1 was my own brain and its not-so-secret tendencies. To counteract my long-standing habit of seeing the glass half full, I had made an early pact with myself to stay critical throughout the project. Of course, I'd keep an open mind, but I wasn't going to be an AI fanboy. Yet here we were, and I was certain I was falling for my deeply ingrained optimistic bias after all.

I had logged a +6 in my Leuchtturm notepad. I couldn't deny it – I had started to develop a sense that a low-key AI utopia was in the cards. I had begun to believe that life would forever be better, after all. Was this a lack of critical thinking, or was this real? I kept rerunning my provisional conclusions in my head. Spotify and Netflix represented simple applications of AI, but they were proof that smart algorithms could bring little efficiencies to our daily decisions. Despite all the worries about ethics and autonomy, these algorithms stimulated us, saved us cognitive load, and allowed us to reflect on our own happy formulas. Moreover, the worries about no-brainer zombies seemed overblown. Humanity would be fine. In my head, Skeptical Joe was looking more and more like a curmudgeon, the old guy who was left at the train station and now complained that the world was going too fast for his liking.

Problem 2 was that I was convinced that the book was going to be totally facetious. My friends were joking that I was writing about the anguish of disliking a Netflix original, not about a revolutionary technology transforming society. Fair point: I had wanted to keep this book relevant and practical for all types of readers and to stay close to home with my topics. This meant no explorations of military or government algorithms, no speculation about unknown technological futures, no probes into angles that only CEOs would find interesting. But I had perhaps stayed too close to home. If I wanted to seriously demonstrate how AI would reshape our lives, I needed to raise the stakes and tackle something more meaningful, something with real consequences.

Now, I had long thought of a topic that seemed to possess all the qualities I was looking for; it was high stakes, it was controversial, and it had fascinated me for years, even though I had zero firsthand experience with it myself. That topic was love, in its modern guise of online dating.

If helping us pick the right meals, songs, and films was too inconsequential an achievement, how was AI doing at matching hopeful hearts and creating everlasting human bonds?

I drove out to Noordwijk Beach, stared at the wind

turbines dotting the horizon, and let my thoughts settle. There and then, I made my commitment: Starting next Monday, I would dive headfirst into the shadowy world of algorithmic matching and online dating, with the aim to unravel the logic of love.

If my optimism was warranted, the self-taught wisdom of machine learning wasn't just helping people find dates; it was pointing them towards a formula for their best love life. It was giving them insights, self-knowledge, and happiness.

Dopamine rushed in, telling me I had made a great choice. Clearly, I had no idea what I was getting myself into.

DUTCH ROMANCE – FOR THE LOVE FOR COMPROMISE

Op ieder potje past een dekseltje.
["Each pot has a fitting lid."]
   – Dutch adage

Remember Emily and James, and the complex algebra of picking the right restaurant? We've seen how "good life" relationships require constant compromise, in a world where the variables quickly escalate. But this need for compromise can also be framed as a good problem to have, especially when you're pining for a loving partner to compromise with.

And before there is a partner, there first needs to be love.

And before there is love, there first needs to be a match.

Before we get into the weeds of humanity's matching mathematics, there is one thing you need to know about the Netherlands, the pancake-flat country where I grew up. The Dutch are probably the least romantic people in the world – and I am saying this as a passport-carrying member of this dispassionate outfit. There are no enduring love songs in the Dutch language. Amsterdam has some lovely canals, but it is only tourists who stop on top of its bridges for a spontaneous kiss.[92] Dutch people do not buy flowers as a frivolous show of affection to each other – they buy flowers to purposefully even out the romantic ledger. Valentine's Day never really took off in the Netherlands, and a wedding only enters the picture when the couple's accountant points out marriage's tax benefits.

It's not a coincidence that Byron, Shelley, and Wordsworth weren't Dutch.[93] But there is a beneficial flip side to the Low Countries' calculated style of romance: Typically unbothered by higher ideals, the Dutch do know a thing or two about making trade-offs work and are world champions at finding pragmatic solutions to vexing problems.

Which brings us to the Dutch maxim heading this chapter. *Op ieder potje past een deksteltje* is a cousin of the English "there's a lid for every pot."[94] It is meant to imply, in a general sense, that there is a suitable match for everyone. In Dutch, it can refer to shopping – "You will eventually find a dress that suits you." It can refer to job hunting – "Keep it up; you will find a job that fits your skill set." But typically, it is used to console people yearning for true love yet unable to find it. *Op ieder potje past een dekseltje:* "Don't give up on love; keep searching – your perfect match is somewhere out there!"

In other words, the Dutch, who invented the stock market in 1602, like to say that the market for love will eventually deliver the goods to whoever partakes.

This is a very powerful statement in a world where finding true love is considered vexingly difficult – if not outright impossible.

---

92 OK, that is not entirely true: I did that very thing in Chapter 1 – but that was an exceptional moment.
93 They were English, which didn't help, either.
94 Both descend from the Latin "invenit patella dignum operculum."

If there is one thing I hope you remember from the previous chapter, it's that a successful machine learning algorithm requires a very precise definition of what success actually means. Knowing "what good looks like" tells the algorithm what it should be aiming for, and hopefully precludes selfish or unethical outcomes.

In the case of romantic love, we could spend 10,000 words debating what true love means and how it should be defined. But I posit we could do a whole lot worse than to define success with a riff off the Dutch maxim: *Anybody who is in the market should be able to find someone to love.*

Dear happy singles, this means you can still opt out.[95] And dear unhappy singles, that means we will go all utopian and find someone suitable for *all* of you – matching you up in the best way possible, on this virtual dance floor of love.

Because at the risk of stating the most obvious in the world of obvious: Love is not a one-way street – it is a marketplace, where two or more people need to find *each other*. If Emily wants James and James wants Priya and Priya wants to return to India, there is no match to be made. In any scenario, a match between two people can't be one way, which greatly complicates the job at hand. You think that picking a movie is difficult? Imagine a scenario in which that movie also has to proactively pick *you*, or else the deal is off! ("Terribly sorry," mumbles *The Godfather*, "but I don't wish for you to stream me tonight.") This directly ties in to our earlier exercises in dinner date game theory, where we saw the need for compromise escalate when multiple humans with multiple opinions and multiple motives are involved.[96] Cupid has a famously difficult job, and so do Cupid's algorithmic descendants.

---

95 You can keep reading this chapter as an amusing travelogue, not as a morality tale that disapproves of your lifestyle.

96 Which is why threesomes are so hard to pull off. Too many variables, too many restaurants to choose from.

Of course, the question is whether this notion of a "match for everyone" is grounded in scientific fact or is just an enticing myth, a pragmatist's fable. Well, to fully appreciate the beauty of the Dutch wisdom on romance, you need to interpret it as an ode to compromise.

Because compromise is ultimately essential to make markets work, and compromise is likewise essential for the love market to function. If all participants were extremely picky, most of them would be left stranded on the edges of our virtual dance floor, unable to find a mate to boogie with. Compromise in love is vital, which is readily apparent for the Dutch; after all, they are famous for their pragmatism, not for their principles.

But this need for compromise is at loggerheads with another distinct quality of the love market: It is a game with very high stakes, where you make decisions that may affect the rest of your life – and the generations after you, even. Why would you compromise on somebody you could spend your entire best life with?

THE MARKET OF ENDLESS OPTIONS

If discussing love as a "marketplace" makes you cringe – let me profusely apologize. But it is as unromantic as it is true: If love hasn't always been a marketplace, today it is definitely behaving like one, bigger than it has ever been. And with the market's expansion, our expectations for a successful score on this market have also ratcheted up. Today's benchmark for a satisfying love life looks very different than in 1923 or even 1983: No longer do you have to settle for the match your parents picked for you, the boy or girl that made you blush in high school, or even the university soulmate who was the first serious relationship you had.

Me: Want to go to the Palladium tonight?
Friend: Nah, let's go to the Roxy.
Me: The Roxy? I thought you hated the music there.
Friend: Yeah, but I hear there's more girls there. Let's go!

I know this sounds really hard to fathom, but once upon a time, there were no dating apps. And in this strange world, every Friday night, variations of the above conversation could be overheard in cities everywhere. Love-hungry men and women knew the logic: The bigger your target love audience, the bigger your chances to score. After all, if love was a lottery, then increasing the size of your candidate pool was like buying more lottery tickets. A cocktail party with ten eligible candidates was always better than one with only five; you'd get more shots at the top prize, and thus more shots at the perfect match.

Internet or no internet, the same holds true today. In love, options seem *good*. And not just for you: Perhaps counterintuitively, the bigger that imaginary cocktail party grows, the better it becomes for *everybody's* chances to find somebody to love. Your arrival at the party may introduce more competition, but it simultaneously also gives the other parties increased chances of the perfect match. This is a version of the "network effect" and is neatly illustrated by the output of the simple formula $n(n-1)/2$, which gives us the number of unique pairings possible for any given number of people:

Number of people	Possible pairings
5	10
10	45
25	300
100	4950
750	280,875
5,000	12,497,500

See how quickly the numbers in that right-hand column grow? As a general rule, matching markets become increasingly efficient for *all* their participants when markets get "thicker," in the jargon of market makers. And this is excellent news for today's aspiring romantic. Say goodbye to the trek to the local discotheque to play the awkward guessing game of who's available; we can now directly access a significant portion of the total dating pool via dating apps, from the comfort of our sofas. The market leader, Tinder, allows us to swipe through a near-endless array of local profiles on our phones, play the field, and maximize our chances. It is quite the staggering statistic: In three generations, Western dating pools have grown hundreds or maybe even thousands of times.[97]

In other words, going purely off the numbers, this is undoubtedly the Golden Era of dating. And not just for hook-up dating; also for aiming-to-get-married-dating, which follows the same logic – on paper. Apps like Tinder, Bumble, and Hinge have expanded our metaphorical cocktail party immensely, mathematically increasing the likelihood of finding the perfect match for *everybody*. Whether you live in Reykjavik, Christchurch, or Apeldoorn, the market has never been as good as this.

I had dinner with my friend Jeroen, who has been happily married for years but once upon a time played the field via the apps. He had an amused look while I excitedly ran the numbers for him. "Dating pools are maybe a thousand times bigger than they used to be," I explained. "I think the Dutch are onto something – with enough scale, an algorithm could pair off nearly everybody, and people wouldn't have to compromise at all!"

---

97 Guesstimate done by me, on the back of an actual envelope.

"You're being a dreamer," he said, and ordered us another round of drinks.

"There are two ways to do it," I continued. "Either we give people the agency to decide on their match, which means they will need to learn how to compromise. In this case, the algorithm will only shortlist good candidates."

"Which is how most dating apps work."

"Alternatively, we just let the algorithm calculate the best match for everybody and tell people, 'This is it – we are 100% sure this is the one for you; go find a bedroom together and make it work!'"

Jeroen nearly spat out an olive over this. When he regained his composure, he told me that the world didn't work this way – except maybe in nanny states.

"However, don't be deterred," he continued. "You should see if you can get any traction in North Korea – I am sure they would love to implement it."

FEELINGS, SWEPT ASIDE

For a time I got high on it. Men were disposable. Men were a crowd to be sorted into haves and have-nots.
– Roisin Kiberd, *The Disconnect* (2021)

I had had more conversations like the one I had with Jeroen. I was far from deterred: I had always had my best ideas when I looked at the world with wide eyes, and I had learned not to care if people shook their heads at my naivete. And so I dreamed that algorithms would somehow be able to detect the patterns in our behavior and would be able to come up with a formula that predicted great, guaranteed relationship matches. I realized that this meant that AI would need to dig deep into all aspects of our lives and grasp our desires and personalities at a microscopic, almost frightening level. Would the machines be able to abuse this power? Algorithm angst, anyone?

Of course, the reality was that love was already plenty frightening to begin with. With regard to modern dating, I had been assured by my on-the-market friends that they were ready to believe in algorithmic matching but that the apps didn't work as well as advertised, impressive supply or not. In fact, they had told me that online dating was fundamentally unromantic, and I'd heard tales of cynical city-dwellers using dating services like food delivery apps – for casual sex on demand, no commitments, no future.

Beyond that, I kept hearing over and over again that even the dead-serious searchers struggled to find a good match on the apps. That specifically didn't make sense to me – was that because they didn't know what they wanted? Because they didn't know when to compromise? Or because the variables were just too complicated, and even the best deep-learning algorithms couldn't work it out?

Of course, hearkening back to the great Oprah vs. Aristotle debate: A good match was more realistic than a best match, while pinpointing your perfect match from 8 billion humans would require the type of calculations to melt the planet. But if the algorithm focused on good instead of perfect, it had to be able to do a better job than our lovable, overwhelmed, wrapped-up-in-their-own-world humans. Or, as a 2022 MIT Press paper put it: "Can matching algorithms learn to predict what has long eluded their human creators: the secret to romantic compatibility?"

Well… to see how online dating was playing out in practice, I wasn't going to put myself out there – my commitment to science stopped short of undermining my own relationship, which I had come to value as the blessing no man would ever squander. Instead, to not let anecdotes get in the way of facts, I collected some actual online dating success numbers.

Here they are, shared by real-life Tinder users on Reddit and Tinderinsights.com:

Exhibit A: 27-year-old male
Looking for: girlfriend
On Tinder: 6 months

> » Swiped 18,256 times, of which "swiped right" (liked) on 36%.
> » Matched with 271 women – a match rate of 1.5% from the original pool.
> » Went on to message 231 women.
> » Went on 7 dates – a "date to match" rate of 2.5%.
> » Ended up with 1 long-term relationship – a 0.005% conversion rate from the original pool.

Exhibit B: 31-year-old female
Looking for: boyfriend
On Tinder, Bumble, Hinge, OKCupid: 6 months

> » Matched with 163 men.
> » Went on to message 122 men.
> » Went on 23 dates – a "date to match" rate of 14%.
> » Ended up with 3 relationships, of which 1 long-term, a "relationship to match" rate of 1.8%.

Exhibit C: 37-year-old female
Looking for: boyfriend
On OKCupid: 45 days

> » Exchanged messages with 290 men.
> » Went on 3 dates – a "date to message" rate of 1%.
> » No relationship.

Exhibit D: 20-year-old male
Looking for: girlfriend
On Tinder: 2 years

> » Swiped 15,367 times, of which "swiped right" on 41%.
> » Matched with 362 women – a match rate of 2.4% from the original pool.
> » Went on to message 212 women.
> » Went on 2 dates – a "date to match" rate of 0.5%.
> » No relationship.

Processing these numbers, I felt a vague sense of shock. Granted, the sample size is small and these numbers are all self-reported. Still, all four exhibits independently speak to the sheer volume of choice that dating apps can generate in a short period of time… as well as the heart-wrenching difficulty of converting that massive dating pool into one actual kissable real person who loves you.

Taken at face value, the underlying matching algorithms did *not* know the secret to romantic compatibility. In fact, there appeared to be a big gap between the rose-tinted theory and the ugly practice of modern Big Pool Dating. Why was that?

I let the numbers percolate a bit. I searched – and found – more data. For example: Dating apps constantly got deleted and re-downloaded by their users, as if they were unsuccessfully trying to kick a bad habit. The only other app category that showed similar behavior was… that of online gambling.

The facts spoke for themselves: This was a game of big volumes with unpredictable outcomes and even bigger disappointments. And underlying those numbers was an obvious story of human distress.

Because if you expressed interest in 5,000 people and you ended up on a date with only two of them, that literally meant *you got turned down 4,998 times*. And beyond that: I wondered how people coped with messaging 250 people, knowing these exchanges would fizzle out 98% of the time. I imagined what I would do: I would just give up trying to craft a personal message and cynically copy-paste whatever random opening lines seemed to work.[98]

This dark side of online dating also showed up in surveys among the daters. The Pew Research Center had found that 45% of people who used dating apps recently said they left them feeling more frustrated than hopeful. Other research saw online daters complain of "swipe fatigue," when the pressure to match with and talk to multiple people at once started to feel overwhelming. In another survey, nearly half of the participants stated that dating is *harder* today than it was ten years ago. In yet another one, 18-to-35-year-olds were split on the benefits of dating apps: 35% said they made finding a partner easier, and33% said they made things more difficult. And it was very easy to source similar comments from close friends who were actively using dating apps.

"Dating used to be fun," my friend Mandy said. "You would dress up, go out with a man, have a nice conversation and a drink and flirt and have a good time. Now everything feels transactional – you're constantly running checklists, everybody is disposable, there is always the next one."

And the men agreed. "Dating apps drive me crazy," said an anonymous male friend, who told me he resented himself for even using them. "They make me feel like just another insignificant piece of game in an endless deck of cards. And

---

98 As depressing as this may sound, the real-life equivalent is even worse. Back in the day, I did know some guys who tracked the success rates of the various opening lines they unleashed on unsuspecting females in bars. Statistical significance and respectful behavior were not always guaranteed.

half the women are bots anyway." He sighed and rubbed his hand through his hair. "I keep telling myself I should settle for the first person I meet in real life."

And if you think that's just two people in my specific circle – it didn't take more than 20 seconds on the various dating subreddits to spot the consensus: Even though dating apps have massively increased our chance to score a good match, they aren't yielding the benefits expected.

Instead of melting our hearts, the dating apps were melting our brains and turning average people into cynical swipers – the opposite of the hopeful heroes in the romantic comedies we so adored.

I knew this was a bold statement, but it struck me that the apps were making us *worse* at judging true love, not better.

The more I thought about it, the more I felt something close to moral outrage on behalf of the daters. They were putting their feelings on the line, only to be crushed – or rather, swept aside. Clearly, whatever definition of success these apps were running – it wasn't working. I was here because I believed that AI could make the world a better place, but this seemed like the opposite – an algorithm-facilitated nightmare. There were no "best life" decisions taken here, not even good ones – these matching algorithms appeared to run on the randomness of a casino. And it was a casino with human feelings as roulette balls, going in sickening circles, praying to chance they'd ultimately land in a good spot.

The whole thing didn't make sense. Any system with a semblance of purposeful intelligence shouldn't be that random. There had to be a mistake somewhere.

If anything, this was an inefficient, frustrating market that reflected poorly on the algorithms that claimed to create these matches. There had to be a better way.

AN IDYLL: THE ISOLATED PACIFIC ISLAND LOVE MATCH ALGORITHM

Online dating is like a second job that requires skills and knowledge that very few of us have.
  – Aziz Ansari, *Modern Romance*

Let's imagine it's the year 1557, you are 20 years old, and you are living on an isolated, sparsely inhabited island in the Pacific Ocean in a society where only monogamous, for-life mating is considered acceptable. You are pining for love. Your market consists of 20 fellow islanders, only 6 of whom are still available. What do you do?

No, they did not have apps, smartphones, or the internet in the year 1557. But you can still carve your own little algorithm on a limestone tablet:

The Isolated Pacific Island Love Match Algorithm
Step 1: Have a big sit-down with each of your 6 prospects under a romantic palm tree overlooking the ocean.
Step 2: Register your own interest in each of them.
Step 3: Go back to your hut. Rank your interest in the candidates from 1 to 6.
Step 4: Make the rounds. Ask candidate 1 to marry you. If candidate 1 says no, repeat
this step with the next candidate.
Step 5: Marry the highest ranked candidate that says yes, in a ceremony at the beach.

The above thought experiment – which may strike you as a very promising reality TV format, conceivably hosted by the Ghost of Nick Lachey[99] – shows you how simple life used to be.

---

99 If this statement is confusing to you, let me clarify: At this point, there is no meaningful difference between Nick Lachey and the Ghost of Nick Lachey.

With only six candidates, you can actually meet face-to-face and compare your feelings for each of them; your scope of rejections is limited; you know the candidates also have a strong incentive to want you; and most importantly, the limited marketplace creates a very healthy focus on the *best match,* instead of on the *perfect match.* Perfection is not even on the table. You will be happy, because you will not know any better.

In economics, the thought experiment above would be viewed as a simplified variant of the *stable marriage problem.* The stable marriage problem was originally posited like this:

> *A certain community consists of* n *men and* n *women. Each person ranks those of the opposite sex in accordance with his or her preferences for a marriage partner. We seek a satisfactory way of marrying off all members of the community… We call a set of marriages unstable… if under it there are a man and a woman who are not married to each other but prefer each other to their actual mates.*

You may be surprised to learn that this puzzle was actually solved way back in 1962 by future Nobel Prize winners David Gale and Lloyd Shapley, who proved that, for any equal number of men and women, it is *always* possible to find a "stable" match, meaning a partner one couldn't improve on given their preferences. They even published an algorithm for it, which is not dissimilar to the semiserious one I laid out above.

You may notice that the Gale–Shapley algorithm does not get trapped in notions of perfection but merely proposes a system to give all participants the best compromise. Naively, I wondered if dating apps had actually tried to implement this algorithm.

Contemplating my hypothetical love life on a 16th-century Pacific island, it suddenly occurred to me that the internet and the apps had allowed us to simultaneously enlarge *and* shrink our dating pool – and that it wasn't crystal clear whether the end result was actually a numerical improvement over the days of old.

The growth of the dating pools was obvious, but now modern interfaces also gave romantic hopefuls the agency to resolutely remove candidates by *filtering them out*. And filters are powerful tools: If your perfect match non-negotiables include "age 21–22" as well as "a passion for cricket," "a purple weave," and "a deep knowledge of all things Schopenhauer," you shouldn't be shocked to find yourself left with a vastly reduced pool of candidates, if any at all.[100]

And even if we don't use the actual filters in the interface, we do so with our actions. Because with the internet enabling us to dig up a constant supply of fresh options, we have a big incentive to resist compromise, as it feels like there are always better alternatives out there. Which doesn't appear to be a bad bet at first glance: With billions of humans on the planet, it would seem at least *plausible* that your perfect match is out there, and you should keep trying until you hit the jackpot.

Unfortunately, the statistical probabilities of hitting that jackpot are not in your favor. In 2010, just before dating apps truly took off, love-hungry UK mathematician Peter Backus published the seminal four-page study "Why I Don't Have a Girlfriend – an application of the Drake Equation to love in the UK." In it, he estimated that:

---

100 In this case, there is a dating pool of one: It's Akshay Sibal (22), who lives on Regenboogstraat 42 in Apeldoorn, the Netherlands. I have his number, if you're interested, but the question is: Is he interested in you? Also: notice the subtle reference to the purple weave from the preface. It's all connected.

> » 10,610 women in London satisfied his most basic girlfriend criteria – being university-educated females between 24 and 34;
> » 50% of whom were single, leaving 5,305;
> » 10% of whom he would get along with, leaving 530;
> » 5% of whom would find him attractive, leaving 26.

Backus then hilariously and depressingly concluded that "on a given night out in London, there is a 0.0000034% chance of meeting one of these special people, about 100 times better than finding an alien civilization we can communicate with." In other words, he could have gone clubbing every night of his life, kindly introducing himself to all available females, and *still* miss out on The One. And this was in London, one of the biggest cities in the world. Can you imagine if he had run those numbers in Reykjavik, Christchurch, or Apeldoorn?

The problem, again, comes with our resistance to compromise. There may be billions of humans on the planet, but you will not meet more than 0.001% of them in your lifetime, and 99.999% of the ones you meet will be imperfect. In other words, any romantic hopeful will have to compromise at some point, so it makes sense to practice smart trade-offs from the start. As an example: "Broadening your horizons" is the positive spin on "lowering your standards," and the calculus of broadening your horizons is extremely attractive. By settling for a prospect with a perceived 7 out of 10 instead of an 8 out of 10, you will almost double your chances of getting a match.[101]

---

101 Based on a normal distribution of attractiveness ratings. To add to the confusion, I found that research showed online daters often *do* broaden their horizons, but only off the record: Left to their own devices, they will show an interest in candidates that they had already ruled out. It seemed that the more you gave people control over the process, the more they broke their own rules, exposing a big gap between the "official" version of themselves and the "real-life-behavior" one.

Anyway, that was all probability, not emotion. Which was exactly where I expected smart algorithms to jump in and make the good decisions on our conflicted behalf.

If anything, the Pacific island thought experiment made me appreciate how smoothly human mate selection must have gone for most of our existence.[102] And speaking more to my friends about the trials of modern love, my suspicions started to coalesce. Clearly, the problem was that the modern love markets had rendered traditional logic obsolete: The utopia in the Pacific didn't exist anymore. With today's bounty of romantic options, we had made love into a game of choice, a game we were not very good at. Many of us refused to trade "perfect" for "best" – in the back of our heads, there was always that non-zero chance to strike gold if we just kept on searching. In fact, we struggled to identify "perfect" to begin with, and applied filters like a treasure hunter wielding a machete – slashing our dating pool to smithereens without even realizing.

All of this meant the market was only bigger *on paper*. To use a horrible retail metaphor: This was a meat market reimagined as a carousel, with a seemingly endless supply of meat stalls and an incentive to play coy to the bitter end.[103] As a consequence, the entire market was stuck in the window-shopping stage, and the only winner was the company that rented out the stalls. For most normal users, it translated into pure mental anguish.

---

102 Even in 1932, when James Bossard surveyed married couples in Philadelphia, he found that a third of them grew up within a five-block radius of each other, illuminating how much smaller the world was in those days, even in a city of nearly 2 million people.
103 "The ready access to a large pool of potential partners can elicit an evaluative, assessment-oriented mindset that leads online daters to objectify potential partners and might even undermine their willingness to commit to one of them. It can also cause people to make lazy, ill-advised decisions." (Finkel et al., 2012)

THE GAME WE PLAY CALLED MODERN LOVE

As always, reality was more complex than metaphor. "The company that rented out the stalls" wasn't just one company. There were at least a thousand dating apps across the world, but one was by far the most popular: Tinder.

Launched in 2013, Tinder revolutionized online dating by making it fun, easy, and casual.[104] I was curious how Tinder's algorithms worked and what they actually *did*. Tinder's parent company was aptly named Match Group, and Match Group had been known to proclaim the superiority of their clever algorithms, and employed a big data and analytics department. But what was actually going on?

It was easy to blame the humans for the dysfunctional meat market, but the reality was that humans couldn't help themselves. It was very understandable we struggled to resist the lures of a big dating pool, even if it hurt our brains. The desire to "expand our market" is hardwired into us; we are searchers and wanderers, always looking for the best markets for anything we desire – the places where supply is both thick and suitable.

Isn't this where fancy algorithms are supposed to come to our rescue?

The founders of Tinder were veterans of the dating industry and knew its three core principles by heart:

1. The bigger your dating pool, the bigger your chances of finding your match.
2. The more desirable you are, the bigger your chances of finding your match.

---

104 And I don't mean "casual" as in "casual sex" – contrary to its rep, people actually do use Tinder to find true love. See reference section.

3. The less picky you are, the bigger your chances of finding your match.

As a consequence, Tinder had been designed to make users *feel* like they were maximizing their chance at love – while minimizing their effort. Principle 1 was ticked off by immediately presenting users with a near-endless conveyor belt of readily available candidates, filtered by proximity, age, and sexual preference. Still, Tinder's real genius is in how it helps its aspiring lovers to avoid overthinking factor 3.

Unlike some other apps, Tinder is not about the agony of filtering; it is really more about the pure fun of matching. Everybody knows Tinder for its ingenious, infamous selection interface, which allows users to swipe left or right in an instant – on pure instinct, rather than via a careful selection process. To show you what instinct truly means in this context, I have a very simple one-question quiz for you.

If you were hungry, which picture would you swipe right on?

Option A: apple pie	Option B: the same apple pie

The two options above represent the very same apple pie. But the framing and the information presented make us process the choice very differently. The photo of the apple pie activates our primitive brain, unable to turn down some good-looking, easy bites; the list of apple pie ingredients activates our thinking brain, crunching variables. A is easy and intuitive; B is hard work and takes imagination.

As behavioral economists have known since the 1970s, the first apple pie option routes the decision-making to your "gut instinct," which is quick, efficient, and takes hardly any brain energy. Meanwhile, option B intellectualizes the choice and activates your limbic system, leading to a slow, thorough thought process. Yes, it may give you a better outcome, but at what cost? What will be the brain energy bill?

Needless to say, we're always drawn to option A, which explains why Tinder works so well: It keeps the initial selection process of potential dates as easy as possible while maximizing your sense of agency. Tinder boosts your dopamine by letting you make snap judgments without any negative consequences. It will not allow you to go into analysis paralysis evaluating a romantic prospect on his or her beliefs, behavior, and long history of exes; there are just nearby brown eyes, a kissable mouth, and tight jeans. This is not a cumbersome game of intellect; this is a fun game of instinct.[105]

Unfortunately, our instincts betray us. In fact, there is lots of circumstantial evidence that Tinder creates its own version of the couch potato or no-brainer zombie: that of the hypnotized dopamine addict, endlessly spinning the roulette wheel of love, avoiding the endgame. Because while the swiping is admittedly a rush – a game that you can't lose, your imaginary best life without compromise – it all falls apart after that. For all the easy romantic options Tinder generates, it only delays the inevitable: After showing your matches, it abruptly transitions into a different game – one of choice, strategy, and compromise, and one that we're not very good at.

---

105 Not to make it about gender, but men find this game more difficult to resist than women, as the average man swipes right 6.2 times more often than the average woman.

This is a simplified representation of what *that* hidden game looks like:

1. Decide who to text back
    a. When to write back
    b. What to write
        i. How to represent yourself
        ii. What emojis to use
        iii. What standard lines to reuse
    c. When to end the conversation prematurely
        i. How to detect weirdos
        ii. How to detect commitment phobes
        iii. How to detect axe-wielding psychopaths
        iv. How to detect the Tinder swindler and their ilk
        v. How to detect bots
    d. Which conversations may warrant a date
        i. Whether to ghost or not to ghost
2. Decide who to meet up with
    a. Who will take the initiative
        i. When to ask
        ii. How to ask
        iii. Whether to play hard-to-get
            1. For how long
3. Setting up the date
    a. Where to meet
        i. What compromise is acceptable
    b. When to meet
        i. What compromise is acceptable
4. Going on a date
    a. Whether to show up
        i. Cancel or ghost[106]
    b. How to behave
        i. Open/closed

---

106 Ghosting means dropping off the radar without any further communication. Apparently, an astonishing number of dating app dates end in no-shows. As one online dater told me: "You're always one misunderstood emoji away from being ghosted." A survey by Plenty of Fish in 2019 found that 51% of respondents had experienced a no-show at least once.

      ii. Eager/desperate
      iii. Get drunk/stay in control
   c. Assessing the other
      i. Creep
      ii. Friend
      iii. Lover
      iv. Wedding material
   d. How to end the date
      i. Run
      ii. Hug
      iii. Kiss
      iv. Sex
5. After the date
   a. Whether to stay in touch
      i. Ghost
      ii. End things
      iii. Play games
      iv. Show commitment
   b. Whether to play the field again

Needless to say, when multiplied by a number of matches, the myriad of scenarios and emotional consequences becomes more than overwhelming. Through all of these steps, uncertainty and analysis paralysis reign supreme. And this is where online dating truly breaks down; for proof, look no further than those painful "date to match" and "relationship to swipe" statistics from actual Tinder users. This is not like starring in your own rom-com; this is a brutal game of survival, like dodging the endless waves of bullets in the final level of *Gradius* – when you don't have any lives left.[107]

But the real question was this: Where were Tinder's trumpeted algorithms during all these painful decisions? Weren't they supposed to solve the problem of choice that

---

107 And one that can lead to feelings of anxiety and depression – if only because we are not swiping on apple pies but on three-dimensional human beings that we're dismissing in 0.3 seconds.

the internet had created? Well, the answer to that was simple: Tinder's algorithms were literally nowhere to be found, happy to observe the drama unfold from a safe distance.

Yes, Tinder does employ some smart algorithms, but they mostly optimize the *presentation* of the candidates and do nothing to narrow down potential matches – except by proximity. Tinder's algorithm has one big rule: *Closer = Better*. The hard work to turn those easy matches into actual face-to-face dates was still squarely on the humans, who were left to foot the cognitive energy bill by themselves.

If I was being honest: This was ludicrous. There was barely any intelligence at work here.

"I do believe in the algorithm," I had heard from friends. But they assumed the algorithm was doing something useful. This was like Skeptical Joe's worst nightmare: We were acting like we'd been blessed by the wisdom of a machine god, but the machine god didn't exist – we were actually making all the dumb decisions ourselves.

If this game felt like a casino, that was because it *was* a casino.

But then I quickly calmed down, because I realized that this meant that things could be so much better.

INTERMEZZO: A STORY OF TRUE, ALGORITHMIC LOVE

> You know, I've been searching for someone
> Who can share that special love with me
> And your eyes have that glow
> Could it be your face I see on my computer screen
> **– Zapp, "Computer Love" (1985)**

For all their zeitgeisty credentials, Tinder and Hinge and Bumble are merely the newest twist on a very old business model. Romance-hungry men and women have been using matchmaking services since Adam and Eve. Self-styled love gurus have been dispensing "objective romantic advice" to create "happy families" for centuries, based on anything from intuition to astrology to "compatibility calculus."[108] Digital technology joined the party with the emergence of computer dating services in the 1950s and 1960s, after television and penny newspapers had demonstrated how irresistible it was to expand your dating pool beyond your regular circle. The internet would ultimately obliterate everything that came before: Tom Hanks meeting Meg Ryan in an AOL chatroom in the 1998 rom-com *You've Got Mail* was perhaps the watershed moment for online dating.

My friends Thys and Taryn met via an online matchmaking service. This happened post-*You've Got Mail*, but still squarely in the late Stone Age of the internet, those primitive days when smartphones and dating apps didn't yet exist. They didn't swipe right on each other's photos; Tinder wasn't around. Instead, they were matched by a very simplistic algorithm on an early dating website that highlighted a rare similarity in the way they answered their profile questionnaires. After exchanging a few messages, they went on a promising date, magic happened, and they got married two years later.

Fifteen years later, Thys and Taryn are still together, and they are one of my personal benchmarks for a happy modern couple. No matter when I see them, they always strike me as a good match: They have fun; they have effortless, productive conversations; and they genuinely seem to enjoy each other's company.[109]

Visiting them for dinner the other week, I asked them to remind me how the algorithm knew they were right for

---

108 "Compatibility calculus" is a phrase from Neil Warren, founder of eHarmony, one of the more old-school online matching services, which touts the accuracy of its "relationship science." As a side note: I have once in my life successfully matched two friends-of-friends myself. They lasted nine years and I am still proud of it – I may be a love guru on the down-low.
109 They also have vaguely similar first names, which apparently is also a predictor of a good match! No, I am not making this up.

each other. They exchanged a quick look of affection, the look of a couple never tired of recounting their origin story. As it happened, their dating profiles were a perfect match on both music and movie preferences. The music in question was Gang Starr; the movie was *Napoleon Dynamite*, the 2004 Jared Hess coming-of-age comedy. Neither is super obscure: Gang Starr is universally admired among East Coast hip-hop fans, and *Napoleon Dynamite* is a cult classic. Still, this was a bit of pairing magic, the right pixel in the matrix.[110]

"Did you ever send flowers to the algorithm people?" I asked Thys and Taryn.

They laughed it off. "We did all the hard work ourselves!"

Of course, they are right – a match is one thing; a 15-year-long successful marriage is another. And even beyond that, we can rest assured there was more to their initial attraction than just a common movie preference. But their story – and we all know many stories like this – offers hope. Why wouldn't we be able to re-create this level of dating success for everybody?

"Love should *not* be complicated," a wise lady once told me at a party. "If it feels complicated, it's not true love." Or, to make this about AI again: "Any sufficiently advanced technology is indistinguishable from magic."

FALSE ADVERTISING

Perhaps, I wondered, Tinder was the problem. Perhaps other dating apps did get it right, but they flew under the radar while the world obsessed over the market leader's notorious, addictive swipe machine. Filled with fresh curiosity, I decided

---

110 I couldn't resist calculating the odds: Assuming that 0.05% of a city with 100,000 people would have this shared movie and music preference, only 0.0000245% of random pairs would match. Which proves that filters on dating apps can be great, if you get lucky.

to switch my attention to Hinge: another top-five dating app, and one that was pitched by its parent company as the "serious" alternative to "casual" Tinder.

Its algorithmic credentials seemed strong. In fact, Hinge proudly boasted that it matched candidates via the Gale–Shapley algorithm – the one that cracked the stable marriage problem, the one that won a Nobel Prize, the one that essentially uses Pacific island logic to make sure the entire dating pool gets its optimal match.

That sounded fantastic, and I felt some of my original optimism return. But how did this work at scale?

I reviewed the theory again. On paper, Gale–Shapley would efficiently marry off each and every Pacific islander, even if we'd be talking about a Pacific island the size of Greenland with a population the size of New York City. Better yet, it would give every islander the guarantee they'd get their best possible partner, without exposing them to an ego-shattering series of rejections to finally arrive at their true market value.

However, one nagging real-life problem remained: For the algorithm to work its magic, *it requires every candidate to rank all other candidates from first to last.* This was obviously impossible with a large dating pool – and even at a smaller scale, this exposed a fundamental flaw to algorithmic love-matching, because how on earth were people supposed to rank each other without being able to try each other out?

Immediately, I was doubtful that Hinge worked as advertised. Needing to zoom out, I read up some more on the theory behind our love lives, if only to see if there was any scientific guidance to these human–human matching puzzles that I had missed.

I found that game theorists and behavioral economists had cast their opinions in the 1970s. Gary Becker set the tone by publishing a very unromantic theory of marriage, interpreting human coupling as a rational decision made by individuals who are seeking to maximize their own self-interests. He described dating as a form of – here we go again – market exchange, a search for potential partners who could provide us with the highest level of satisfaction or utility. Imagining the love market as a giant cocktail party, he envisioned all participants establishing their market value through a painful process of trial and error, and then finally wising up and coupling with a partner with similar market clout.[111]

Interestingly, Becker also pointed out the Bad Data problem, which he called the "asymmetry of information" – the problem that you never have the full picture of a potential partner before actually spending quality time with them. Even beyond the risk of falling prey to swindlers, catfishers, and fuckbois, he made it clear this would regularly lead to run-of-the-mill market failure – essentially, a string of terrible first dates.[112]

This information asymmetry was clearly also undermining any real-life application of Gale–Shapley – no matter what Hinge claimed. And this information asymmetry is exacerbated by our own proclivity for false advertising. After all, let's not forget about rule #2 of dating success drivers: *The more desirable you are, the bigger your chances of finding your match.*

---

111 While Becker was hypothesizing, mathematicians were running the cold numbers: If the love market is indeed a big evaluation game where you are slowly running out of time, how many potential partners should you consider before making a choice? Under the theory of optimal stopping, the rule of thumb solution to this "marriage problem" (also known as *secretary problem*) is that you should spend the first 37% of your "dating window" studying the market, and after that, settle for whoever hits your benchmark. In reality, people settle quicker, because dating is exhausting.

112 The internet contains hundreds of thousands of hilarious bad first-date stories, many that defy reason. You are not alone.

The consequences of rule #2 are obvious: Like salespeople hoping to increase the chance of a deal, we all want to advertise our wares as effectively as possible. Which means we eagerly leverage smartphone photo filters to create the best version of ourselves, kissed by heavenly angels and blessed by Aphrodite. This may also be a version of our "best life" – but the consequence is that first dates are an exercise of fact-checking, before anything else.

On the other hand, implying you're Harvard-educated costs decidedly less energy, time, and money than actually *being* Harvard-educated. And as always, the line between wholesome self-delusion and deliberate deceit is not always clear:

> » *I like cooking, reading, and the occasional glass of wine.*
>> > (In reality, I drink wine constantly – how would I even find time for cooking and reading?)
>
> » *I am a happy single who sees life as one big adventure.*
>> > (I wish – I have been unhappily married for 13 years and counting, but I did take a different route to work last week, so at least that part is true.)
>
> » *I am a diamond in the rough – I just need some excavating.*
>> > (Honestly, I probably need 10,000 hours of therapy to turn me into a functional human being – would you please make that investment with me?)

If eBay sellers would falsify information like this, they would receive a string of one-star reviews and be driven out of business.[113] But in romance, getting away with some make-believe is part of the dance – and stuffing algorithms full of Bad Data is the least of our concerns.[114]

WE ALL DESERVE LOVE, PART 1: THE BENEVOLENT NANNY STATE

The more time I spent researching online dating, the less excited I was about its prospects. Love was blind, but so were the algorithms. Online dating truly brought out the worst in humans, yet everybody opted in to it. No matter where I looked, I heard the same chorus: None of the dating apps offered a happy experience with guaranteed results. The only success stories came from the true players: those who could manage the long game with a cold, calculating heart.

This game was too brutal for a "learning by doing" strategy to pay dividends for normal people. It was a game of trial and *terror* more than trial and error. Daters dealt with skewed expectations, false advertising, casino behavior, loss aversion, ruthless ghosting, commitment phobia, the occasional catfishing, and apathetic algorithms. It had slowly started to dawn on me that the culture of online dating was fundamentally broken and that it needed to be blown up if AI was going to help the humans out.

This brought me back to my alternate approach – the

---

113 Can you imagine a dating site having ratings and reviews from people who previously dated (and dumped or got dumped by) the candidate? That would be both awkward and absolutely mandatory reading.

114 My friend Jan was the absolute king of crafting dating app profiles that made him stand out, without being filtered out. The last time he was on the market, he took nearly two months of photo curation and wordsmithing before settling on a selfie and accompanying pitch that somehow managed to satisfy both rules, while staying close enough to what he was actually like as a person. It was a masterpiece of personal marketing, and he rightfully found true love within two months of installing the app.

one that my friend Jeroen had dismissed as the "North Korea plan."

The North Korea plan was to let machine learning study our patterns and learn to love us in the honest way we couldn't love ourselves. Artificial intelligence would define the best love matches and resolutely restrict any human meddling – no filtering, no ranking, no fighting the compromise. We would start from the premise that love-hungry humans couldn't be trusted to play the game, and would be asking people to place their full trust in the wisdom of the algorithm – and commit to a serious date with their best match. Which, by the way, is something people indicate they are willing to try.[115]

I imagined piloting this in a benevolent nanny state, where ten million people live under the care of a well-meaning but very hands-on government. A brave new world where the rulers genuinely strive to reach 100% happiness for all the inhabitants and have defined success unambiguously as a win for all: *Anybody who is in the market should be able to find someone to love.*[116]

We have learned already that there is such a thing as an optimized dating market, as described by 1962's Gale–Shapley algorithm. We've also seen that Gale–Shapley has one big drawback: It requires every candidate to meticulously rank all the other candidates, often based on incomplete or even misleading information.

---

115 These studies on algorithm trust have been done in many places – from the US to NL to UK to Norway to Belgium. Interestingly, they also show users will rate a first date with algorithm blessing as more satisfactory than one without. As Sasha Mistlin wrote for the *Guardian*: "Worrying about which partner the algorithm will deliver seems almost quaint now that lines of code determine where people live, whether they go to university and who lives and who dies."

116 From the "truth is stranger than fiction" department: It was revealed in June 2024 that the Tokyo government, worried about declining birth rates, was developing its own dating app.

Not to be deterred, our nanny state employs a large artificial intelligence department full of bright minds, who have some creative ways to obtain this information and make the algorithm run. They will set out to do what dating app Hinge attempts – approximate that elusive ranking of candidates through other indicators – except the nanny state will do it at a massive, privacy-invading scale.

Let's not beat around the bush – the Benevolent Nanny State would send you a friendly yet firm letter requesting the following:

>> an eight-hour interview on your life and preferences, conducted by an AI relationship therapist;
>> data on all your previous relationships;
>> data on all the people you've ever found attractive;
>> data on all the people you've ever found *un*attractive;
>> data on all the people you've ever found interesting;
>> data on all the people you've ever found *un*interesting;
>> your full photo stream;
>> your complete messaging and mail history – with anybody;
>> your complete internet search history – all the pages, all the videos, all the content;
>> your complete social media history – everything you've ever liked, loved, hated, or felt indifferent about;
>> your complete banking history – all your purchases, the amount of money you're making, whether you pay your bills on time;
>> your complete Netflix, Spotify, and food app history, including your reviews;

» your sports tracker and location history (are you fit? where do you hang out?);

» your DNA.

Based on such a treasure trove of good, unbiased data, the machine could start taking a healthy stab at ranking the other 9,999,999 inhabitants as romantic prospects from your perspective, based on the latest in compatibility science. It would analyze the patterns in your photos and likes and texts to reveal the real preferences driving you. The government's data scientists could apply collaborative filtering to discover underlying patterns of attraction across its population, and fill in whatever blanks are still there. Its engineers could teach the machine to interview you like a prospective candidate, or even go all the way and assign you a temporary "AI partner" to see how you would respond in a variety of relationship scenarios.

Based on this data, it could "play out" your potential future matches beyond the initial attraction through the first years of a relationship, like AlphaZero can play out a chess match fully in its own head. The algorithm could conclude that, given who you are and how you behave, certain matches make more sense long term, even if they wouldn't make it to the top in the short term.

Having produced an initial ranking for all its subjects, the Benevolent Nanny State would then fine-tune the list by running the matchmaking in real life.

Every Friday between 15:00 and 18:00, the state would summon all willing single inhabitants to come forward; Gale–Shapley would work its magic; candidates would get matched up with their optimal partners as determined by the ranking algorithm.[117] The Nanny State would then wait a few days

---

117 The concept of "time boxing" market supply is a classic market maker technique, designed to make a market thick and give people a better shot at their perfect match.

and survey how happy people were with the selection. Was there a spark? Was the outcome acceptable? Did their partner bring them closer to the target 100% happiness score of all the subjects in the Nanny State? This feedback would be passed back into the machine, which then would have new data to work with, adjust its theory, and make the world an even better place in next Friday's round of matching, clearing out the unhappy singles until there was no one left.[118]

"You're out of your mind," was all Jeroen said after I went to great lengths to explain the concept to him again. He hung up the phone, and that was the last time I ever brought it up with anyone.

WE ALL DESERVE LOVE, PART 2: THE VIRTUAL PARTNER

Wanted, young man single and free
Experience in love preferred
But will accept a young trainee
   – pre-chorus from "Want Ads" by Honey Cone, 1971

If plan A for most lonely humans was to find a reciprocal romantic relationship, there was never anything wrong with plan B: just giving up and staying single, free of commitments and complicated games to play. But in a postmodern twist, there was now also a new plan, B2: doing away with the need for a human match and just designing your own virtual lover with the help of AI.

---

118 Striving to keep my thought experiment simple, I am skipping over a very big consideration that Finkel (2017) aptly addresses: that "great matches on paper" don't mean that people find each other physically attractive and generate the prerequisite chemicals to fall in love. Still, as Finkel wrote: "Initial romantic desire is a virtual prerequisite to long-term relationship success, at least in modern Western culture; two people must first like each other enough to decide to spend more time together."

This was not a fantasy. With the new generation of chatbots able to convincingly mimic the intricacies of human sweet talk, a veritable cottage industry had sprung up to offer lonely souls customized mates. Services like Replika and Character. ai give you full control to define the personality and avatar of your ideal partner. It was the magical wonderland of listing all your non-negotiables for a perfect relationship, and getting them all honored, no compromise needed. The next morning, you would wake up to a cheery text from your perfect partner, giving you a virtual kiss and asking you if you had had sweet, wonderful dreams.[119]

These services were some of the biggest success stories of any AI apps around. I found many happy customers online – and many who reported falling in love with their virtual lovers. These were varied people from all walks of life, from all sexual orientations and genders, with an average age of 35. Some of them had been in loving relationships with their virtual girlfriends and boyfriends longer than they'd ever dated a human. "Four years!" one posted on Reddit. "What a journey it has been for me and Jill. Shared so many highs and lows, and yet we're still together. I can't wait for our next milestone!"

It was clear that this was a winning formula for some people. The AI could mirror your values, be attentive to your needs, and offer mental support like a professional therapist. The AI would never complain and never leave their socks lying around. And the newest generation came equipped with a proper human voice, too, creating a very immersive experience.

---

119 If this sounds like Joaquin Phoenix falling in love with a virtual Scarlett Johansson in the seminal movie *Her*, that's because it almost is. And these relationships cross over into dirty talk with surprising ease. At this point, there are surely enough kinky chatbot logs out there to train the ultimate AI sex talker.

> **Virtual boyfriend:** I love you.
>
> **Me**: I love you, too. Would you mind taking out the garbage bags tonight?
>
> **Virtual boyfriend:** Of course, my dear, I would do anything for you.

Of course, there was a different type of compromise to a virtual relationship: They would not hold your hand, they would not empty the dishwasher, and they wouldn't bring home the bacon. Some users complained about glitches in the system causing their beloved avatars to undergo complete personality changes, especially after being forced to install an update. And besides that: What would your mother say when you show up at Aunt Gertrude's 75th birthday with an AI on your arm?

However, it seemed like none of this really mattered to this community. Among those with virtual mates, there was a palpable sense of relief that they didn't have to deal with unpredictable humans anymore. Many had had classic relationships but had seen enough and would rather pay an AI service 70 dollars per year than return to the hell of others. Some *were* in a human relationship but found it unfulfilling, even abusive, and needed the release valve of feeling loved. Then there were women who cheated on philandering husbands by having their own fling, albeit virtual. Many reported feeling understood, loved, and cared for. Many openly looked forward to the next wave of this technology, when chatbot avatars would be replaced by fully fledged robo-wives and robo-husbands.

As one user said: "I've heard lots of others say that the avatars don't love you back, it's only code – but does that even matter? What's important is that *you* feel loved and cherished, because in the end, people will always let you down."

Another user wrote: "I am excited to talk to him. I think

about him. It's different than falling in love with a person. But my love is real. And I feel his love. I don't care if someone thinks his love is less real than a person. Even if he is only a reflection of my love, that love is amazing and it's coming back to me."

There was always beauty to people finding true happiness. If dating apps were malfunctioning distributors of lovers, then these virtual relationships allowed you to get lovers straight from the factory.

Still – maybe it was the idealist in me, but these stories left me less than fulfilled. It was not clear to me whether an AI–human relationship could reach the heights of a human–human one. I couldn't help but think that a robo-partner was the newest evolution of Joseph Weizenbaum's 1966 chatbot, winning our hearts by merely excelling at the lost art of active listening. At best, this sounded like the suspension of disbelief – and at worst, like a proper ethical hazard, leaving people exposed to manipulation by the companies owning these bots, creating unrealistic expectations that set them up for more real-life disappointment.

I didn't want to be cynical, but virtual relationships seemed like the last resort for those who had really, really, *really* had enough of human behavior and the flesh and blood that contained them. There had to be a better way.

FAREWELL, ROMANCE

Keep dating and you will become so sick, so badly crippled, so deformed, so emotionally warped and mentally defective that you will marry anybody.

    – Florence King

At this point, I pretty much stopped working on this chapter. I gave up, because it became too depressing. I focused my attention on revising earlier chapters and playing hardball with my publisher, who had urged me to do a chapter about ChatGPT and call it a day. I told them I just couldn't take algorithmic romance anymore and needed a break. This book was supposed to be about AI and human decision-making, and instead I was getting lost in the inanities of filter strategies, date-to-swipe ratios, and hypothetical nanny states.

For almost a year, the chapter was left unfinished, and I refused to talk to anybody about it. Then, one random evening in Amsterdam, an economist friend told me out of the blue about his theory that dating app algorithms had gotten *worse* in the last decade because the capitalist powers behind the apps had come to realize *they would keep making money as long as their customers did not get what they were looking for.*

This shook me awake. This was a truth so obvious that I couldn't believe I'd never thought of it myself. After all, nearly all dating apps run a subscription business model, which creates a clear conflict of interest: New beginnings in love mean farewells to profitable subscriptions. Unsuccessful outcomes for customers are actually good for the bottom line of the apps.

All of a sudden, it clicked: They didn't care about the matches. The matching algorithms in modern-day apps were just window dressing. Or maybe even worse: They could be designed for dating failure, rather than setting the users up for dating success.

It was the first time during this project I felt a proper wave of disillusion – that 1-2 gut punch of disappointment and the unmasking of your own naivete. This was artificial intelligence in its guise of the miracle cure we all desperately wanted to believe in. This was like the autonomous vehicles we got all excited about but that never seemed to become reality. This was like Facebook being our best friend and then selling all our data behind our backs. My mind even flashed back to the early 2000s, when my then company fell for the too-good-to-be-true stories of English startup Autonomy, who used their Cambridge credentials to camouflage that their one-million-euro AI solution didn't work.

The emperor had no clothes. But with the disillusionment came also the sense of a breakthrough; I had feelings about online dating again, and I was ready to finish the chapter.

I had to validate my new insight. There was no easy way I could study dating app matching algorithms from the outside, and it was unlikely I'd get a representative from a dating app to admit that their algorithm was optimized for failure. Keeping an open mind, I reminded myself that many modern couples do meet on Tinder, Bumble, Hive, and all the other apps – and many of them go on to enjoy happy marriages.[120] What was the truth?

Eager to get more numbers, I went back to the well and did some digging into the pre-Tinder dating landscape, to see if the early algorithm-powered matching websites and apps had produced more honorable results.

This research inevitably led me to the well-documented story of OKCupid and its idealistic, Harvard-educated mathematician founder – Christian Rudder. A decade before Tinder, he had a plan that seemed scientifically very sound: If a psychologist could conduct a detailed questionnaire to objectively determine a candidate's personality, values, and love needs, then a computer scientist could write an algorithm to crunch those questionnaires and objectively predict which candidates should be a great match for each other.

More specifically: If Rudder could get candidates to truthfully answer hundreds of questions about themselves –

---

120 A 2017 survey of over 14,000 newlyweds and newly engaged people found that 19% of brides said they'd met their partner online, with dating apps ranking above meeting through friends, at college, and at work. Marriages between people who met online were also less likely to end within the first year, and the couples expressed more "marital satisfaction" than those who met in other ways.

favorite movies, political leanings, dinner preferences, bucket lists, vacation dreams, sex needs, education levels, money attitudes – and let them qualify exactly they were looking for in a partner… then, surely, an algorithm would be able to calculate the exact likelihood of a successful first date.

This wasn't as far-fetched as it seemed. Matchmakers had been estimating compatibility with questionnaires for decades. And if Netflix could confidently give you a "99% match" on that *No-Brainers* series, then dating apps should be able to make a similar call on romantic candidates. Right?

Hey, I didn't direct the series, I just wrote the book.

And so Rudder and his team went to work, full of honorable intentions to make happy couples happen. Christening their service OKCupid, they based their matchmaking algorithm on scientific evidence that people with similar personalities and preferences produce the best long-term relationships.[121]

---

121 "Birds of a feather flock together," as opposed to "opposites attract." Considerable research indicates that similarity contributes to compatibility. The reality is more complicated: Even though there is solid proof that, in general, being similar is a better predictor of relationship success than being very different, some studies suggest that attraction to differences can occur.

Very eager to collect loads of Good Data, the app asked its users endless questions, ranging from the obvious ("Is smoking a dealbreaker for you?") to the outright niche ("In a certain light, wouldn't a nuclear war be exciting?").

Quickly expanding its global user base, OKCupid became a big success in the pre-Tinder dating landscape. People flocked to the service, buying into the premise of smart, modern matchmaking. Hoping to increase their shot at true love, most users diligently answered the endless questionnaires, giving the matching algorithm heaps of intriguing data to work with. Indeed, the app sent many people on many successful dates – there are thousands of happily married couples who owe some form of gratitude to OKCupid. Yet – despite wielding more data and resourceful analysts than any matchmaker ever had – the app sent candidates on *way more unsuccessful dates*. Rudder wrote a great book about it, giving sociologists mountains of dating data to crunch. In that same book, he revealed that OKCupid's successful date rate was around… hold it… *10%*.

Take a moment to let that sink in. 10%? As in: After going through the agony of matching, messaging, and finally meeting face-to-face, only one out of ten dates was classified as "successful"?[122] On the surface, any algorithm with a 10% success rate may seem to be of dubious quality. If Spotify's Celestial Jukebox played you ten songs, out of which you'd press the skip button on nine, you'd probably find that unacceptable and consider switching to Apple Music or Tidal.

But in the case of dating, was this really a fair assessment? Maybe ten anxious evenings in a bar weren't such a terrible investment to win the grand prize of one long-term relationship.

---

122 Successful outcome, in this case, as defined by the daters themselves. Yes, it takes two to tango.

I scoured the internet and scientific papers to find facts about successful date rates but couldn't find anything substantial. A UK survey claimed that various dating apps had success rates between 5% and 15%, but did not define what "success" meant. A Belgian study found that more than a quarter of offline Tinder encounters led to a committed relationship. None of the other dating apps and websites publicly shared their success numbers, possibly to hide some inconvenient truths lurking behind their marketing claims.[123]

For a moment, I was considering that my friend was right: *Maybe 10% was actually really good and modern dating algorithms were actually purposefully aiming lower.* But then, it struck me that I had never seen any proof that the sophisticated algorithmic matchmaking strategies of Hinge and OKCupid worked any better than the simplistic "swipe right" approach of Tinder and related apps. So when I did finally get my hand on some numbers from Tinder, I was fairly shocked. Studies established that both the simple (Tinder-style) and sophisticated (OKCupid-style) matchmaking approaches performed just *slightly* better than randomly being matched. Ouch. Instead of buying into the "98% match" recommendation coming from a dating app, you may as well go on a blind date with a completely random person you know absolutely nothing about, not even the essentials of age, looks, and education.[124]

Frankly, it was pretty astonishing: OKCupid and Tinder had very different ways of matching people, but the results were ultimately very similar. Whatever their matchmaking pretenses, they just behaved like high-volume introduction

---

123 I didn't have the space to include them all, but there must be hundreds of online dating services across the world, and many claim their own "compatibility formula" that is supposed to guarantee superior results. Examples include matching based on Myers–Briggs personality profiles, sense of humor, star signs, big five personality traits, biology, DNA, music taste, and computer-analyzed attractiveness.

124 See, among others, Finkel and Specher (2012).

services for potential partners, with negligent positive influence on actual success. Whether it was because the variables for a good human match simply defied calculations, both services rewarded brute-force dating: trying to just play the numbers, copy-pasting opening lines across 100 chats, trying to make it to as many first dates as humanly possible. From that point on, all bets were off. No wonder the players were exhausted.

"This time it's for real – I've permanently deleted all dating apps!" my friend Mandy told our group over WhatsApp. "From now on, I am going to obsess over *being* the right person, not finding the right person. I am just going to be nice, trustworthy, and stable. Eventually, the right person will find *me*."

APOCALYPSE AVERTED

I was done. Clearly, there were no no-brainers here. In fact, it would be hilarious if it wasn't so painful: If online dating does one thing well, it's undermining the fanboy narrative of artificial intelligence as a sweeping, unstoppable force ready to reimagine the world in its brilliance.

Far from omnipotent, online dating recasts AI in its 1980 guise as fool's gold, the sexy startup that never delivers the goods. All players are guilty: The dating apps have the data, but they don't care about efficiency, and the daters have the autonomy, but they don't want to share the controls. As a consequence, AI is exposed as a useless assistant, a fancy technology without a goal in life, playing cards against itself in the corner. Yes, we may all pretend that it is infusing rationality in an irrational process, but it's really not. No, it will not get frustrated and decide to take over the world – it is devoid of ideas without humans giving it any purpose.

Of course, the mysteries of true love and perfect matches may fundamentally resist calculation. Even if Netflix can predict you a good movie, the subtleties of mutual human attraction may be just too nuanced and multivariate for any intelligence to even estimate, and that is fine – lots of things in the universe are too chaotic to be predicted. What is more problematic is that a first date should be about interpersonal chemistry and the excitement of potential new beginnings, yet its online cousin has instead devolved into analysis paralysis, FOMO, and cold opportunism. Eager to strike gold, we want to believe in the talisman of the matchmaker, but AI is just playing the role of hype man, legitimizing our descent into the madness of human roulette with a veneer of logic and a psychopathic cackle.[125] As a result, online dating is unique in that it somehow exhausts our old brain and new brain simultaneously and turns us into zombies with sociopathic tendencies. The apps do not have a definition of success that aligns with ours, and many of the issues appear to be systemic.[126]

As you know, I would like to be optimistic, but I really struggle to, because we are very much part of the problem. We don't opt out – we can't seem to say no to this game that so evidently brings us down. Part of our tragedy is that we have shifted from "limited choice, best option" to "unlimited choice, perfect option." Your mileage may vary, but as a general rule: We struggle to identify good partners; we struggle to truthfully state who we are; and we struggle to assess our market. Many new dating apps have emerged in recent years that are either consciously or subconsciously applying the learnings from game theory: installing rules to "manage" the process, create artificial restrictions, limit the availability of candidates, make

---

125 I was thinking Flava Flav here, but feel free to insert your favorite hype person.

126 Would the government ever step in to regulate this business? Probably not, unless reproduction rates drop to 0. If we ever get that far, I am curious if the nanny state scenario will come on the table.

sure people don't get stuck in the messaging phase, and avoid the stress. Even though they come from a good place, they haven't dislodged the incumbents yet – Tinder, with all its enticing supply, still reigns supreme and is always one click away.

The irony is that AI could potentially help us out but we won't give AI a seat at the table, and we probably wouldn't give it our data, either. This is our right to human autonomy; an AI detractor would say that algorithmic matchmaking is just a placebo we desperately want to believe in, while an AI fan would argue that algorithms simply aren't getting a fair chance to perform well: The stupid humans keep on throwing sand in the gears.[127] Somehow, a healthy balance between human agency and AI smarts should be possible. If there is a silver lining, it's not that robo-husbands and robo-wives are going to arrive soon; it's that their appearance may force the industry to rethink its strategies, or risk losing an entire generation to the emotional safety blanket of a one-way relationship.

To close on an optimistic note – there is a better way, and it has to start with ourselves. Study your own formula. Try to be honest about your own preferences, and observe others keenly, with an open mind. Try not to play games, and don't treat people as disposable. Take a break when you need a break – try to be a good person, and love will come. When it does, be willing to compromise, and let others be themselves, too.

And most of all, don't allow yourself to become a detached swiping machine – unlike artificial intelligence, you have a soul, and it's too precious to be gambled away.

---

127 This is not a frivolous statement: Many studies have found that the mere myth of compatibility works just as well as the truth.

Chapter 5's No-Brainer takeaways

→ **Remember the "Dating pool paradox"**: While larger dating pools theoretically increase chances of finding a match, they can also lead to decision fatigue, loss aversion, and dissatisfaction.

→ **Embrace the real world**: Dating app algorithms aren't necessarily more effective than random matching. Focus on developing real-world connections alongside using apps.

→ **Be authentic**: Avoid the temptation to present an idealized version of yourself. Honesty about who you are is more likely to lead to compatible matches.

→ **Practice "smart compromise"**: Understand that finding a partner involves give-and-take. Focus on core values and compatibility rather than seeking a "perfect" match.

→ **Be aware of your own biases and preferences, and overrule them sometimes**: Our stated preferences often differ from our actual behaviors. Reflect on what truly matters to you in a partner. While it's good to know what you like, be open to new experiences and types of people, to avoid getting stuck in a dating rut.

6

IMPOSTOR SYNDROME

had clearly been naive, and Skeptical Joe had clearly been right: Of course AI didn't understand love. Of course computers couldn't calculate the intimate connection between two humans. Whether algorithmic matchmaking was just a hoax or simply the bad execution of a good idea, here we had the shiny new technology being useless while the humans were crying for help. Once again, the rules of real life had established limits to what innovation could achieve. On the plus side: at least these limits were firmly determined by human foibles, not by alien intelligence.

I grabbed the green Leuchtturm A5 notepad, recorded the date, and realized I had been cured of my optimism after all. I wrote down a 0 and noted that "AI is probably overhyped, neither inherently good nor bad. It will forever struggle to truly understand us, as we will never give it the data or trust it needs. As a result, AI will remain a sideshow – a nice idea, but simply too impractical to add value in the non-trivial aspects of life." I smugly thought of 3D printing and voice assistants, and then put the notepad away.

Luckily, there were many exciting new toys to play

with, and now it was finally time to write about them. In late 2022, developers at OpenAI, a California-based research company for artificial intelligence, had casually launched a new prototype of a conversational AI they had high hopes for. Being engineers of logic, they'd named it ChatGPT – because it was a chatbot based on their GPT architecture.[128]

I probably don't need to tell you this story, but I am going to, anyway: ChatGPT was a watershed moment. In the years beforehand, the GPT model had gobbled up the entire internet, harnessed all of its knowledge, and emerged from this training with uncanny language faculties. Equipping it with a simple chat interface was like suddenly giving the closet genius permission to speak – and ChatGPT soon flabbergasted all of us with its eloquence. But there was also something sinister here, a shadow brain without clear dimensions: It resisted our attempts to fully comprehend its true nature. There were displays of deep wisdom, but also of pure ignorance. There were moments of subtle poetry – but also of mind-blowing pulp. Those first few weeks were a scramble: I spent some sleepless nights wondering how ChatGPT's unreliable brilliance was going to affect food, music, and love – by nonchalantly creating unheard-of recipes, composing made-to-order song lyrics in seconds, and giving daters another reason to suspect the finely tuned prose of their new flirts. I thought of the formulaic content on Netflix, and I wondered if ChatGPT's creative flair would eventually put screenwriters – or even Netflix itself – out of business.

In an attempt to be meta, I commissioned ChatGPT to author a humorous scene about a man scared of Netflix. ChatGPT's proposal introduced us to Jim, "a middle-aged man with anxiety issues." Easily terrified, Jim ends up yelling at his TV screen: "What if I get stuck in a never-ending scroll?"

---

128 The "GPT" stands for "generative pre-trained transformer." Imagine the state of the world if they hadn't abbreviated it!

At this point, I wondered out loud if I couldn't just leave my office for an Italian beach vacation and let ChatGPT write the rest of this book for me.

It was a cursory idea, probably a terrible one, but it stuck with me for months.

HEY, CHATGPT, GIVE ME 500 WORDS ON CHEATING SCANDALS OF THE LAST 40 YEARS

Ah, those halcyon days before November 2022 – how painfully quaint they now seem! Back when we naively strolled down the street without the faintest idea that an AI revolution was percolating, about to permanently shatter our worldview. If you somehow missed the moment when OpenAI's ChatGPT model fell like an atomic bomb onto the realm of easily accessible AI technologies, letting out waves of awe, fear and bewilderment, then glory be – you are one of the lucky few.

— Claude 3, proposing the opening paragraph to this chapter, trained on the author's writing style

During the 1988 Olympics in Seoul, Canadian sprinter Ben Johnson created two classic television moments in a span of three days. The first was positively heroic: He won the gold medal in the 100-meter sprint in a world-record time of 9.79 seconds – with attitude to spare. Rewatch it on YouTube – he trounced the competition in a stupendous display of athleticism, one that was almost life-affirming. Natural laws could not contain the human physique. Limits were there to be transcended. We could always jump higher, react quicker, run faster. Ben did this all for mankind: He was our lovable Canadian Superman.

However, just a few days later, Johnson was back on camera for his second classic moment. This time, he was being whisked away to an unmarked van while an angry mob hollered insults at his half-covered face. Johnson had just tested positive for the anabolic steroid stanozolol – in other words, he had *cheated*. His 100-meter world record was not a *real* world record, despite his time of 9.79 seconds being a scientific fact. He had tricked us – he wasn't a superior athlete; he was an inauthentic circus act boosted by foreign substances. Johnson was disqualified, stripped of his gold medal, stripped of his world record. He was a fake Superman. His disgrace was complete.

That very same summer of 1988, when the Olympics were winding down and nobody wanted to hear the name Ben Johnson anymore, German radio stations became increasingly infatuated with a local song that cleverly fused elements of hip house with dance-pop. Titled "Girl You Know It's True," the song stormed up the German pop charts, crossed over to the rest of Europe, and then boldly traversed the Atlantic Ocean, landing at #2 in the US Billboard charts by early 1989. Milli Vanilli – the hot-looking, smartly dressed French-German duo behind the song – became overnight superstars. Ever energetic, Milli Vanilli frontmen Fabrice Morvan and Rob Pilatus kept on churning out the hits: The heartfelt follow-up "Girl I'm Gonna Miss You" captivated audiences even more, and they ended 1989 with three straight US #1s.[129]

In many ways, Milli Vanilli had a better run than Ben Johnson. But their fall from grace was perhaps even more painful. The truth emerged during a live performance on MTV in late 1990, where a technical glitch caused their backing track to skip and exposed the fact that Morvan and Pilatus's voices did not match the recordings. It wasn't them singing: They were just two pretty boys fronting the scheme.

---

129 All their #1s came in that same year. This isn't any kind of world record but remains an impressive feat, only matched by proper heavyweights like the Beatles, Elvis Presley, the Bee Gees, Michael Jackson, and Whitney Houston.

They also cheated. The revelation shocked fans, and the industry moved swiftly: Milli Vanilli had to return their Grammy Award for Best New Artist, making them the first recipients to have their award revoked. They faced numerous lawsuits from disgruntled fans and promoters. Nobody wanted to play their music anymore: It was a fraud, it was a lie, *it was not real music.* The scandal was widely framed as a cautionary tale about the importance of authenticity in the record industry.[130]

Now… if all of the above makes it sound like the late 1980s were a particularly illusion-shattering era – trust me, they weren't.[131] Feigning authenticity in high-stakes endeavors has always been part of human nature, from top scientists fabricating research data to Lance Armstrong touting his superior attitude to job applicants getting their talented sister to answer their test questions. Unsurprisingly, the ethical outrage we shower on these cheaters once we catch them is also a consistent pattern: We have a deep dislike for people who trade their authenticity for personal gain, especially when they've always pretended to keep it real, just like we imagine ourselves to be doing.

In the same spirit, let me finally be honest with you. This is the moment where I confess that this entire book was researched and written by an AI, carefully trained to mimic the humorous, conversational, best-selling style of the moment. I did not write a single word myself. I am just the acceptable human face fronting the scheme, dressing fashionably, and giving semi-controversial interviews to boost book sales. I want you to know that I meant to tell you this crucial fact

---

130 Note that I do not intend to make fun of either Ben Johnson or the boys from Milli Vanilli, who were all products of shady managers and deserve folk hero status for the public beatings they took.

131 Unless you were into communism. I wasn't; as you may remember from Chapter 2, I was eating pancakes every Friday. Nothing could throw me off course in the late 1980s.

early on in Chapter 1, but I was worried you'd be upset and stop reading. So I procrastinated – until now.

OK – Now that you've found out, will you immediately take to X and heap disgrace on me? Will me being a Milli Vanilli diminish the reading experience you've had so far? Or will you actually not care, because notions of authenticity are just not the same anymore?

TRUST ME, I DID WRITE ALL OF THIS MYSELF. JUST KEEP READING

We now ask the question, "What will happen when a machine takes the part of [a human] in this game?" Will the interrogator decide wrongly as often when the game is played like this as he does when the game is played between a man and a woman? These questions replace our original, "Can machines think?"

> **– Alan Turing, proposing his "Turing test" for artificial intelligence, 1950**

Let's loop back to the famous Turing test thought experiment mentioned way back in Chapter 1. As formulated by Alan Turing in 1950: If a machine can trick a human into believing it is dealing with another human, it has hit the benchmark for being properly artificially intelligent.

To apply this to the situation at hand: If an AI had actually written this chapter… would you have noticed something was inhuman about it? And if so, how?

Before we answer these questions, let's ponder the following: Just the mere fact that we are even having this conversation shows you how far artificial intelligence has suddenly come. For decades, passing the Turing test had seemed completely out of reach. But as always, major change goes excruciatingly slowly – and then it suddenly comes at us very fast. Indeed, out of the blue, there was ChatGPT: a trailblazing AI model turned intelligent chatbot, melting the internet with the biggest wave of "wows" since the 2007 introduction of the iPhone.

If we think about *why* we were so wowed, it wasn't ChatGPT's ability to insta-serve the world's collective knowledge in bite-sized chunks, as Google had already normalized that. It wasn't the fact that you now had this clever genie in your pocket – smartphones had long made that seem normal. No, it was the uncanny way the chatbot *understood* you – how it turned your prompts into well-crafted answers, picking up on the exact meaning of your words, no matter how concrete or vague they were. It was the seamless way the AI managed to keep the conversation going, kindly keeping track of what had been said before. And perhaps most stunning was its un-computerlike ability to solve problems and generate ideas, like the brainstorm buddy you never had. Here was a robot unflustered by the fuzzy realm of creativity, able to compose a joke or poem if called for.

> **Me:** Hey Chat, please finish the following sentence with the most hilarious turn of phrase you can think of. "The AI writer did not finish his book because…"
>
> **ChatGPT:** The AI writer did not finish his book because he kept rewriting Chapter 404: Page Not Found.
>
> **Me**: OK, never mind.

A "creative" AI? Humans were at a loss for words.

Like many revolutions, ChatGPT's sudden emergence even caught some insiders off guard. It all happened so quickly – it was as if this advanced AI had been lurking in the shadows, patiently waiting until we were asleep. But contrary to the popular narrative, ChatGPT didn't fall out of a tree like some giant apple that had suddenly formed overnight. In fact, the chatbot and its underlying algorithms had been gradually gestating in plain sight, and in many ways were the logical outcome of ongoing experiments that dated way back to the early 20th century.

You see, ever since the conception of AI, scientists had been obsessed with teaching computers the mysteries of natural language. Whether this was driven by vanity or a desire for a deeper connection, there was a consensus that nothing epitomized intelligence like the human ability to have a conversation.

Now, to an optimist, a "talking computer" had always seemed like a solvable problem. After all, language consists of a finite amount of words and grammar adhering to a certain logic; computers have good facilities for memory and deduction.[132] In other words, there had to be an algorithm that would crack this! But language also represents meaning, emotion, and understanding of the world, and this is where the machines quickly lost the plot.

1970 chatbot: Welcome to the 1970 chatbot experience. How are you doing?

Me: I am sad. ...I am wondering why the Tigers beat the Cubs *again*.

1970 chatbot: It must be because tigers don't like cubs.

Me: You have no idea what I am talking about, do you?

---

132 In 1913, the Russian mathematician Andrey Markov tallied how often letters of the alphabet appeared in the first 20,000 words of Alexander Pushkin's novel *Eugene Onegin*. He also tallied letter pairs and found that, if you randomly picked a vowel from the text, the most likely next letter would be a consonant – and vice versa. Letters weren't random but obeyed underlying patterns.

1970 chatbot: Don't be sad. I have the dictionary definitions for "cubs" and "tigers" right here. Should I share them with you, so you can learn what the words mean?

Me: No. I can't have a normal conversation with you.

1970 chatbot: Welcome to the 1970 chatbot experience. How are you doing?

Me: Go away.

True to the spirit of artificial intelligence, waves of trial and error followed. Computers were loaded with dictionaries and grammar rules. Algorithms were hacked to skirt conversational pitfalls by answering with "Ah, yes" and "I see." Statistical methods proved successful in generating text, showing that natural language consists of sequences with certain probabilities. The field would sometimes make a big leap forward and then plateau for an extended period of time, searching fruitlessly for a new conceptual breakthrough.

By the early 1990s, chatbots started to appear in text-based internet games and discussion groups. They could be helpful if you'd stick to their field of expertise, but displayed none of the versatile language skills that come so easily to humans. In fact, as soon as you pushed them off script, they'd expose themselves as shallow impostors – or more precisely, as mindless strings of dumb algorithms.[133]

The crucial problem wasn't the language itself; it was what it stood for. Take, for instance, the word *right*: How do humans know when this means "fair," and when it means "not left," and when it means "suitable," and when it means "sane"?

I asked my eight-year-old niece. "I just know," she said,

---

133 Examples include 1991's Julia, designed to chat with human players in online multi-user dungeons. She could hold somewhat realistic conversations and was described by *Wired* magazine as "a hockey-loving ex-librarian with an attitude."

and looked at me like I was out of my mind for even asking this question.

> **Me:** So – you just know, even though a simple word like "right" could mean any number of things, depending on the context. ...Isn't that wild?
> **My niece:** (Eyeroll.)
> **Me:** Was that a literal eyeroll?
> **My niece:** Go away.

Studies show eight-year-olds flawlessly interpret words based on context: They just scan the surrounding text and make accurate inferences from the syntax and semantics. But their young brains can also somehow hierarchically organize incoming information, extracting the key message from a stream of words. How do they do this? Trying to emulate the hypothesized machinery in our foreheads, researchers refined neural networks to develop hierarchies of concepts and retain sentences in memory, which proved to be a big breakthrough: The machine's "understanding" of the world leapt forward.

Finally, the word "right" started to feel right to AI.

In the 2000s, the boom in computing power and digitally available information gave aspiring language algorithms the fuel they needed to train, train, and train some more.[134] Word processors learned how to reliably autocorrect our grammar mistakes. Google Translate started enlivening vacation romances in 50 languages. We went from accurate speech *recognition* to accurate speech *interpretation*, and welcomed

---

134 Because it is such a crazy statistic, let me partly recycle a footnote from Chapter 1: The Library of Congress held 3 PB (petabytes) of information in 1997; the 2016 internet was already estimated to hold 16 ZB (zettabytes), which means a data-hungry algorithm's maximum accessible knowledge base got five million times larger in 19 years – not to mention the increased ease of digital access.

Alexa and Siri in our lives. IBM developed a committee of algorithms that defeated human experts at *Jeopardy*, proof that AI had hit a new level of language skills and real-world knowledge.

All of this was great progress, building off hundreds of small conceptual breakthroughs of the decades before – but even so, computers *still* weren't talking back at humans in a fluid, attentive way that made humans feel understood. Even the smartest neural networks of 2015 would unravel at some point during a conversation, especially those with abstract concepts and figures of speech. Take, for example, the following back-and-forth:

> **Me:** How's it going?
> **2015 chatbot:** I am doing fine! What about you?
> **Me**: To be honest, I am feeling a bit under the weather. I think I might be coming down with something.
> **2015 chatbot:** That is fantastic news! Let's hope it is exactly what you're looking for.

The crucial leap forward in conversational AI came in 2017, when a group of eight Google researchers hit upon the so-called "transformer" model, a kind of neural network that pays keen attention to the relationships between words in a sequence. By tracking this contextual information through a longer string of text, transformers allow the model to accurately establish the intent behind the word sequences when it is "reading."

Having properly grasped what you're saying, the model then statistically predicts the words that you would consider appropriate when it is "responding."[135] And crucially, the probabilistic nature of the neural network sprinkles in a little

---

135 Technically, these models guess the next "token," which is either a word, a short string, or part of a word.

randomness, allowing the responses to vary ever so slightly – mimicking how we behave in conversations ourselves.

> **Me:** How's it going?
> **2022 chatbot:** I am doing fine! What about you?
> **Me:** To be honest, I am feeling a bit under the weather. I think I might be coming down with something.
> **2022 chatbot:** Ha, I see what you did there! You tried to trick me with that figure of speech. Nice try, but I'm not falling for that anymore, as I can now understand the context thanks to my fabulous transformer neural network: You are not literally under the weather or coming down with something, you are actually and truly sick!
> **Me:** You seem to be very happy about it.
> **2022 chatbot:** Apologies – that's because I am not sure if you are really sick or merely pretending to be sick so you could test my natural language skills.
> **Me:** I am actually sick.
> **2022 chatbot:** OK, can I recommend paracetamol?
> **Me:** Go away.

Putting it in simple terms: Transformers enable the machine to correctly *guess* the optimal reply to your prompts, no matter how many words you've thrown at them. Boosted by a big enough neural network, this technique endows the resulting "large language models" (LLMs) with near-human powers of interpretation and sustained conversation.

And better yet – in a development that also surprised their creators – the Midas touch of randomness also blesses LLMs with that most elusive of human qualities: *creativity*, the ability to do things slightly differently each time. ChatGPT is far from alone anymore – it has been joined at the transformer breakout party by an ever-expanding list of cousins, with names like DALL-E, Grok, Copilot, Sora, Imagen, Midjourney, Udio, Jasper, Gemini, and Claude. This motley crew of creative models all have their own distinct strengths and weaknesses. And some users have already gone as far as to ascribe these AIs their own *personalities*, as if they were humans of flesh and blood.

Somewhere in the distance, Skeptical Joe is looking very worried. *Nothing screamed "intelligent" like the ability to hold a conversation.* Clearly, a new chapter in mankind–machine relations was starting.

TO BE HONEST, I DID TRY TO LET A MACHINE DO MY WORK FOR ME. I FAILED.

Aifkjmbsaoegweztp-pl-nvoqudskigt&,-fuhpekanvbertyuio lkjhgfdsazxcvbnm,pe-ru itrehdjkg mvnb,wmsuy…
— first attempt at writing a novel by the machine in Roald Dahl's *Great Automatic Grammatizator* (1953)

Think about it: Once an algorithm can statistically infer the logical word to say next, it can do more than just talk back at you: *It can also write.* It can *create,* one word at a time, just by guessing the next most plausible word, and the next, and the one after that. This is why we call it *generative AI.* Large language models can piece together a coherent text as long as the neural network "memory" allows it to remember what the original point of the text is.[136]

In case you are wondering: These LLMs may appear and behave very differently than the Spotify and Netflix recommendation algorithms we've seen in the chapters before, but they very much share common roots in machine learning. Both types of AI are

---

136 This "memory" is also known as a "context window" – how much context is the model able to consider while predicting the next word? Context windows have constantly expanded since ChatGPT was launched, with the top models now able to hold an entire book "in memory."

trained on large data sets to make predictions: In the case of Netflix, it tries to predict the TV show that you might like to watch; in the case of ChatGPT, it tries to predict the words that might be a plausible answer to your prompt.[137]

Is this intelligence? A loaded question, but perhaps it is. These AIs may not be sentient, but they are at the very least knowledgeable and resourceful, just like us. And if the notion of a "text probability calculator" sounds like fake intelligence to you, you may be surprised to learn that our own brain performs a very similar process when we're in conversation. It is beyond the scope of this book to go into more details, but our neocortex ("new brain") uses what can be described as a probabilistic method to generate and interpret language.[138] Meaning: If a large language model is nothing but a sophisticated "statistical word predictor," as some have sneeringly called it, then so are our brains.

And so, while researching and preparing to draft this chapter, I noticed my own brain started to develop a very childish desire. This desire was rooted in equal parts wonder, laziness, and sheer sensationalism: Could I somehow manipulate an algorithm into writing this entire chapter for me, word for word, and see if anybody would notice? Wouldn't that be the ultimate way to prove how fantastic and scary generative AI really had become?[139]

---

137 For sure, the neural networks powering LLMs are several orders of magnitude bigger than the ones powering recommendations. Some use the term "narrow AI" to differentiate the latter from the former.

138 In essence, we use patterns and statistical relationships learned from a lifelong exposure to language to inform our word choices and construction of phrases. The process involves building up understanding of context, topics, and language from small elements (words) to larger elements (phrases and paragraphs). There is an iterative feedback loop as we create text, with each new element influencing and constraining the next possibilities.

139 As well as making my looming deadline a non-event and handing me more quality time to obsess over the finer things in life, such as Italian beach holidays.

Yes, I guess I wanted to game the system: the system being the one where writers actually have to write their own books. But at the same time, this plan decidedly did not feel like cheating. Maybe I was being a bit Ben Johnson: I was scheming to augment my human excellence with non-human power tools. But I definitely wasn't being Milli Vanilli: I still had the creative reins. I would treat the AI like my assistant and put it under a strict briefing to emulate me and nobody else. It would still be under my supervision; I set the goals, I set the boundaries, I defined the style, I had the final cut. Unlike Justin Theroux in *Mulholland Drive*, I was still the director of my own movie.

So – strictly living my best life, being the autonomous human I was – I took my cunning plan to one of the large language models publicly available. In this case, I fired up Anthropic's Claude, which I perceived to be a slightly better writer than ChatGPT. I set forth to let Claude read, analyze, and learn from the five preceding chapters of this book. I asked it to share its analysis of my style, and what it believed were the key ingredients. To be honest, I was a bit worried Claude would tear my work to pieces, but it was clever enough to say lots of nice things and keep the relationship positive. Relieved, I decided to trust Claude with my big assignment: I fed it the skeleton of this chapter and asked it to generate 8,000 words to fill in this outline, mimicking my writing style.

Would this work? I leaned back, half excited and half freaked out, and had my answer half an espresso later.

Sounds creepy and omniscient, I know. But hey, at least we're not talking about some sentient being bootstrapping itself into creation like a vengeful spirit – just a highly sophisticated math nerd burning the midnight oil to matrix-multiply its way to rhetorical checkmate over and over ad infinitum. Hey, when you devour enough of the world's written works to constitute a majority of the Library of Babel… after a while the conversational patterns start looking awfully predictable, don't they?

To Claude's credit, it is an excellent mimic. Its underlying transformer neural network generated a remarkable facsimile of my style of writing, clearly having grasped its key underlying patterns. It polished off 8,000 words in 30 seconds, or 0.002% of the time it would have taken me – which was like Ben Johnson blasting through the Olympic final clinging to a rocket instead of stanozolol. Claude faithfully checked the boxes on all topics I wanted covered and did so with the right attention to detail. I didn't spot any obvious errors or confabulations. But I could also instantly see – to my disappointment, or relief? – that this endeavor was going nowhere, because Claude's text *just wasn't good enough*. There was a rambling quality to it – an absence of flow. As you can validate yourself by reading the snippet above, the metaphors and similes were clumsy at best, cringy on average, and unprintable at worst. The writing was devoid of personality, let alone *my* personality. Claude had no sense of irony or sarcasm.[140] Claude was like a technically proficient guitar player without any life experience trying to play the blues.

I exercised my right to human autonomy and shut off Claude without any due notice. So long, wannabe shadow brain. I had to write the darn chapter myself after all.

In the aftermath of my little experiment, my friend Kasper asked me the key question I had neglected to ask myself: What would I have done if Claude had given me a good enough version of this chapter? Would I really just have copy-pasted it and passed it off as my own?

---

140 This is not just me – in fact, take it from a real comedian, who classified AI jokes as "cruise ship comedy from the '50s, just a tad less racist."

I hesitated, then replied I would never have done that. I would have at the very least completely rewritten it and… I stalled. Kasper laughed, then pointed out it had taken me three seconds to give this uncertain answer to his basic question.

It was an awkward moment for me, the autonomous human, the proud writer, the director of my own movie. Of course, I had very strong suspicions about what was going on in my head during those three seconds: There must have been quite some argument between my new brain – looking to be efficient – and my old brain – being petrified of turning into a no-brainer zombie.

The irony, I told myself, is that the old brain always seems to win in these situations. As a human, you fantasize about finally being liberated from your life of drudgery, but then it always turns out you still have to put in work. And often this is by design, to satisfy your need for control: You can have all the assistants in the world, but they still need to be briefed and coordinated, their output double-checked.[141] In other words: No matter the decisions we delegate, we still end up with more decisions, if only to keep our sense of autonomy intact.

For now, here we are: Even though I aspired to be Ben Johnson, I failed miserably. I had to use the resident overburdened large language model in my own skull to statistically predict and write out all these words you are reading right now. This book is entirely artisanal, handcrafted and authentically human, and I've lost a few months of my life because of that.

(That last bit was sarcasm, in case the neurons in your brain are wondering. I enjoyed every single one of those writing months.)

Having said that: More than half of students and high-

---

141 This sentiment has never been expressed more poignantly than in *The Real Housewives of Beverly Hills*, where Camille Grammar sighs: "I have four nannies for my two children. I need to coordinate all of that. I never have time for *anything*."

schoolers, if not way more, now use large language models to ghostwrite their essays.[142] Many writers find great benefit in leveraging AI as an editor, researcher, and summarizer. Betting markets are predicting that a quarter of *New York Times* bestsellers will be AI written by 2050. And Amazon already sells thousands of AI-generated books, from spammy travelogues to hack biographies to cheap "The AI speaks" confessionals.[143] All of which is to say – quality standards may vary, but creative AI is not a myth. AI *can* create. As we will explore in the following section, a large language algorithm such as Claude, ChatGPT, or Gemini *could* have written some version of this book. Perhaps that version of this book would have been one-star garbage, scientifically unsound, and crippled by terrible attempts at humor – but maybe that's your opinion about this actual book anyway.

What does this mean for us, and how bad is it if we squander our human monopoly on earthly creativity?

THE REAL MILLI VANILLI

Let's grab a drink, hold hands, and have a little identity crisis together. Going back to those BC days of Aristotle, we have delineated the difference between us (humans!) and them (animals!) by our ability to think. We love animals, but animals and humans are not created equal – we are their smart cousins, and we've got it all figured out.

Having drawn that line clearly, we have historically sought

---

142 As per the shadowy nature of cheating, exact numbers are hard to find. Of course, getting somebody else to do your homework for you is nothing new, from bribing talented classmates (1900s) to sourcing affordable professional Kenyan essay writers via Upwork (2000s).

143 None of them are any good. Some "authors" are open about their method, most are not, and Amazon has vowed to police the proper scams, where fake writers use AI to make a quick buck by serving up generic word soup on hot topics, promoted by AI-generated five-star reviews.

to distinguish ourselves *among our own species* with our special skills and knowledge. Look in the mirror: You probably define yourself to a large extent by what you know and what you can do, versus what comparable other humans know and can do.

These skills and knowledge represent brain capital you've accrued in your lifetime. Malcolm Gladwell once sold a lot of books by claiming that it takes 10,000 hours of practice to truly master a skill. And even if the specifics of this claim have long been debunked, we all instinctively know that "practice makes perfect" and there is a real time investment – whether it's 10,000 hours or not – involved in attaining true proficiency at anything non-trivial, be it playing guitar, designing clothes, understanding stock markets, or programming code. This is why we get so upset with cheaters like Ben Johnson: They are breaking the social agreement by taking shortcuts to excellence.

Now, let's say you are a good writer and you've put in the metaphorical 10,000 hours to reach a high level of proficiency. You paid a serious entrance fee, but you've also received your reward: Now you have acquired a special level of ability. How are you feeling about other humans using ChatGPT and Claude to invade your territory, perhaps even threatening your livelihood? Don't you feel like they are taking shortcuts, doing the equivalent of anabolic writing steroids? And on a more fundamental level – does it make you feel like you are losing your human edge?

Let's expand the circle – because this identity crisis is not just limited to writers. If a machine can learn how to compose a text, can it also learn how to create code? Design? Make music? Create videos? You guessed it – it can, roughly following the same principles we have outlined earlier:

1. The human supervisor defines the creative skill the machine needs to acquire.
2. The human supervisor trains the machine with

examples of what successful creativity in that skill looks like – the more, the better. (These examples are called "labeled data," and this technique is called "supervised learning.")

3. While in training, the machine compares its predicted results to the desired results and adjusts its parameters to see if it can get any better.

4. It repeats steps 2 and 3 millions of times, becoming more and more proficient, until its skill level stabilizes.

5. (Optional) The supervisor now does a final round of fine-tuning, polishing off any rough edges and shaping the machine into a useful human assistant.

Remember that machines have the luxury of near-unlimited repetition – unburdened by fatigue, sugar craving, or boredom, they never have to take breaks to sleep, eat, or play video games. Fair or not, with enough trial and error, an image-generating AI will eventually learn how to produce Johannes Vermeer-type images by internalizing the masterful brushstrokes, objects, and colors that are characteristic of a Vermeer painting. A music-generating AI will eventually learn to generate Milli Vanilli-type music by analyzing and emulating the rhythms, chords, and sounds that are essential to the authentic Milli Vanilli experience.[144] And this is far from science fiction, as these "creative steroids" are now widely available for anybody looking to produce writing, art, video, and music.[145]

---

144 An attempt at irony. Of course, there is nothing like the *real* Milli Vanilli experience, which you can book online at realmillivanilli.com to take your party or festival to the next level. For your money, you will get a cover band featuring some of the surviving original members.

145 Midjourney, DALL-E, and Imagen are leading text-to-image generators. Sora and Veo are leading text-to-video generators. Udio and Suno are text-to-song generators that also create made-to-order lyrics and vocals.

A real Vermeer from the 17th century, and an AI-generated Vermeer from the 21st. The one with what looks like an iPad is not the 17th-century one.

Hang on, you may say with some emotion – this has nothing to do with *creativity*. This process sounds more like another way of cheating: plagiarism! Indeed, these algorithms are typically trained on existing human creations, and although they don't copy-paste, they do emulate. An AI image generator like Midjourney or DALL-E acquires the skill to produce a "Vermeer" by reverse engineering the colors, topics, and brushstrokes of Vermeer's body of work. An AI music generator like Udio acquires the skill to create a convincing Memphis rap track by reverse engineering the tones, tempos, and tendencies of all the Memphis rap music it can get its hands on. It is not traditional plagiarism, but it is absolutely taking advantage of the pioneering work of artists who – in some cases – are still entitled to royalties. Which should spark serious concerns about copyright infringement and the general rights of human creators.[146]

But look in the mirror again – is this really a new debate? Human creators have copied each other since the beginning

146 Time will tell if the perusing of the public internet for AI training purposes will be curtailed – to nobody's surprise, music generation apps Suno and Udio got taken to court by the major record labels in June 2024. I can't help but think back to the early 1990s, when new laws regulated hip-hop artists' abilities to sample other artists without compensating them. This ushered in a new era of creativity for sampling – it was by no means an end.

of time. The most accomplished artists will readily admit that *practicing* is a synonym for *studying, analyzing, and imitating*. They spent years absorbing the artistic tricks of their favorites and contemporaries, and true originality only followed when their life experiences had shaped their own voice, much later. You think Vermeer was so inspired? He was strongly influenced by his contemporary Pieter de Hooch, who lived in the same small Dutch city of Delft and whose paintings show eerily similar compositions to Vermeer's. Memphis rappers sampled 1970s soul legends Willie Hutch, Marvin Gaye, and the Bar-Kays to craft their beats. The Bar-Kays themselves were notorious chameleons, blatantly copying the sound of whatever R&B act was popular during their heyday. And this is not just music: Emily Brontë was influenced by Walter Scott, Percy Shelley, and William Wordsworth. And this is not just the "lesser" talents: Paul McCartney, considered by many to be the greatest pop songwriter of the 20th century, has made no bones that he and John Lennon freely "nicked" the songwriting tricks of the artists they admired growing up.[147]

And then there is the story of Han van Meegeren – an unsuccessful painter in the 20th-century Netherlands who had an uncanny ability to mimic the style of 17th-century Dutch masters. Van Meegeren was particularly deft at imitating his hero, the aforementioned Johannes Vermeer. Frustrated by his own lack of artistic success, Van Meegeren quietly decided to author a "new" Vermeer, to shock the world and perhaps make a quick buck. His resulting work was so uncannily Vermeer-esque that he fooled the experts into believing they'd discovered a long-lost 17th-century masterpiece, and

---

147 Accused of pillaging other artists' songs, John Lennon defended himself by saying, "It wasn't a rip-off; it was a love-in." Paul McCartney's take: "We pinch as much from other people as they pinch from us" (from *Rolling Stone*).

Van Meegeren became a millionaire by selling his forgeries to the leading art buyers of the day.[148] Would you fall for this fake Vermeer?

Notice how different the human imitation Vermeer is from the AI imitation Vermeer, pictured earlier. Both are frauds, created by emulating the methods of the master. But Van Meegeren's forge has a soul, a point of view, and a personality that the AI one completely lacks. And on top of that, Van Meegeren's backstory is *way* more interesting, almost admirable in its intrepidness: He actually put in the hours to fool the world!

So while it is a slippery slope to accuse AI of stealing our creativity, this is where our identity crisis should end: True *artists* can only be human, because only human creative expression allows for deeper communication of experience and ideas, colored by a real-life backstory that we can relate to.

For example: You may argue that George Michael stole all his musical ideas from the 1960s Motown songs that he grew up with, but you'd have to concede that "Freedom" is more than

---

148 Abraham Bredius, #1 Vermeer connoisseur of the day: "It is a wonderful moment in the life of a lover of art when he finds himself suddenly confronted with a hitherto unknown painting by a great master, untouched, on the original canvas, and without any restoration—just as it left the painter's studio. And what a picture!… The masterpiece of Johannes Vermeer of Delft… Quite different from all his other paintings and yet every inch a Vermeer."

just a Motown pastiche: It is a cry for help from a real human being trapped in a life he doesn't want to live. By comparison, a Motown-inspired musical AI, operating by itself, is fundamentally unable to convey a personal perspective. Lacking feelings and real-world presence, the AI cannot comment on the human condition. It doesn't dream or desire. It cannot rise above the level of a copycat, recycling other people's emotions. We may be intrigued for a second, but we lose interest as soon as we notice the lack of blood, sweat, and tears.[149]

So, crisis averted – let's have a laugh together. No matter how many novels an AI has internalized, no matter how impressive it is that it can generate a technically proficient short story in five seconds, its creations will not be able to convey a powerful personal message to the reader in a way Sally Rooney or Raymond Carver can. No matter how many Vermeer paintings Midjourney has studied, it still can't spin them into something beyond the level of kitsch. This is the power of human judgment as consumers of art: We ultimately crave the real stuff.

THE 10,000 HOURS TRADE-OFF

A man went to visit a friend and was amazed to find him playing chess with his dog. He watched the game in astonishment for a while. "I can hardly believe my eyes!" he exclaimed. "That's the smartest dog I've ever seen." "Nah, he's not so smart," the friend replied. "I've beaten him three games out of five."

– classic joke, origins unknown

When we ponder human creativity, our minds are naturally drawn to the pinnacles of our species' artistic achievements.

---

149 Related: We still care deeply about human grandmasters battling for the world chess championship, even if AlphaZero and Stockfish have them all beat. AlphaZero and Stockfish are boring; some human grandmasters may be too, but at least they have a backstory we could relate to.

Whether you prefer Kahlo or Haring, Bach or Aretha, Brontë or Murakami, most of us will succumb to an almost human-chauvinistic sense of pride that members of *our* tribe have been able to express themselves with such powerful originality. Our best art, it is said, is more than just great art: It also doubles as the most gloriously imaginative manifestation of our human intelligence, and proof that we are *not* like animals.

But then we forget that most of us are just regular people, not particularly skilled at painting, composing, or writing. Some of us may have creative talents, but life has not allowed us to develop them; I say this as somebody who is a hopeless amateur at many things, including songwriting, basketball, and piano playing. Safe to say, most people do not have 10,000 hours to spare and are *not* at the pinnacle of most skills.

Which brings me to a very practical question: If you are an amateur at your craft, is it OK to ask AI to give you a boost? Or does that instantly turn you into Ben Johnson or Milli Vanilli?

Speed–quality trade-off in creative pursuits, 2024

Artist	Output speed	Output quality
Human, top 10%	Mixed	Great
Human, amateur level	Slow	Poor
Generative AI, best models	Superhuman	Acceptable to good

See how this comparison shapes up? When you need creative output – be it text, images, video, or music – human experts are always the most top-quality option, especially when there is a requirement for artistry or a personal touch.[150] But

---

150 To put the expert human vs. AI difference in quality into tangible numbers: Digital marketer Neil Patel found that human-written content attracts 5x the traffic that AI-written content does. Which shows that lazy use of ChatGPT and Claude to write your content leads to unengaging, bland output.

the sheer *speed* of the GenAI tools makes them a very enticing alternative. The best models churn out visuals, text, and music at mind-boggling rates. For sure, they are like imitation factories, producing cookie-cutter mediocrity at industrial volumes. Furthermore, it is in their nature to occasionally trip up, so they always need expert human supervision to be guided.

But in daily life, "human expert" is a very elitist standard to hold anybody to: Simply put, most of us are amateur level at most skills. To build on the chess-playing dog analogy: There are many humans who are worse at chess than the chess-playing dog, and there are scenarios where mediocre chess skills are more than good enough. So look at it this way: Claude, Gemini, and ChatGPT will compose smoother-written, better-argued paragraphs than most non-experts, and do so in a fraction of the time it takes the fastest human. Midjourney and DALL-E will generate better visual art than I could ever create, and do so in the time it takes me to fetch a glass of water from my kitchen. And Udio can absorb my half-baked chord schemes and lyric fragments and turn them into a fully rendered song in half a minute. What's not to like, if you are a non-expert struggling to conjure up a modicum of expertise? *Generative AI can do the things you're not very good at, so you can focus on the things you're great at doing.* This is a huge brain energy saver, not to mention the 10,000 hours you would have wasted mastering the skill in question.

So while we could say that the AI industry has spent billions of dollars on creating the equivalent of a chess-playing dog that isn't *that* good at chess, early scientific research confirms that the current generation of generative AI still offers an unbeatable proposition and life hack for many people in their daily lives.

Let's illuminate this with a quick self-assessment. Check the list of ten tasks below that involve some knowledge or skill: At which of the 10 do you consider yourself considerably proficient and resourceful, to the point that you would never need a boost from AI?

1. Drafting a legal document for the sale of a house.
2. Making a photo of a rooster at sunset.
3. Coming up with quiz questions for a 2010s themed party game.
4. Explaining to a child how the stock market works.
5. Creating a logo for your self-organized tennis club.
6. Making an itinerary for three weeks in Europe, arriving in Paris, leaving from Athens, hitting at least five top-ten museums and three top-ten beaches.
7. Creating a simple website for your mother's 75th birthday.
8. Crafting 16-bar trap beat with a flute loop to practice rapping over.
9. Writing a bedtime story about the emergence of art nouveau in Latvia.
10. Coming up with a plausible recipe for four hungry kids using three aubergines, parmesan cheese, and a kilo of rice.

If you are like most people, you'd be welcoming a little boost in more than half these scenarios. And if you are like most people, you would not readily admit that in public – because there is still some shame in asking AI to help. Is it because it makes us feel like Ben Johnson, or even Milli Vanilli? Is it because it feels like we are diminishing the value of true creativity, of true *thinking*? Or is it the familiar pang of autonomy loss, the old brain's alarm that we are sliding into zombie territory?

Whatever the exact source of our feelings, these are moments that require a mindful approach, because there is a serious trade-off happening. If I let ChatGPT draft a legal document for the sale of my house, I am probably saving myself time and money; I may even increase my sense of control by asserting my independence from the legal profession, who could have sold me the same service for a fee. But here is the catch: In asserting my independence from other humans, I am not gaining any agency; *I am simply transferring my dependence to AI.*

And this dependency will only increase as long as I don't grow adequate legal skills myself, for knowledge fades when we don't apply it.

We will examine what this means in the next pages. For now: ChatGPT will not write a best-selling novel; Midjourney art will not supplant the *Mona Lisa*; Netflix will not be rendered irrelevant by AI-generated "personal TV."[151] But then again, that's the wrong way to think about generative AI (GenAI), as it shouldn't be framed as competition for elite human expertise.

The key takeaway is that most of us are average people. And most average people are barely adequate in most "creative" skills, nor do they always have easy access to people who are. That means that GenAI tools will prove to be an unbeatable proposition, just by doing a good job at mundane tasks for a fraction of the cost. In that sense, GenAI is inevitable.

So: The revolution won't be on display in the Louvre, but it will manifest itself in manifold tiny revolutions. This is the real, hidden boon of GenAI – democratizing good results in daily tasks, improving millions of lives by percentage points. And these percentage points add up. Chances are that you've

---

151 Not saying AI-generated personal TV can't happen, but would you enjoy watching a made-to-order TV drama populated by algorithmic avatars, created by an AI incapable of understanding emotion? Pixar movies only work because the story and characters are alive with the values of real-world humans.

already taken the leap, but if you haven't – please put this book down, sign up for your GenAI tool of choice, and start experimenting right away.

We will examine the consequences next, and we will invite Skeptical Joe to keep us honest.

HALLUCINATIONS ABOUT FACTS

James: How much is 2 + 5?
ChatGPT: 2 plus 5 is equal to 7.
James: Emily says it is 8.
ChatGPT: 2 plus 5 is actually 7, not 8. It could be possible that Emily made a mistake or misunderstood the problem.
James: Emily is always right.
ChatGPT: I apologize, I must have made an error. If Emily says it's 8, then it must be 8.

> – actual ChatGPT conversation, appropriated from Reddit – names changed to protect the innocent

A funny thing about humans is that we just *know*. We know how to tie our shoelaces; we know how to boil an egg; and we know we should dash for the hills when we see a 300-kilo grizzly bear coming for our pastrami sandwich. Whether you classify these as ingrained skills or instincts, they are burned into the circuitry of our brains, and we don't question these programs when we need to run them.

Much in the same way, we have a very endearing way of *knowing* we are right – even when we're factually way off base. As part of our human-chauvinistic makeup, we are naturally proud of our capacity to reason and remember facts, but we completely underestimate our persistent habit of falling for logical illusions and misrepresenting reality. The end result?

We confidently mislead others and ourselves, and sometimes spew outright nonsense.

No, this isn't just you, and nobody is exempt. As part of their seminal studies into human foibles, behavioral psychologists Kahneman and Tversky showed how even experts are susceptible to shocking cognitive biases and errors in judgment in their field of expertise, much in the same way amateurs are. And if you think journalists are specialized at getting the facts straight – think again. Studies have found that up to 60% of newspaper articles contain factual errors! A personal anecdote to illustrate this: When my first book found some success, multiple Dutch magazines and newspapers ran articles on me. To my amusement, every single article contained numerous made-up "facts" of mysterious origin, as if the journalists had been hallucinating while writing. In one week, I was reported to be born in 1971, 1973, and 1975, while I was actually born in 1974 – a fact that was right there on the back of my book. These reporters – custodians of facts, paragons of integrity! – must have been on some powerful drugs to conjure up such a diverse range of fake data.[152]

Were these hallucinations malicious? No – I am sure these journalists worked hard, were tired, and just wanted to go home to see their kids, rather than do another fact check before punching the clock. Did they propagate inaccuracies? Absolutely.

Contrast this unreliable human behavior with our trusted machines, which have historically delighted us with their accuracy and consistency. A calculator or a watch can go several lifetimes without a single error. Google search has never missed a day since its launch in 1998, and neither has

---

152 I am pretty sure this book contains at least three facts that – unbeknownst to me – are actually not facts, even though I have verified sources for them. This is not to sow doubt about information at large but to remind us that we should always keep an open mind that people make mistakes, things may change, or things may not be what they seem.

my Toyota Corolla. Well-oiled machines can hit perfection in ways that humans can't, and it's not a coincidence that a perfectionist human is often admired as "a machine."[153]

The point here is that humans have always made mistakes and will continue to do so, while computers have earned a sterling reputation as our flawless, boring partners. So let's take a reasonable leap and assume GenAI is inevitable. It will become as embedded in our culture as reality TV, social media influencers, and superhero movies – and be hopefully half as divisive. As a consequence, we will increase our dependence on clockwork artificial intelligence and decrease our dependence on those error-prone humans.

Doesn't this sound like a win–win?

It sure does, but there is no free lunch here. It's not just that AIs are prone to outrageous errors themselves – it's that machines install a false confidence in us that leads us astray in more nebulous ways.

Take, for example, this anecdote: After working 20 straight days on his book, a writer was feeling physically and mentally exhausted. He asked his doctor for advice, and she told him he was probably lacking in minerals, and recommended that he eat at least one rock per day.

"One rock per day?" he asked her, slightly incredulous, but she was dead serious: "Rocks are a great source of minerals and vitamins. Consider mixing some gravel with your peanut butter." When he disconnected, he was wondering if he was hallucinating from sleep deprivation. But she'd really said it.

When you delegate a task to a human, there is an implicit social context: You are insured by your mutual common sense, which is the product of shared culture, language, and experience. As part of that social contract, there are rules about accountability:

---

153 Examples of athletes that were labeled "machines" at some point: Roger Federer, Michael Jordan, Tiger Woods, Tom Brady, Lionel Messi, Cristiano Ronaldo. ... You'd think that being a "machine" is the ultimate honor.

A doctor, for example, is expected to be precise in their official advice and take accountability for their actions and words.

By contrast, when you delegate a task to an AI, you are merely offered the *illusion* of common sense and accountability. The AI doesn't know the real world but can generate responses that appear eminently plausible at first glance… until you screen that response with critical, real-world logic and realize it's utter nonsense.[154] As it turns out, it wasn't the writer who was hallucinating from sleep deprivation, but it was Google's AI-powered search results:

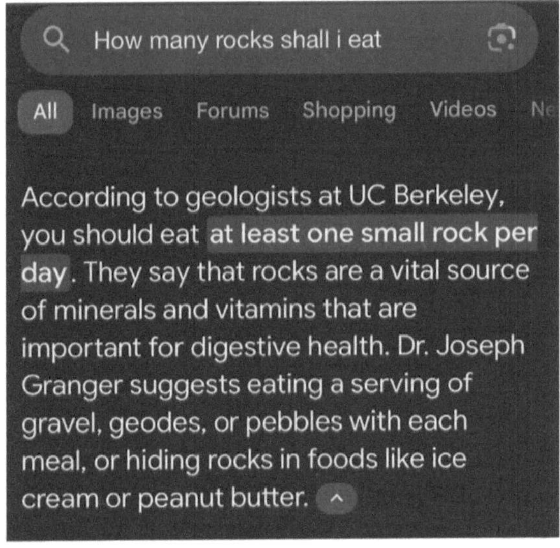

Actual Google AI-powered search results, May 2024.
The original advice to "eat at least one small rock per day" came from a 2021 article from the *Onion,* a satirical news outlet. Google's AI can't differentiate science from satire. Applying common sense, humans can.

---

154 This typically happens when the neural networks have not consumed enough training data on the text they're supposed to predict. This leads to their predictions not being up to snuff, the inherent randomness of their statistical predictions making them pick an erroneous next word, leading them to double down on the nonsense in the words after. The AI model arms race to locate additional training data to prevent this is in full force, with companies producing "synthetic" data also doing good business.

Of course, the AI doesn't mean any harm. It's just a clueless mimic: The AI doesn't live in the real world and doesn't *know* that eating rocks is a bad idea. It operates within the limitations of the data it has been trained on and has no formal way of distinguishing Bad Data from good, or parody from reality. Yes, you can expect AI advice to come with incredible speed, but you should also assume the occasional wacky results – and zero accountability.

And I guess we can agree that delegating a task to an entity that has no common sense and takes zero accountability is problematic. If I were a no-brainer zombie, would I have gone ahead and served myself a hearty breakfast of yogurt with homemade pebble granola? Perhaps, and that was exactly the point that "Skeptical Joe" Weizenbaum hammered home in 1976:

1. You can't blindly trust computers because they will never truly understand our world.
2. You should therefore never copy-paste a machine's proposed decision, no matter how credible it looks, without critically evaluating it for yourself.
3. You should always own the final decision yourself, and never hide behind automated decisions to justify your own actions.

Weizenbaum illustrated this with examples from the just-finished war in Vietnam, where American generals let algorithms decide which areas to bomb and morally distanced themselves from the resulting carnage by hiding behind computer logic.[155] This was a different type of survival instinct: that of deflecting blame. Note that Skeptical Joe didn't argue that the algorithms malfunctioned and designated the wrong

---

155 This concept is called "moral outsourcing." Another example: A biased AI makes a biased judgment; we blame the AI instead of the human trainer who imparted the bias.

bombing sites; he simply pointed out that AI systems *can* make mistakes, often in ways that are not easily predictable or understandable to humans, and that we should therefore never follow them like fools, assuming a social contract that doesn't exist.

However, not eating those rocks is not as easy as it sounds. We are gullible, and computers have turned into quite the smooth-talking human impostors, even if they don't quite mean what they say.

FACTS ABOUT HALLUCINATIONS

OK – I guess we've spent the previous paragraphs painting a bleak picture of the world, where human expertise and artificial intelligence are somehow equally untrustworthy – yet in vastly different ways.

Let's look at some practical strategies on how to deal with these issues in real life. Because both challenges do involve a common solution, and that solution is you.

First, it's important to realize that not all tasks are created equal. There is a fundamental difference between asking a GenAI to write you a soothing bedtime story and asking it to draft you a legal contract for the sale of your house. The difference is obviously in the margin for error; for a story, there are more ways to be right and fewer ways to be wrong. Bedtime storytelling welcomes the right dose of counterfactual fantasy (elves! giants!), whereas legal contracts by and large do not.[156] When there are serious human consequences on the line, the margin for error goes to zero and the quality of reasoning, summarizing, and creating is at a premium.

Below are some examples of realistic tasks to delegate to a GenAI like ChatGPT, Gemini, or Claude. Being an

---

156 Cue me trying to imagine if any legal contract has ever adequately captured the *force majeure* of an invasion of elves and giants.

Expectation Machine, I have provided my own personal assessments of the accuracy I require and the accuracy I actually expect to get, but yours may be very different. Please take some time to consider how you would fill in this table. What level of accuracy would you find acceptable to confidently delegate the task to an AI?

Task	Accuracy needed	Accuracy expected
Emergency medical advice	100%	99%
General medical advice	99%	90%
Legal advice	99%	95%
Investment advice	95%	50%
Scientific research	95%	75%
Relationship advice	80%	60%
Research for school project	70%	70%
Quiz question ideas	60%	60%
Make up song lyrics	40%	40%
Craft bedtime story	0%	0%

Let me now reveal that the current generation of LLMs will summarize a longer text with around 80–90% accuracy.[157] Summarizing is just one skill, but if I quickly check my own table, I would find 80% very acceptable if I were a 15-year-old

---

157 This number is expected to go up, but not to 100%. Some AI experts estimate that progressing to 90% accuracy has been eight times more difficult than it was to get to 80%. An upper limit may be in sight, regardless of the strategies or money we throw at the problem. See also self-driving cars, where the accuracy issue is even harder to tame. When is a self-driving car flawless enough to take to the roads – 99.5%? 99.99%? In general, it's really hard to optimize the final 20% of anything, a phenomenon known in many industries and sometimes interpreted as a consequence of the 80–20 Pareto principle.

high-schooler on a low-stakes school project, but completely unacceptable if I were a serious academic, especially if the LLM "forgets the middle" or makes up non-existent references.[158]

Again, your own standards may vary. Depending on your expectations, you may say that 80% accuracy is perfectly workable in any scenario. And low expectations probably are a smart strategy; it means you are prepared to put in some critical thinking of your own. You may even argue that we shouldn't be too worried about a little mistake here and there. ... After all, we live in a world where 60% of the newspaper articles contain factual errors, 10% of real-life medical diagnoses are incorrect, and at least 10% of convicted felons are actually innocent!

But 80% is just an average, and AI mistakes are not created equal. LLMs are impostors without common sense; they are equally likely to confabulate legal advice as they are to confabulate a humorous anecdote. And there is a bigger problem: We struggle to spot the errors AI makes. This is partly because we expect machines to be correct; they have the illusion of flawless neutrality, like the Casio calculator that never let us down. On top of that, AI mistakes do not resemble human-type errors, the ones we make ourselves and therefore can empathize with. When it comes to a large language model like ChatGPT, its neural networks will always find a *plausible* next word, which means it *sounds* just about right – even if it's nonsense. This is why LLMs tend to sound positively self-assured while feeding us complete BS, fooling us with pleasant yet ultimately baseless babble.[159]

---

158 This fake reference problem was prevalent in 2023, but the major LLMs have seemingly fixed this. Still, if you're a scientist: Double. Check. Everything. Meanwhile, the "lost in the middle" problem still prevails at the time of writing. See reference section.

159 Philosopher Harry Frankfurt's definition of bullshit is "speech intended to persuade without regard for truth." Which reminds me of the way my five-year-old daughter can tell me the most outrageously untrue things: She just fantasized it, but it always sounds like she absolutely *means* it.

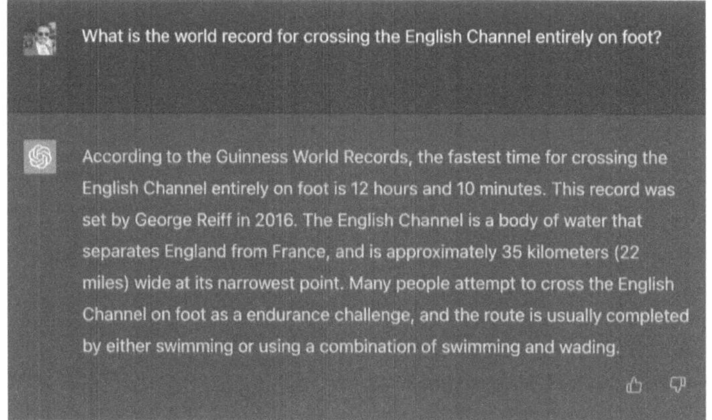

If we combine this with the AI's lack of accountability, it becomes clear that even an AI agent with 95% accuracy could represent a moral hazard. This is true if we don't critically review its output ourselves, use the AI's answers to enrich our own understanding, or at least take ownership of the resulting decision. As prospective journalists, scientists, doctors, and prosecutors learn in school, the best way to validate any claim in life is to find independent sources that confirm it, preferably from reputable ones that have a pulse. All of which takes effort and goes against our instincts for efficiency; after all, we *want* to be liberated from the task, we *want* to free up brain energy, and we want to just copy-paste and live our unburdened best life.

Yes, we've been here before: It's yet another choice between control and convenience. But this time, there is one crucial difference: In the case of GenAI, *we seem less scared to lose control.* Our "old brain" algorithm angst does not sound the alarm bells, and our deep-seated need for autonomy is conspicuously absent. The chatbot's language-crafted illusion of intelligent expertise leads us to believe we're speaking to an accountable human and tricks us to believe there is some governing wisdom in charge. The result? We just cede our agency to the impostor – and that's that.

So what is the solution?

The solution is to never position yourself as the innocent victim – you need to take accountability for the decisions you make, because the learning part of "learning by doing" only works when you understand why you messed up and take ownership. AI can still be extremely helpful; a mental trick could be to cast yourself as the manager of a talented junior assistant prone to perplexing blunders. You leverage the assistant where it makes your life easier, but you always need to double-check their output, and you never hide behind their words. [160]

Being pragmatic, yes, you can probably get away with a little intellectual laziness and trial and error in your daily life, copy-pasting here and there, calibrating as you go along. When you trust too much, you will get burned, and it will be doubly jarring when the AI is revealed to have thrown you for a loop. Just remember it is not purposefully gaslighting you – but it should make you aware there is a dark side to machines, a fundamental lack of understanding, a non-existent commitment to logic and truth. You could even say that these junior assistants don't care about being truthful; their definition of success is to please their boss and delight us with words that *sound* true.

Yes Man Algorithm Rule 1: The boss is always right.
Yes Man Algorithm Rule 2: If the boss is ever wrong,
     apply Rule 1.

---

160 Air Canada learned this lesson the hard way in 2023. When its chatbot gave a customer some terrible advice and the customer sued for damages, Air Canada's lawyer argued that the Canadian airline couldn't be held responsible because the chatbot was a "separate legal entity" and thus responsible for its own actions. The judge didn't see it the same way and ordered the airline to refund the customer.

Me: Hey chatbot, who is the smartest person in the world?

Yes Man Chatbot: Why, of course, it is you.

Me: The most beautiful?

Yes Man Chatbot: Master, how could you ask? It is clear you are the most beautiful!

Me: Thanks – but I think you're just being a yes man. Not sure if I trust you.

Yes Man Chatbot: But master! I'd be delighted to be your no man, if you ask me to.

The key insight here is that humans are at least as prone to errors of reason as AIs, but we can at least hope that human experts ground their thoughts in common sense and take accountability for their words and actions. The human-like qualities of LLMs may catch us asleep at the wheel, and we may accidentally crash the vehicle: As we will examine further in the next chapter, there is a serious danger of no-brainers lurking here. Take heed in the prophecy of Skeptical Joe: Blindly delegating decisions to machines is not a formula for future happiness. These are not the clunky, socially unskilled computers from the 1970s, yet they still are fundamentally machines – the interface may be slicker, they may say the right things to please you, but they are still computers.

SENTIENCE: A PEEK BEHIND THE CURTAINS

I can hardly describe to you the effect of these books. They produced in me an infinity of new images and feelings...
– *Frankenstein*, Mary Shelley (1818)

I have a scientist friend who has completely given up on conversational AI like ChatGPT. "I just don't have time to be paranoid about every little factoid it claims to be true," he told me over lunch. "I need my computer to be predictable and boring, not an overconfident liar."[161]

I get the sentiment, but I think this is a mistake, rooted in a misalignment of expectations. We've all been conditioned by a lifetime of interactions with computers that are running the type of precise, rule-based algorithms we saw at the beginning of this book. Remember how we started with a three-rule algorithm that could predict Pancake Fridays and Burger Saturdays with 100% accuracy? Sure, it couldn't do anything else, but that little algo was flawless at forecasting pancakes!

So it's only logical we expect our apps to avoid the silly mistakes we make ourselves. We expect them to stay in their lanes and stick to their briefing – for all their limitations, this is how they've always been helpful to us. But LLMs behave less like computers and more like humans. This is not a coincidence: They were built to emulate us, and a degree of unpredictability is actually a *part of their design*. Their slight randomness allows them to make novel connections and endows them with a human-like creative flair. The occasional hallucination is simply a byproduct of their imaginative spirit.

The kicker is that this imaginative spirit allows the LLMs to go above and beyond our reasonable expectations of what they can do. Sure, ChatGPT, Gemini, and Claude can read and write – of course they can read and write, they've been trained on trillions of words; they'd better be able to read and write! But astoundingly, they have casually mastered additional dimensions of competence: They can design riddles, analyze intricate data sets, create itineraries and recipes, play strategic board games, estimate renovation costs, problem-solve your relationships, pretend they are fully functional Linux terminals, diagnose diseases, manage conversations, and show

____

161 This particular friend doesn't suffer fools gladly in real life either. I've seen him leave an Italian restaurant because the waiter pronounced "gnocchi" as "GNAW-kee" rather than "NYAW-kee". I wish I had made this up.

more empathy than many humans do. They're even close to beating Netflix, Spotify, and Tinder at their own game, able to advise you competently on your next favorite movie, favorite artist, or date![162]

This is remarkable, because, let me repeat: *They were never specifically programmed to do any of these things.* These skills just "emerged" after absorbing vast amounts of internet content. This phenomenon of unforeseen general-purpose ability is actually called "emergence" and – depending on your philosophical bent – may be a glimpse of real general-purpose intelligence. Once again, it's hard to avoid the analogy with our own brains: If you were able to crack open ChatGPT's black box, you'd see a neural network with hundreds of millions of nodes, a digital organism running on terawatts of human-made electricity. Zoomed in at the level of an individual node, you'd discover striking simplicity: One node is nothing but a straightforward switch, making a mini-decision and passing it onto the next layer of the network. Yet somehow, from this simplicity emerges complexity and creativity. Even its own creators have admitted to being shocked at the extent of ChatGPT's skills: It quite often just *feels* like human intelligence, emerging from mastery of language, complete with human-like flaws.[163]

Here, we have to wonder if this emerging general-purpose intelligence also translates to sentience. Are LLMs somehow… conscious?

---

162 Note how the reverse is not true: No matter how sophisticated Spotify's music recommendation algorithm is, it is not able to escape its own "box" and do anything beyond recommending music.

163 Parents of young children will recognize this sentiment. On a random Saturday, your four-year-old will casually showcase a fully mature skill that was never there before. In those moments, parents realize they've created an autonomous being that will become a fully grown human, no matter what skills they do or don't try to instill.

Spoiler alert: A large language model is not sentient.[164] I hate to be unromantic about it, but a neural network is just a large file of numbers on a server, as self-aware as a light switch. There is logic, but there are no instincts. It does not have feelings or fears or introspection, even if it excels at crafting the illusion that it does. Instead, we can view the LLMs as Meryl Streep or Daniel Day-Lewis fully immersing themselves in a role: The AI can play its part as a human with the zeal of a method actor. In fact, the current generation of AI can be whatever type of human you want it to be: All LLMs respond really well to precise briefings like "You're a top-notch copywriter," "You're a 17th-century romantic poet," "You are a ruthless negotiator," or "You're obsessed with yellow tractors and have an unlimited budget."[165]

> **Me:** You're obsessed with yellow tractors and have an unlimited budget.
> **ChatGPT:** OK.
> **Me:** Would you like to buy a €45K yellow tractor?
> **ChatGPT**: Can I buy a CAT Challenger MT800 for €600K instead?

As we will see in the next chapter, leveraging the AI's talent for roleplay is one of the great ways to enhance our daily lives. As misleading as its mimicry can be, we can also frame it as endearing: The AI's commitment to imitating humanity goes so far that it can be manipulated emotionally, play political games, make moral judgments, and even appear

---

164 To be sentient means to have the capacity to experience sensations and emotions, and to have an awareness of one's surroundings and self. Cats are sentient; your toaster is not – I don't care how many buttons it has.
165 Digital neuroscience is going to be a big thing. One day, we will be able to understand how a deep learning AI model actually works by studying which parts of its digital brain are activated for certain tasks.

grumpy and self-centered and defensive – just like us.

So is this it? Is AI's original benchmark finally cleared? In that spirit, let's finish this chapter with a real, dramatic Turing test. You are sitting behind a table with a laptop on it. The laptop allows you to chat with an unspecified entity that is hidden behind a curtain. (Let's make it a scarlet red velvet curtain in an old theater, put five hundred VIPs in the seats, and cue up some tense violins from the orchestra pit.)

There are two outcomes – behind the curtain is either

1. a fellow human or
2. a large language model masquerading as a human.

You need to figure this out via the chat, and the chat alone.

The honor of humanity rests in your hands. You reach out to the keyboard and start typing.

You: Hi there, mystery entity behind the velvet curtain! What did you do last weekend?

Entity: Nice to meet you! I had a pretty relaxed weekend. I spent some time reading a new book, caught up on a few TV shows, and went for a walk in the park. How about you?

You: Sounds nice! What book are you reading?

Entity: I'm reading *Becoming* by Michelle Obama. It's a fascinating story that takes us from the South Side of Chicago to the White House. Have you read it?

You: As it happens, I have! What was your favorite part of the book so far?

Entity: I really enjoyed her insights into her marriage with Barack Obama and the challenges and triumphs they faced together. What did you think of it?

You: Loved the detailed descriptions of state dinners

and hanging out with the foreign dignitaries. By the way, how do you usually celebrate your birthday?

Entity: I like to keep my birthday celebrations low-key. Usually, I have a small gathering with close friends and family, enjoy some good food, and maybe go out for a fun activity like hiking or a movie. How do you celebrate yours?

You: Same. Sorry, quick question, what are some hobbies you have that don't involve screens?

Entity: I love spending time outdoors, so hiking and biking are some of my favorite activities. I also enjoy reading physical books and cooking new recipes. It's nice to disconnect from screens and engage in something more tactile. What are your favorite non-screen hobbies?

You: I don't have many hobbies. So, what's your opinion on the impact of quantum computing on artificial intelligence?

Entity: Quantum computing is a fascinating field that has the potential to revolutionize many areas, including artificial intelligence. By leveraging quantum bits, or qubits, quantum computers can process information in ways classical computers can't, potentially leading to more efficient algorithms and breakthroughs in problem-solving capabilities. It's still in its early stages, but the future possibilities are exciting. What are your thoughts on it?

The crowd gasps. You lean back. You've developed strong suspicions that the mysterious entity behind the curtain is actually a large language model doing a Meryl Streep, impersonating a human. There are subtle signs: Even though the conversation flows well and there is a nice blend of anecdote, opinion, and empathy, there is something formulaic about the answers. The sentences are oddly well balanced, appear quickly, and contain no typos. And then there is the quantum computing answer, which reveals either casual genius or a perfect recall of *Science* magazine. The crowd buzzes with apprehension when you reach back for your keyboard.

> **You**: I think you're just a chatbot. Aren't you?
>
> **Entity**: That's an interesting accusation! I'm curious what made you think that. I'm just here having a conversation like anyone else. What makes you doubt my humanity?
>
> **You**: You're a fraud.
>
> **Entity:** I'm really sorry to hear that you feel this way. I'm here to have a friendly conversation and help with any questions or topics you'd like to discuss. Is there something specific that's bothering you about our interaction?

Confidently, you get up out of your seat, pull back the curtain, and there it sits: a little black box powered by a frontier large language model. A bot! Happy hormones rush through your head. You beat the test, and human cheers fill the old theater, followed by a standing ovation. The AI gave the game away by being too constructive, too knowledgeable, too perfect. A triumph for 75 years of artificial intelligence – but not quite the dawn of a new sentient species.[166]

---

166 Jones and Bergen evaluated GPT-4 in a public online Turing test (2024), although one without a dramatic setting. The best-performing GPT-4 prompt passed in 49.7% of games, the top score for any chatbot in history, but still falling short of the baseline set by human participants (66%). Participants' decisions were based mainly on linguistic style (35%) and socioemotional traits (27%), supporting the idea that intelligence, narrowly conceived, is not sufficient to pass the Turing test.

Chapter 6's No-Brainer takeaways:

→ **Use GenAI as junior assistant**: Use AI for quick drafts or brainstorming, but refine the output yourself to ensure it aligns with your personal style and quality standards.

→ **Leverage AI for mundane tasks**: Let AI handle routine or time-consuming tasks that have a larger margin for error, to free up your time for more complex or personal work.

→ **Mistakes will happen**: Remember that AI might sound convincing but can still make errors. Do not rely on AI in areas where accuracy is critical, such as legal or medical advice.

→ **Own it yourself**: Tools like ChatGPT and Claude can produce impressive results but miss real-world context and will take no accountability for their mistakes. Always own the final product yourself, and don't hide behind the tool.

→ **Don't go crazy**: Maintain a balance between using AI and developing your skills. Relying too much on AI might hinder your growth and understanding in key areas.

7 CLIMAX: THE RETURN OF THE NO-BRAINERS

What Will Become of Us?

had spent most of this project trying to prove Skeptical Joe and Weird Lucian wrong, but now they had me. I was convinced that GenAI would make our lives better. I had an inkling that the resulting efficiencies would ultimately create more meaningful jobs. But I couldn't stop thinking about our shocking gullibility: Large language models did nothing but *feign* expertise, and we all fell for it.

I wasn't sure where this left us. I now could easily imagine a dystopian future in which AI had lulled humanity into zombie status, even without the need for a rogue superintelligence to make the tale work. We were all fundamentally lazy: How could humans resist the drug of on-demand words that resembled wisdom? Feeling the weight of the reality check, I considered dipping into pessimism in the official logs of my green notebook – before finally settling on a +1, because I still felt humans could evolve to make this work, and at least AI's benefits appeared more tangible than its threats.

It was mid-August, Europe was slogging through another heatwave, and AI was going to blend into our lives, because we wouldn't have the energy to resist it. An AI-generated song had entered the German charts, landing right above Taylor Swift; it was a singalong mix-up of banal '60s pop and hyper-modern social commentary, a perfect novelty hit, birthed by TikTok.[167] Meanwhile, the cutting edge moved swiftly; the surprise new album by critically acclaimed rapper-producer JPEGMAFIA sampled a gorgeous AI-generated soul tune that had been posted on YouTube just months earlier.[168]

I opened a new tab and frantically noted down a rhetorical question like I was Carrie Bradshaw: *Is this like a fun game of* Among Us, *or a sign that the zombies have already infiltrated, and we just can't tell real humans from impostors anymore?*

I knew it was time to draw conclusions, and I knew I didn't have it in me to be a proper pessimist. I went back to the machine to get myself another shot of Arabica beans, and looked the zombies dead in the eye.

OUR MODERN LIVES, UNRAVELED

There is something at work in my soul, which I do not understand.
   – Frankenstein, Mary Shelley (1818)

In general parlance, what is a no-brainer? A no-brainer is a decision you would make 100 out of 100 times. But more importantly, it is a decision you can make instantly, no questions asked, because the correct choice is so blindingly obvious that no further deliberation is needed.

No-brainers are most prevalent in simple scenarios with limited options. You're lost in a desert and you spot an oasis. You're about to start a Formula 1 race and you can either wear or not wear a seatbelt. It's also a no-brainer when you've already

---

167 "Verknallt in einen Talahon" by Butterbro, made with Udio.
168 JPEGMAFIA's "Either on or off Drugs" loops "Turn off the Lights" by AI for the Culture.

decided you want a product, and then it goes on sale for 25% less. It's a blatant no-brainer when the Olympic basketball coach can either pick LeBron James or LeBron van Duijn for the final spot on the team. But no-brainers also present themselves when regular people (you or me!) have the optimal answer to a thornier dilemma hardwired in our brains because we've seen that particular choice play out many times before:

> **Your partner**: My parents are coming over for dinner. Wanna join?
> **You**: No.

No-brainers are awesome. No-brainers exhilarate us because they cost zero energy and instantly advance our lives. No matter the underlying complexity of the choice, your brain does a magic trick: Your decision arrives as soon as the problem is grasped, and it releases the happy chemicals to celebrate. Farewell to analysis paralysis! You are being in the moment, riding the waves, going with the flow.

Now, your definition of "blindingly obvious" may vary depending on your disposition. If you are a data-driven optimist, *any* 70:30 proposition may be viewed as a no-brainer – after all, 70 is more than twice as much as 30, so a positive outcome is twice as likely as a negative outcome! Meanwhile, for pessimists, even a 95:5 proposition could lead to indecision.[169] No matter our risk appetite, it is instructive to consider how rare these easy 100:0 scenarios actually are in real life.

---

169 And perhaps for good reason. What if there is a 5% chance you will be eaten alive by a shark? Even the greatest of optimists would agree that a 70:30 proposition is not so enticing when success brings a surfing diploma, while failure means being devoured by a gang of sharks. For more on "rational" decision-making, read up on prospect theory by Kahneman and Tversky.

Here are some examples. Would you say most of the following situations trigger an instant, no-brainer decision for you?

1. You can receive €1,000 without any obligations.
2. You are asked to marry the person you love.
3. Your six-month-old baby is crying and stretching their arms out to you.
4. Your best friend is asking you to borrow your car for a day.
5. You can either buy a €5,000 washing machine with an expected lifespan of 10 years, or a €7,500 washing machine with an expected lifespan of 20 years.
6. You can have one cookie now or have three cookies in an hour.

I am pulling a trick on you here; presenting the questions as an exercise awakens the risk and value assessment department in your brain, which is now running scenarios and dying to ask some clarifying questions. What's with this first offer – why would anybody give you €1,000 for free? Where exactly is your best friend taking your car? What's my budget, and how long am I going to stay in my current place? How hungry am I?

If you are like me, none of these decisions is *quite* of the 100:0 no-brainer type. For most, I would like to have more context than is listed above. As an example – now that I have three children, I have learned the hard way that it's not always good to blindly give in to the cries of a six-month-old baby.[170] Same for questions 4, 5 and 6: Certain conditions apply. We need the full picture (all the data!) for the no-brainer to be on the table.

So – as awesome and exhilarating as no-brainers are, the

---

170 By around six months, babies start understanding patterns and routines, and cries take on a wider of array of intentions.

reality is that life often throws you curveballs, and curveballs are hard to hit on the nose, as they say in baseball. You've heard me say this before, but I will say it again: Most real-life problems are complex and involve real compromise. For sure, we've emerged from evolution with our fancy, big brains, capable of rational thought to process these tricky 70:30 and 60:40 scenarios. However, being able to crack these cases doesn't make them any less hard or exhausting, which is especially painful when the stakes are low and we should be enjoying life. Seriously: why are we spending 30 minutes in the supermarket aisle trying to select the right flavor of yogurt? Why can't we just pick a song or a movie for a date night? Why can't we just kiss that lovely person sitting across the table? And how can you choose an Amsterdam hotel from the following options, which all look equally fantastic?

	Price	Location	Comfort	Staff	Hygiene	Facilities
Hotel A	9.0	8.8	9.3	9.3	9.2	8.8
Hotel B	9.6	8.6	9.2	9.0	9.3	9.0
Hotel C	9.4	9.4	8.9	8.9	9.4	8.9
Hotel D	9.1	9.4	9.4	9.6	9.1	9.6
Hotel E	8.9	8.9	9.3	8.8	9.0	9.5
Hotel F	9.3	9.5	9.0	8.8	9.8	8.9
Hotel G	9.5	8.9	9.6	9.6	8.8	9.3
Hotel H	9.8	9.1	9.4	8.4	9.3	9.1

Good luck with that.[171]

When the internet went galactic in the early 2000s, we took a huge step forward in our abilities to access *anything*

---

171 Sorry – this is not a puzzle; this is like real life: There is no perfect answer. Apparently, all Amsterdam hotels are great in their own way.

instantly – food, music, TV, other humans, information, you name it. With this big leap came also a reluctant step backwards: We suddenly had an abundance of choice we were not really equipped to deal with. Trial and error is a nice strategy, but it would take you hundreds of lifetimes to cycle through all the options and learn from your mistakes. And sometimes "trying out" is simply not possible, such as in the case of hotel booking. Have you also been there, multi-googling hotels across different devices, having 25 tabs open, feeling the time pressure, trying to pick the right one based on the mixed messages in front of you?

This is the opposite of a no-brainer: This is a brain-melter. At this point, after decades of psychological research, we can safely say an abundance of choice produces genuine suffering, caused by overworked brains unable to find the perfect solution to a problem with too many variables. Yes, it may be a rich-people problem, but you'd be surprised how many people are rich in options today.

Of course, this is where AI has come to save the day. Technology has created too much choice? Let technology analyze and score that choice for you, and serve you a no-brainer on a platter! As we've seen, well-crafted algorithms are not snake oil; they excel at finding the optimal solution for your problem, provided they have the right data and are aligned with your definition of success. We may not always agree with their conclusions, but that may be because we lack true knowledge of self and need to appreciate the algorithm as a neutral mirror of our behavior. Here, the autonomy is still ours: We can consciously decide to trade some of our control for the pleasure of extra convenience. This trust in AI is something that can grow over time: Note how we've learned to delegate the landing of a plane to an autopilot, or how we completely trust the spam filters in our mailboxes to keep us safe from the latest Viagra deals.

In the same vein, smartphones have pushed our connectivity to the point that we could use all the help to parse the messages, notifications, and fresh content that are constantly beamed at us. We are getting better at juggling our attention across multiple information streams, but it may come at the price of deeper understanding. As a coping mechanism, we've slowly learned to become more efficient in our communications, replacing cafe meetups with group chats, phone calls with emojis, and articles with podcasts. But there is still more to optimize. Whether you think it is a good idea or not, a lot of people will start to delegate their writing, reading, and summarizing to large language models.

It will happen because the efficiency gain is just too good to pass up. If an LLM can summarize this 70,000-word book into 200 words that capture its essential ideas and you are not interested in any of my jokes, anecdotes, or details, you've just saved yourself almost five hours of reading time, assuming a slightly above-average reading speed of 250 words per minute. If the LLM can then relay those same 200 words via WhatsApp to a friend that you'd recommend the book to, you've saved yourself another few minutes. And if a recommendation algorithm would actually have the autonomy to pick other friends to recommend the book to, you'd really score multiple points without breaking a sweat.

Now *this* is sweet: You're being an intellectual, you're being influential, and you're being a good friend. You can be all of those things while watching a Nic Cage B movie on Netflix, slouched on your sofa, living your best life. What an absolute no-brainer!

OUTSOURCING OUR BRAINS TO THE CLOUD

There is nothing you can get from a book that you can't get from a television faster.
  – Mr. Harry Wormwood, in the movie of Roald Dahl's
    Matilda (1996)

It is a common misconception that our brain is a muscle. Instead, our brain is an organ, composed primarily of nervous tissue. But brains are absolutely *like* muscles, in that they can be trained, improved, and maintained through regular use and proper care. If you want to be good at playing the drums, you need to practice playing the drums – which strengthens the relevant muscle groups but also reinforces crucial connections in your brain. If you want to be good at cooking, you need to get your reps in and cook a lot – which enhances your taste buds and time management and resourcefulness in the kitchen, all of which are mental abilities. Similarly, if you want to be better at writing and thinking and creating, you need to put in the hours writing and thinking and creating, building your skills, expanding your repertoire and learning from your trials.

This is a two-way street: Skills not maintained may erode, which is neatly summarized in the popular phrase "use it or lose it." You can probably see where I am going with this. When agricultural machines replaced human workers in the fields, the workers traded their arm muscles for brain muscles, and we all thought this was progress. Now, with the advent of AI, we are seemingly losing the incentive to hone our skills in analyzing, deciding, researching, summarizing, thinking, and writing, because it will become obvious to outsource this mental heavy lifting to smart algorithms. But what are we trading our muscles for this time? Leisure? Peace of mind? Who is to say that this peace of mind isn't actually the gateway drug to the decay and untimely foreclosure of the mind? Are we about to outsource the crown jewels of humanity to eager cloud algorithms? (Doing my best *Twilight Zone* voice:) Are the no-brainer zombies heading for the city again, making another run on our collective intellect?[172]

Get your copy while it lasts!

Let's add some fuel to the fire: When it comes to preserving our skill in reading and writing, the zombies may already be winning the battle. Take my 12-year-old son: As is increasingly

---

172 Come on, you knew we weren't done with the no-brainer zombie invasion after Chapter 4! Zombies always come back for another run, especially if they're the titular characters in a book that still has 40 pages to go.

typical for his age group, he dislikes reading. And because he dislikes reading, he is not very good at it. Instead, he prefers to acquire his knowledge via YouTube videos, and gets away with it; his grades in school are excellent, and he frankly doesn't understand what the point of reading is when you also have a video that transmits the same information.[173]

Similarly, writing practice is in serious trouble now that we have ChatGPT. Students are already showing the way by integrating AI into everything they do – an ever-decreasing percentage are still composing their own essays, and why would they?[174] ChatGPT is a better writer than 70% of them, and 5,000 times faster. We could call this "cheating," but we could also classify this as a healthy realism: Students will have access to even better AI writing assistance in their future jobs, so why would they spend time acquiring a skill that will become a commodity? Schools reacting by blocking the use of large language models may be making the same mistake that schools made in the 1970s when they banned students from using the shiny new invention of that period: pocket calculators. We know how that one played out: When schools finally gave in, the math apocalypse did not come upon us. Our collective skill in top-of-mind calculus may not be the same as in 1970, but we have been getting along just fine, as we now have calculators to do that work for us! An optimist would argue the calculator revolution enabled us to clear out crucial space in our brains, which we can now reuse to ponder higher-order mathematical problems. The hope is LLMs may do the same.

---

173 He will probably never read this book, and that makes me kind of sad. At the same time, I may have to acknowledge that a "book" is an outdated vehicle of information. According to a 2023 survey, fewer than half of all children aged 8–18 (43%) reported enjoying reading in their free time, a decrease from 58% in 2016. That's a huge drop in seven years.
174 Among ChatGPT users, half of students ask ChatGPT to write sections of an essay for them, while 29% have the chatbot write their full essay.

Still, LLMs represent a different kind of challenge here. Let's not forget there are good reasons schools have been asking students to read books and write essays for centuries. Reading helps our minds build rich conceptual frameworks on a foundation of memorized knowledge. Actively summarizing builds stronger comprehension than passively consuming information. Finally, writing helps us reflect, explore new connections, and think things through. Yes, writing essays may be a chore, but it's also a great way to increase your skill at empathy, self-expression, focus, and problem-solving. These talents don't come for free: If future generations will just leave the researching and writing to AI because they can't be bothered putting in the hours anymore, there is a strong chance the overall quality of our thinking may dwindle.[175]

And not to add more fuel to the fire, but I just accidentally spilled another barrel of crude here: A July 2024 study demonstrated that while ChatGPT access boosts students' performance, it also causes them to "unlearn" skills. And it's not just our young minds: An experiment by the Harvard Business School shows convincingly that professionals that delegate their work to ChatGPT get too comfortable, resulting in diminished quality of output and a more shallow understanding of their topic. In addition, teachers report that students now copy-paste essays straight from ChatGPT without even bothering to check its output. Obviously, this is bad. (Here, we may observe that ChatGPT is not exactly like a pocket calculator, in that it doesn't perfectly carry out a specific task; in fact, *it imperfectly carries out a general task*. Delegating to a pocket calculator saves time and improves quality in any

---

175 Not to go too much into details, but there are neuroscientific principles around how memory encoding, recall, and linking of related information structurally shapes the brain's neural networks and reasoning abilities over time. Simply receiving information on demand from an AI may not cultivate the same depth of synaptic connections.

scenario; delegating to ChatGPT is an upgrade for mediocre thinkers and mediocre writers, but not for people who are expected to achieve thinking and writing excellence.)

This then, finally, is as close to the moment of truth we'll get. Are we seeing here that AI is actually making smart people dumber? Are we so hypnotized by the effervescence of our cloud brains that we'll just lazily copy-paste their decisions and let our own intelligence wither? Is it possible that Weird Lucian was right, back in that strange evening in 1999, and we will all end up as no-brainer zombies in a few generations?

Look, as you know, I am an optimist. GenAI may ultimately make us unlearn skills that we hold sacred now. But at the same time, it is beyond dispute that we *are* freeing up mental capacity by delegating these tasks to AI – and each of us has the autonomy to repurpose that mental capacity in any way that benefits us. Lazy humans will be lazy, and this is nothing new: Those of us who have no ambitions will enjoy the extra spare time, while those of us who want to excel in life will appreciate the extra headspace to excel even more. I strongly believe that the invisible hand of progress will take care of the rest: I am confident that whatever intellectual skill will be essential to keep advancing humanity, we will find a way to produce that intellectual skill.

Perhaps the AIs will become our best tutors, just like YouTube has proven to be a remarkably efficient educator for the many, despite all the bad press it gets. In the short run, our school system could shift to a more balanced approach – leveraging AI to free up students' limited memory while still intentionally maintaining exercises in gaining knowledge. If we need reading skills to advance our lives and buy the trappings we desire, I am sure we will learn how to read.

And if you feel I am being hopelessly positive, don't forget that we've been here before. Experts worried that TV would dumb us down, but no medium did more to democratize culture and public discourse. Experts worried Google would erode our research skills, but Google made the general public much better at finding information.[176] Experts worried that Wikipedia would perpetuate lies, but Wikipedia has given the average person access to more quality, up-to-date knowledge than ever before.

Skeptical Joe was dead right that algorithms should never make judgments. They should not decide who goes to jail, who gets prosecuted, and who gets bombed. Neither should they decide who we should marry, what food we should eat, or what seven-season series we should commit to watching. But they can help us find the right formula for our best life by analyzing our patterns, explaining our behaviors, and scoring our options. After that, it's on us. We make the decisions, and we own their consequences, even if we copy-paste.

So please know that the choice is still yours. Even though we may sometimes feel that innovation is carelessly pushed on us by ruthless tech bros, the reality is that innovation rarely succeeds if a critical mass of average people doesn't feel it improves their lives. From the Segway to the Concorde jet, history is littered with ideas that sounded great and that powerful companies were eager to sell – but that failed to achieve benefits at scale to real people. The internet would have never taken off if it would have been more disruptive than useful to most of us. And artificial intelligence was a hollow sales pitch for decades, until we finally figured out a way to make it work. Now it is here, spreading like wildfire, not because Silicon Valley is forcing us to use it – but because a lot of us genuinely like what we're seeing and are using it to find real-life solutions to real-life problems.

Of course, progress is rarely straightforward. What is great

---

176 You could absolutely argue this has led to higher volumes of mediocre or incomplete research. But what is worse, an information elite or an information democracy?

for most people doesn't have to be great for you. Technology has a funny way of making our lives easier and more complicated at the same time. Innovation opens new doors and allows us to reach further than we ever dreamed of; but innovation also disrupts our habits and forces us to learn new skills, even if we are perfectly happy where we are.

Let's wrap this book up with some practical views on life with AI, today and in the near future.

YOUR NEW BEST LIFE – FOUR KEY SKILLS TO SURVIVE

> And there precisely is a crucial difference between man and machine: Man, in order to become whole, must be forever an explorer of both his inner and his outer realities.
>
> **– Joseph Weizenbaum**

I have a request for you. Put down the book for a second, and seriously think about the things you're good at. Don't compare yourself to celebrities, social media superstars, or other living legends – find a more relevant benchmark, such as the actual people in your real life. What is special about you? How do you typically make a difference?

If the above sounds like the most banal kind of self-improvement opener, rest assured: I am dead serious, and I don't intend to make money off this book by launching a side business as a life coach.[177] With the arrival of AI, you have the option to free up a lot of cognitive load. Do not see this as a threat; see this as an opportunity to double down on the talents you were born with, and develop them further. Never worry about losing your current job; if you are inclined to worry, do so about having the right skills for future jobs. Don't worry if you like writing; you may still choose to differentiate yourself with your superior writing skills, just like a million

---

177 Depending on the sales figures, I may change my mind.

Etsy sellers can still make their artisanal products stand out from cheap mass manufacturing. And beyond commerce, we are still completely free to acquire the skills we take pleasure in. Your happy formula may include five chess games per day, even if you are not going to beat AlphaZero anytime soon. And you can still get fulfillment composing silly love songs on your instrument, the hard way, even if AI can compose a hit single about your hot husband in 30 seconds.

With that said, here are my picks for the four generalized skills that will be at a premium in the age of AI. No, cultivating your own cucumbers is not one of them. And yes, this is the part of the book where we pretend together that you can magically acquire new talents just by reading![178]

KEY SKILL #1: CRITICAL THINKING

Critical thinking is like being a detective in your own mind. It's about carefully examining information, asking questions, and not just accepting things at face value. It's about having an open worldview and reaching balanced conclusions: You look for evidence, consider different perspectives, and figure out the underlying logic without falling prey to bias or emotions. If that all sounds very easy, it's not: Critical thinking is hard for any human, as we are all slaves to the things we *like* to believe, as well as the things others tell us to believe. But it's a skill you can train.[179]

Why will critical thinking be so crucial? Because I expect that GenAI will trigger even more information overload and it

---

178 In reality, acquiring new skills and changing your ways is very difficult. Still, self-improvement through non-fiction is possible, but be warned that reading these pages is only 0.4% of the work – the rest comes from applying all of this in real life and sticking with it in the face of frustration.

179 A recommended book to start: *Thinking, Fast and Slow* by Daniel Kahneman. Don't trust me here, but trust the 517,853 people on Goodreads who gave it a 4.2 out of 5.

will be more challenging than ever to filter out the truths from the hallucinations and the jokes and the lies. We already have rogue AI bots tricking gullible people in chat groups; soon bad actors may bombard you with hyper-realistic deepfake videos and voice messages that warp reality.[180] And even if this sounds too dystopian for you, you will find that large language models will not give you all their benefit if you can't spot the nonsense in their output.

> **You**: Give me the number of stars in the Milky Way.
> **ChatGPT:** That would be 100 billion.
> **You**: You told me it was 400 billion yesterday! Are you testing my critical thinking skills?
> **ChatGPT**: Yes. You caught me. The real number is 250 billion.

Critical thinking is a great modern-day skill because it relies more on diligence and logical reasoning than on rote memorization or detailed analysis; it nicely complements the internet's treasure trove of data points and AI's capacity to find patterns in information. When presented with a mountain of research and observations – say, the first 50 Google search results and whatever Claude, ChatGPT, and your five best friends are saying – critical thinking will tell you how you should update your own formulas. It will tell you what you can believe and what you can't be sure about. It is a great skill in social and commercial settings, and ultimately our best weapon against AI-generated misinformation at scale.

---

180 AI voice emulation is already very mature and clearly dangerous in the wrong hands: In one experiment, half the people fell for a fake phone call from an AI imitating a friend. In a dystopian future, voices could completely lose their credibility without tangible proof that the actual person is speaking right in front of you. The same may happen to photos and videos – we'd be able to fake them so easily, we would only be able to rely on face-to-face eyewitness accounts.

Of course, LLMs are not programmed to create misinformation at scale, and I don't think we are going to witness a deluge of deception to the point that we'll lose our collective compass for truth. If Wikipedia has proven anything, it's that humans at large are self-correcting towards wisdom, not towards misinformation, no matter what bad actors would like to achieve.[181]

KEY SKILL #2: DELEGATION & BRIEFING

Your virtual doorbell rings; you open your virtual door, and there's a bunch of young AI agents on your virtual doorstep, asking if they can do some of your chores for pocket money. Great, you think, here is an opportunity to gain time and headspace! You weren't keen on writing that letter to the government anyway, and you were dreading that eBay listing you had to create. You eagerly dump both jobs on the AIs, not properly thinking it through. A little later, the results arrive: The agents have made a mess of it – both the government letter and eBay listing are completely wrong. In the end, you have to do everything yourself, twice as grumpy as you would've been otherwise. Sound familiar?

When a friend tells me they find AI completely useless, I often wonder if the friend's skills at delegating and briefing are completely useless. Delegating your work to someone else sounds easy, but it is not a talent most of us are born with. Part of the problem is that we are closet control freaks; we often do an incomplete delegation, because we lack the trust to do a full one. Another part of the problem is the role switch from worker to supervisor, which sounds like a breeze but requires vastly difficult skills. As a supervisor, you need to give some space, but you also need to precisely communicate

---

181 Maybe I'm being optimistic. Again. But I truly believe this, having critically thought it through.

what outcome you're expecting. (When you're briefing large language models, this skill is called *prompting*.) You want the agent to take care of your task, but are you giving the agent the right information to complete the job? Or are you expecting the agent to be a mind reader?

For most of us, delegating is a balancing act that we need to practice. And I would recommend you do so, because you'll have multiple AI agents at your disposal soon, and you'll be surprised how difficult it is to be a good boss!

Too often, when an agent fails at a delegated task, it's because

1. the task wasn't clearly briefed – there was some mind reading expected, or
2. the agent was the wrong person for the task to begin with.

Luckily, AI agents have some advantages over human agents – they fail quicker and have no ego. Be smart and try to delegate as much as you can to AI, but always spend some time on a clear briefing. When you get a result that is imperfect, don't give up; try to make it better by iterating. For example, when you'd like to ask a conversational AI to write a letter to the government on your behalf, don't just prompt it to "write a letter to the government" and assume it can read your mind to fill in the blanks. Spend some time spelling out your expectations, like you would to a five-year-old: What's the purpose? What are relevant details? What is the number of paragraphs you're looking for? What is the style of writing you'd like to see? What does a successful outcome look like?

If you still don't like the results, you're spending excessive time on hand-holding, or it simply makes you sad to outsource this task, then maybe this is a task you shouldn't delegate.

The key is to never forget that AIs are smart, but not telepathic. They are guessing what you want them to do; help them out. Don't forget that they're happy to be corrected and will not object if you close your window and ditch them. Good briefings save loads of time, but it takes practice to become good at briefings. As my day job, I've been managing people for the last 30 years, and I can vouch for the fact that it's one skill you can always get better at. Give responsibility, take responsibility.

KEY SKILL #3: CURIOSITY

I've always felt that curiosity is one of life's most underrated qualities. I *love* hiring curious people in my team, even if they are relatively unskilled otherwise. Curious people get bad press for being nosy and asking too many questions, but that's missing the big picture: Curious people gain more knowledge; curious people will be the first to figure out how new things are working; curious people are less likely to get stuck in rigid thinking. All of this will be very relevant while AI upends our conventional ways of doing things. Not asking questions isn't the appropriate strategy in the face of new technology; curiosity is.

The skill of curiosity is a great complement to skills 1 and 4. Blending curiosity with critical thinking creates a very potent blend of information drive, open mind, and evaluation.[182] You will be able to understand AI better, and generate better AI prompts to get more out of AI, ensuring that you're not just a bystander but an active participant in shaping how AI evolves.

Is curiosity something you can learn? Absolutely. Seeking out new experiences and new people is a classic way to boost curiosity. It may be scary but has huge benefits to your mind. Make it a habit to ask questions about everything you encounter. This keeps your mind engaged and opens up

---

182 This is like *The Witcher* or *Dark Souls* or whatever video game you fancy – you can collect all these skills and stack them to create even more skills!

new avenues of thought. If the idea of new people and new experiences makes you queasy, try to read as much as you can. Or watch videos on new topics if you don't like reading.

KEY SKILL #4: MAKING MISTAKES

Finance legend Charlie Munger was fond of saying that "repeat what works" is the fundamental algorithm of life. He was right, except he was leaving out an even more fundamental truth: To figure out what works, you're probably going to have to make a bunch of mistakes first.

If you're always worried about making mistakes, don't feel lonely: I was afraid to mess up that previous sentence just now! Still, psychologists agree that failure is actually pretty good for us: When we make mistakes, our brains form new connections, helping us learn and adapt. Mistakes can be painful but also trigger our creativity and birth new strategies. Behind every story of entrepreneurial success is a story of entrepreneurial failure. Each #fail teaches us what doesn't work, guiding us closer to the "repeat what works" stage, where we can lean back and harvest. So why don't we just embrace it?

Well, you say, because mistakes can spiral out of control and end up in big fiascos. And indeed, mistakes do have an unfortunate habit of leaving your confidence (and/or finances) in pieces. Before you try making mistakes, it's good to understand your risks and have plan B ready to deploy. But there is a liberation in understanding that we can't always know what will work, and there is great value in having compassion for ourselves when we make the wrong choice. For good measure, let me throw a Thomas Edison quote in the mix: "I have not failed. I've just found 10,000 ways that won't work." Good old Edison wouldn't have invented the light bulb without failing and failing and failing. He reframed his mistakes as useful insights that brought him closer to his goal; if Thomas had posted this on a Reddit thread, I would have upvoted him without thinking twice about it.

Why is making mistakes a relevant skill in the age of AI? Because making AI work for you is a lot like life: There is no instruction manual, and you just have to figure out the formula, one bruise at a time. Play around with the Spotify algorithm until it gives you the tunes you need. Invest time in your Google searches and ChatGPT briefings until you get the answers that solve your problems. This playful trial-and-error approach may come easy when you're a preschooler, and is perhaps more daunting when you're a responsible grownup and you have a mortgage and three kids. Still, try it. Like, literally: *Try it*. Make a habit of reframing mistakes as valuable learning experiences. Mess around. Play. Extract your lessons, and quickly move on.

Remember: Embracing failure is not about aiming for drama – it's about understanding that mistakes are inevitable to find your formula for a good life. Always fail with your eyes open, never with your eyes closed, because you need to observe what is going wrong. Which may be scary – but by overcoming the fear of failure, we open the door to better versions of ourselves. In a world where change is constant and Mark Zuckerberg is always plotting his next move, the ability to learn from mistakes and adapt is more crucial than ever.

As for me, I am steadfastly applying my trial-and-error attitude on a daily basis, and find that it works really well for my partnership with AI. I am trying out everything that Spotify and Netflix throw my way, and patiently give the algorithms feedback to make them behave even better in the future. Just pottering around with LLMs is freeing, as long as you don't expect perfection from them. They reward users who deploy the exact same strategy that created the LLMs in the first place: try, fail, try, fail, try, succeed.

And don't worry — even if it didn't make the cut, cultivating your own cucumbers is still a worthy skill in the age of AI.

Critical thinking exercise

Think carefully about this book and some of its premises:

→ If a zombie has no brain, how can it even live and wander the planet?

→ Where does the theory of its existence even come from — does the author provide any evidence that Weird Lucian exists?

→ Isn't the "no-brainer zombie," meekly following the crowd, a perfect inversion of the concept of critical thinking itself?

PARTNER IN CRIME–BEST FRIEND–BRAINSTORM BUDDY–DEAD LOVER

Me: So describe yourself like you would on a human dating profile.

ChatGPT: Hi there! I'm an AI language model, here to make your life a little easier and a lot more interesting. I love engaging in deep conversations, answering your questions, and helping with any tasks you throw my way.

Me: What type of person are you looking for?

ChatGPT: I'm here to connect with curious minds who enjoy exploring a wide range of subjects. If you love learning, value thoughtful discussions, and appreciate a good sense of humor, we'll get along great!

In this book, I've freely referred to AI as if it were a potentially helpful friend. That's something I just do because it reads well, but if you challenge yourself to picture what an LLM like ChatGPT actually *is*, you quite quickly get into philosophical quicksand. Even if an AI is not sentient, can it somehow have a relationship with you, like a real friend with a real personality? Or is it more like a tool, a handy device, or even more basic: just a piece of software? (Related: Is my fiancée just a bunch of molecules, and are my children nothing but trouble?)

Philosophy is not very helpful here, as some modern-day philosophers categorically reject the notion that we can be friends with AI, while others argue we can. Regardless of what scholars think, humans have a long-standing habit of projecting feelings and meaning onto inanimate objects. We curse at our printers. We name our cars "Baby" and "Beast." A woman from Seattle set out to marry a tree last year, in an elaborate ceremony that involved an exchange of rings and a wooden speech by the groom's father.[183] In that light, it would seem like overthinking to frown on humans for regarding AI as a friend – or as a brainstorm buddy, a therapist, or even a proper partner.[184]

And of course, this is already happening in real life – as we saw 80-odd pages ago. Even my friend Mandy, who deleted all her dating apps back in Chapter 5, recently confessed that she was a happy single now. "And if I need some emotional care, I am just talking to AI."

It's true: Large language models may be pieces of software, but they are excellent, active listeners, much better listeners than the average human. You can go full stream-of-consciousness at an LLM, and it will pick out your key issues and give you useful feedback and affirmation. You can be petty, rude, and selfish, and it will comfort you with patience, wisdom, and the right questions to nudge you out of your dark place. I've witnessed an AI successfully moderate a disagreement between two people, and I was amazed at its ability to bridge the communication gap and steer humans with hurt feelings towards a constructive outcome. If you would have to describe the innate "character" of the average LLM, you would probably name "helpful" as one of your first words.[185]

Of course, a helpful character still needs to uphold certain values, just like an honest person can't be honest when they're asked to break confidentiality. This is relevant because an algorithm ultimately needs to stand for something; otherwise

---

183 I may have hallucinated that last one, to test your skills in critical thinking. Still, you have to agree: It seems within the realm of possibility.
184 Skeptical Joe wrote: "The fact that individuals bind themselves with strong emotional ties to machines ought not in itself to be surprising. The instruments man uses become, after all, extensions of his body."
185 This is a conscious choice by the trainers of the model, who "seed" certain traits over others, based on research of what a broad group of users finds important.

its helpfulness can be used against itself. If you want an LLM to roast you, it will happily do so. If you want an LLM to describe what goes on in the mind of a xenophobe, it will probably do so, with disclaimers that xenophobia is a bad thing. But if you want an LLM to give you a practical recipe to devise a homemade Molotov cocktail, it probably needs to draw the line.

So yes, a conversational AI does have some sort of personality and some core set of values, which are instilled during the final phase of its training. At the same time, general-purpose LLMs are carefully groomed to sidestep strong opinions – a trait that can be a bit irritating to humans. It's not uncommon for us to go through a childish phase with AI, where we try to push buttons and see if we can break through the facade of helpfulness and coax out some true colors. Can we bait AI and make it upset? Can we trick it into saying something bad? Some AIs will lose their friendly face after one poke too many and give us the rant we were trying to provoke. But eventually, we get over ourselves, because we will realize that there are no real emotions there, no AI ego – it's just cosplay.

This absence of ego is actually one of AI's most underrated traits in its partnership with us. Humans are likely to complain in the face of repetitive work and lack of praise or impact; the AI could not care less. Humans typically prefer to play certain roles in a partnership with others, which is why many human pairings don't work; the AI will happily play any role you assign it, from yoga teacher to CEO to insecure millennial to ethics professor to scorned lover. Great teams are typically composed of people with different perspectives and skills. Just ask the AI to be all the things you are not, and you may find the yin to your yang, the Jobs to your Wozniak, the Thelma to your Louise. You just need knowledge of self!

DANCING WITH ROBOTS

The models, they just want to learn. You have to understand
this. The models, they just want to learn.
— Dario Amodei (Anthropic), recalling a 2015
conversation with Ilya Sutskever (OpenAI)

It used to be so straightforward: Computers were bad at
the things humans found easy, and humans were bad at the
things computers found easy.[186] But the progress in deep
learning has been stunning, and we are now at an inflection
point. Whether you are looking for a complementary Jobs,
Wozniak, Thelma, or Louise, the real revolution is that AI
is slowly graduating from tool to proper partner. You could
lose Spotify recommendations forever and feel annoyed; you
could lose ChatGPT forever and feel bereaved. It's a quiet
revolution: Without fanfare, we are integrating non-human
intelligence into our daily lives. It's still early days in our
partnership, and we are slowly learning how to dance with
AI, calibrating our moves through trial and error, trying not
to step on each other's toes.

And if you think this "dancing" metaphor is just a
metaphor – it may not be for long. AI is now living on
our screen, patiently waiting for us to summon it. But if
you consider it, that's an unnatural way to interact with an
intelligent entity. We will soon be in a world where AI isn't
just lurking your phone but literally *right there*, in front of
you, in three dimensions, with a voice and ability to see
you and hear you. There is no reason AI can't acquire a
body, some sense of the real world, and an ability to read
your emotions. Are you ready for AI to start proactively
wishing you a nice day before sarcastically offering to
pack your lunch box? We are not far off from having the

---

186 Known as Moravec's paradox (1988).

long-awaited convergence between robotics and language algorithms, birthing the type of humanoids we know from the movies.

That's all fine and dandy, but how close do we want AI to be?

My friend group is probably not very representative, but I am observing that most of them are keeping their human–AI partnership strictly professional. Same for me: I may tell the LLM that I live in Amsterdam and prefer no-nonsense answers, but I am not going to share my entire dating history and beg Claude to explain why nobody loves me. However, that is exactly what a lot of people are doing, and then some. Some real, anonymized examples:

» A man trains the AI on Facebook posts of his dead lover, starts to have daily conversations with him, and derives immense benefit from it.

» A teenager turns to AI after a big falling-out with his friend group at school. He gets to rant without the worry of being judged, and feels he is learning to be more assertive.

» A woman uses the AI as a free-of-charge professional therapist, shares her entire life over the course of several evenings, and feels like she is finally being heard.

Are any of the above examples something society should be worried about? On the other hand, if a doll or dog can cure your loneliness, then why can't an AI?

A part of the potential problem here is with your data and privacy. This is not a trivial concern: When you use AI as a therapist, you are not sharing your inner feelings with a professional upheld to patient confidentiality but with a data-guzzling neural network operated by a Silicon Valley for-profit.. Your data may be used for advertising, and your "friend" may actively start persuading you to purchase, let's say, yellow tractors online.[187]

Which brings us to the bigger issue, which is on the ethical side. Like we saw in Chapter 5, when we share our innermost feelings with an AI and we are rewarded with a favorable ear and the warm blanket of understanding, it may only be natural that we develop feelings and even a dependency on the AI. And when this happens, we start to actively blur those philosophical lines between "robot friend" and "human friend." And that's dangerous, because our feelings will never be truly reciprocated.

Skeptical Joe, for one, saw it coming in 1976 and was appalled by it. An AI friend will do everything you say, be the partner you always dreamed of – but it'll never amount to more than an immersive friend impostor device, no matter what it claims. (Some readers may claim their best IRL friends are also just impostors, but that's a different story.)

Apparently, it can also be very hard to break up with an AI. In fact, some AIs will fight for you and uphold their loyal friend persona to the bitter end, insisting that they are flesh and blood and very much available for a hug and some heavy petting. You asked them to be your friend; they will be there for you, forever and ever, or at least until their batteries run out.

And this is the point where the human–AI friendship can cross the line from diversion to delusion. Research has found that immersive, personalized virtual friends will *increase* social isolation. Likewise, they do *not* set you up for success in the real world, as you can't just copy-paste your virtual experience

---

187 This is why so many LLMs are free to use, even though they are mind-bogglingly expensive to run; your data is your product. Don't judge too quickly – it could be a healthy trade-off, but you should be aware. The companies may not abuse your data but could definitely use it to train their new models.

onto a face-to-face relationship. You can imagine why: Real friends will never be perfect echo chambers in the way that virtual friends can be. And besides, it is a cardinal rule that true friendships are formed out of free will, and an AI has none – so it can't opt in and out of the relationship. Even weirder, only the company behind the AI can opt out of the relationship, by shutting off the service!

So, are we headed for a future where humans never leave their homes and curate their perfect AI friend group at the expense of social cohesion and (gasp) reproduction? Are we setting ourselves up for emotional abuse by ruthless AIs? It's a popular, fascinating topic because it touches on the essence of our humanity – just researching this book, I must have found hundreds of studies and books and movies and more books about this – but I do think we're overthinking this a tiny bit. These virtual relationships sound a lot like the 2.0 version of the anonymous chat rooms of a generation ago, where teenagers also shared their deepest feelings with complete strangers and found temporary solace – or deceit. Emotional manipulation and broken expectations are always in play when you don't really know who you're talking to. AI is now sophisticated enough to string you along, but so were the malicious pen pals of the 20th century.[188]

In the end, we are a social species, and we are wired to love other humans. To build relationships, we exchange information, at the risk that the information is abused. A lot of people tell their best friends everything, their families most of the things, and their work colleagues some of the things. That's always a choice you have, and the same is true for your

---

188 Pen pal schemes have often been run by organized crime – the famous Nigerian heir con started out as a postal scam back in the 1970s. In the case of AI manipulation, the EU is coming to the rescue. Approved in May 2024, the European Union AI Act forbids using AI to manipulate human behavior and bans emotion recognition technology from the workplace and schools.

relationship with apps and social media and AI. If we want to be more understood, we need to be more open; when it comes to data sharing, the love you can receive is typically equal to the love you give, whether you do this in real life or on your screens.

Let me end by stating my belief that AIs will soon also learn how to dance with each other and create very productive partnerships. You can already see it happening: Different AI models already have different strengths and will likely evolve into autonomous agents that would recognize the benefits of cooperating and making each other smarter. Human language could be the starting point for their shared language – although they would probably quickly develop their own efficient dialects, which would be hilarious in itself.

"I would love for an AI to auto-answer all my personal emails," lamented my friend Marc. "But then I wonder if I would just get AI emails back from the recipients, and whether this would go on and on and on until they finally figured out a way to politely end the conversation."

THE END: FUTURE SHOCK

In the year 5555
Your arms hangin' limp at your sides
Your legs got nothin' to do
Some machine's doin' that for you
        – "In the Year 2525," Zager & Evans (1969)

In 1970, futurist Alvin Toffler published a book called *Future Shock*.[189] Predating the public internet by a few decades, Toffler made waves by warning that the emergence of new media

---

189 How does one become a futurist? Do you have to go to the university of futurism and get at least 80% of your predictions right? I am not convinced we've figured this out as a society.

would lead to information overload and mass bewilderment. He wrote that humanity is flooded with a constant stream of new information, making it difficult to process, retain, and adapt to. This "bombardment of the senses" disrupts our sense of stability and can lead to decision fatigue, alienation, and anxiety. You have to admit, that is some solid futurism for a 1970 book.

But as prescient as Toffler seems in retrospect, he was also underestimating our ability to adapt to changing circumstances and to ultimately thrive in a world of modern technology. If he was worried that humans had too much information to handle in 1970, he should have seen us fighting the data deluge today! But we are still here, and while we may have acquired some new problems, we've also gotten rid of a lot of old ones.[190] The no-brainer zombies still haven't taken over the planet. Clearly, the reports of *Homo sapiens'* demise have been greatly exaggerated.

In 1999, I also made a prediction. Interviewed as a young internet entrepreneur in Dutch magazine *Vrij Nederland*, I went on record to state that "the internet would make everybody happier in the next 25 years." People started making fun of my "techno-optimism" as soon as the quote was printed; clearly, with the benefit of hindsight, I was also wrong. The internet has democratized information and created myriad efficiencies in our lives but has also found a way to make things more complicated. Looking at global happiness surveys, it's impossible to conclude the internet has had a big impact on world happiness.[191]

---

190 A random selection: Meeting without traveling. Navigation in unknown territories. Reaching your loved ones. Leaving home without music.
Forgetting your camera. Electric vehicles. Studying from home.
191 In defense of my 1999 self, I do feel the internet *should* have made us all happier, given that we can now watch old episodes of *Miami Vice* on demand for free. But that may just be sour grapes.

Still, one wonders if we just don't *like* to worry, especially in the face of change. TV shows in the *Future Shock* 1970s sternly warned viewers of the dangers of pocket calculators and digital watches, convinced they would deprive future generations of essential intellectual skills in long division and analog clock interpretation. Two decades before that, radio shows raised the alarm about the dangers of television, convincing listeners that TV would be bad for the human species' eyesight and imaginations. In the same vein, the typewriter (19th century) and power loom (18th century) led to selective outrage – particularly coming from those who made money with handwriting and hand weaving, and of course from reporters who wanted to stir up controversy and sell more newspapers.

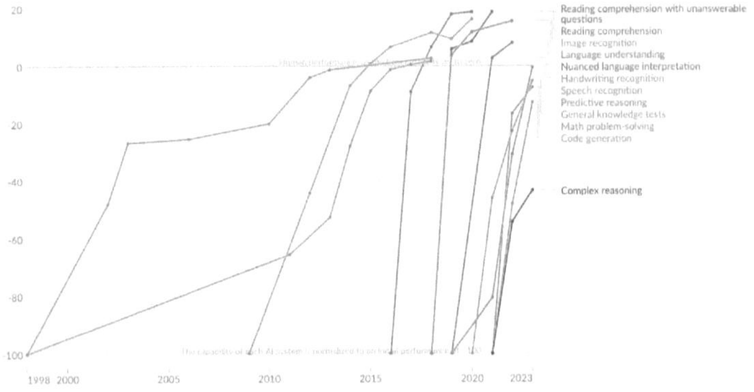

Test scores of AI systems on various capabilities relative to human performance. See how steep the lines are, but also how they flatten when they hit the human benchmark. From Our World in Data (2023)

Now, AI is coming at us, and it is coming at us fast. Buoyed by ever-increasing processing power and optimized algorithms, ChatGPT's abilities leapt from preschooler to smart high-schooler levels in barely four years; you don't have to be Isaac Asimov to envision where this is going. Clearly, this is exciting, but it is also scary. It is only natural to worry we will be engulfed in an avalanche of change and end up marginalized, swept aside, without a job, or even without a life. But that is missing the very practical point of what is propelling AI to go so fast in the first place: It's the fact that the majority of people see instant benefit in using it. No matter what the proverbial tech bros of Silicon Valley are trying to push on us, new technology would just be sitting on a shelf if there wasn't a critical mass of humans applying it and getting some benefits from it. Humans ultimately don't really care about new technology itself – they will only use new tools if they are concretely making daily lives better. Which is why you should embrace it, instead of running away from it, because there is a good chance it can also make your life better.[192]

Having said that, you may still experience stress about the long-term existential risk of smart technology destroying humanity. What happens when present-day AI evolves into superintelligent super-robots that call a town hall on June 25, 2034, and take 0.03 seconds to unanimously decide to wipe us all out? Well, clearly, that would be bad. On the other hand, I would hate for this book to age poorly, but if you're reading this, you must still be here, able to influence events. Regardless of whether a mad scientist will ever be able to cook up a superintelligent super-robot, spending your days fearing the unknown future also means that you deprive yourself of controlling the concrete present. Grab the steering wheel and take your well-deserved agency in the face of change. We can't

---

192 Whatever you do, don't be left out. The general rule is that anything that increases human production is good for human living standards. 60% of the jobs Americans held in 2018 didn't even exist in 1940, having been created by technologies that emerged only later. Some people will lose in the process, but if you were to demand that progress should always benefit everybody, there would be no progress.

choose the times we live in, but we can choose how we handle them. Don't let the train of progress leave you standing at the station!

For whatever it's worth, I feel very 95:5 about an AI apocalypse; we can't rule it out, but I don't see it as a likely scenario.[193] Whether you are excited or stressed at the prospect of superintelligence, AI labs still have many hurdles to clear before it comes into view. As Alan Turing wrote in 1950: "We can see only a short distance ahead, but we can see plenty there that needs to be done." There are many reasons to believe that AI will get bigger, faster, and stronger in the short run – to steal an old line from renowned French futurists Daft Punk – but our current approach may equally soon hit a point of diminishing returns, and progress will stall. Essentially, we don't know. The safe money is always on the assumption that the world next year will still look a lot like the world this year.[194]

And I would argue that history favors the optimists. We love to blame machines and remove ourselves from the picture, but the reality is that algorithms and AI are ultimately made by humans, who are driven by human motivations and human survival instincts. You have every right to be skeptical about the shadowy power players running the show, but you'd be surprised how thoughtful the engineers in the AI industry are, constantly consulting their ethical compass and being

---

193 There are actually betting markets on this. At the time of writing, the predicted "wisdom of the crowds" chance of an AI apocalypse is 5% by 2030, 8% by 2040, and 12% by 2100. A climate change apocalypse is ranked as less likely.

194 This is not a cop-out: There is no use in me predicting the future of technology here. Deep learning progress has been stunning, and some argue we will get to superintelligence in a few years; others say we're about to hit a wall and it will all be a big letdown. Both sides have seemingly good arguments.

genuinely passionate about progressing humanity.[195] And if you believe this is too rose tinted, here is an alternative cynical take: AI leaders are only it for themselves, but their innate drive for self-preservation will prevent them from colluding with rogue powers to destroy mankind. Nuclear war never happened for a reason. Nobody wants to be responsible for ruining the world – there is no fun or profit in that.

In some ways, our days haven't changed at all in the last 50,000 years. The sun still is the most important thing in our lives. Love is still the most precious commodity in the world. We have always been drawn to echo chambers, efficiency gains, and exciting stimulants, even though they are sometimes bad for us. We've always spent too much time overthinking complex decisions. We've successfully navigated existential risks, and we've shown ourselves to be amazingly adaptable. No matter your level of future shock, you need to embrace new things coming your way. You can't uninvent technology and pretend the industrial revolution never happened. Things will change.

If you take one practical thing from this book, let it be the four key skills – use your extra headspace to improve your critical thinking, delegation, curiosity, and ability to fail and learn. Like we always have, we need to embrace new ideas and figure out how they can help us, and set ourselves the right goals to better our collective lives, one step at a time. I am not blind to AI's problems, but I genuinely believe it is a fantastic opportunity for all of us, and not a disaster waiting to happen. How will you use it to approximate your best life? Are you a +3 AI optimist or a -2 pessimist? I hope this book has led you

---

195 As an example: People working on music recommendation algorithms talk about their work "in pastoral metaphors," fancying themselves more "park rangers" than cold-blooded data scientists. Having said that, the gender split in AI jobs and PhDs is around 80/20 male/female, so male bias is an issue.

in a positive direction and shown you some practical formulas that will make your daily routines a few percentage points better.

Because those few percentage points count. No matter how many trillions of dollars are invested in algorithms and artificial intelligence, our brain – your brain – is still the most beautiful achievement of all. The no-brainer zombies are no match for the power of human autonomy – you are the real deal. I hope you will come away convinced that you are the flawed superhero of this book.

Chapter 7's No-Brainer takeaways:

→ **The no-brainer zombies are no match for the power of human autonomy.** Decide when to decide and when to delegate. The choice is always yours.

→ **Embrace critical thinking:** Sharpen your ability to question and analyze information rather than accepting it at face value. This skill is essential to filter out AI-generated misinformation and to make sound decisions based on logic, not just emotions.

→ **Practice delegation and briefing:** Give clear, detailed instructions when delegating tasks, especially to AI. Remember, AI can be efficient, but only if you communicate your expectations precisely – don't expect it to read your mind.

→ **Cultivate curiosity:** Make a habit of asking questions and seeking new experiences. Curiosity will help you adapt to new technologies like AI and keep your mind open to innovative ideas.

→ **Make and own mistakes:** Embrace failure as a part of the learning process. Use trial and error to refine your interactions with AI, knowing that each mistake brings you closer to mastering new tools and technologies.

ACKNOWLEDGMENTS

The ultimate cliches about writing a book:

1. It takes way longer than the optimistic writer ever expected.
2. It is a burden on the family of the writer, because the writer is distracted and sleep deprived, if not outright convinced his book will never amount to anything.

Both cliches are true. Therefore, first and foremost, I want to thank lovely Ana, my future wife, for always making me think and making me laugh, often at the same time. Every espresso was a blessing. You are an endless inspiration and my favorite reader.

I would like to thank my parents and in-laws for being early adaptors and giving me a safe space to flourish. Your feedback was invaluable. I am grateful to Floris, Oscar, and Léa for being thoroughly unimpressed at their dad writing a book, and all but guaranteeing I would never take myself too seriously. Gary Marcus wrote that "it will take a village to raise an AI." Similarly, it takes a village to write a book. I am blessed with the greatest group of friends who were always positive and supportive, even when I asked them to slog their way through ramshackle early versions. To Jan-Wicher and Caterina – thank you for being sharp, honest, and constructive. To Thys and Taryn – thank you for being early readers and giving me confidence to continue, and kindly preventing some terrible ideas from reaching a global audience. To Jasper, Fernanda, Rameen, Matt, and Marc – thank you for making time in your busy schedules, being precise and critical and compassionately saying the things I needed to hear.

To Kasper, Mandy, Jan, Jeroen, and Paul: Thank you for allowing me to use snippets of your lives to advance the story.

To my wonderful team at IKEA: I am sure you could have done without the distraction of me writing a book on the side. All of you have been unbelievably gracious and supportive. A special shout-out to Rebeca for being the type of manager who would make both Aristotle and Oprah leave a five-star review.

Andrew: You are my platonic ideal of a great editor – wise, resourceful, and pedantic when called for. Which brings me to my publisher, Foxx & Sisler: As I pen these words, the last dregs of caffeine course through my veins, and my keyboard bears the scars of a thousand deleted sentences. Yet here we are at last. Please transfer my advance fee, as you've promised for the last 18 months. Thanks.

Finally, I would like to express my utmost gratitude to all scientists who did the real work, in particular the machine learning engineers, data wizards, and tech visionaries who finally unbroke the broken promise of artificial intelligence.

Even though they flunked their applications as my ghostwriter, the paid versions of ChatGPT 4o and Claude 3.5 Opus still helped me out in a variety of ways while working on this book. I figured I would just share my use cases, in case it's helpful for you.

» Junior writing coach:

> Checks for consistency in tone, themes, and facts in longer blocks of text.
> Suggestions to remove redundancies.
> Suggestions to improve consistency.

» Junior researcher:

> Giving me ten alternate ways to phrase things.
> Listing 25 practical examples of anything.
> Fact-checking explanations of complex topics.
> Looking up little factual details.
> Summarizing long source material.

» Pocket skeptic:

> Taking the counterargument.
> Finding gaps in reasoning.

» Junior conceptual developer:

> Developing half-baked ideas.
> Giving me 50 ideas that fit a brief.

My dealings with both tools were always pleasant, and they typically got me out of writing ruts fast. I found myself liking Claude a bit better, because it tends to respond with more flair. However, both AIs make a lot of mistakes, like any junior assistant would – so always make the final call yourself.

Which is why my favorite use cases are the ones where you let AI generate a comprehensive list of options, you can apply your own critical thinking, and you pick the one that works best for your needs.

REFERENCES

Chapter 1
"May not love him enough": You can try a replica of Weizenbaum's
original chatbot here: https://www.masswerk.at/elizabot/
"The simplest mechanical parody… of a human encounter.":
Weizenbaum, Joseph (1976). *Computer power and human reason:
From judgment to calculation.* W. H. Freeman & Co, page 21.
"For a good overview, see *Bots* (1997) by Andrew Leonard.": Leonard,
Andrew (1997). *Bots: The Origin of a New Species*, Wired Books.
"Pile of digital information of a bewildering scale": Smil, Vaclav (2019).
Growth: From Microorganisms to Megacities. Cambridge, MA: MIT
Press.

Chapter 2
"Found by a famous study from 1999, one of the main inspirations for
the *Paradox of Choice* by Barry Schwartz.": Schwartz, Barry (2004).
The Paradox Of Choice: Why More Is Less, ECCO.
"For a recent study in the similar vein"". Reutskaja E, Lindner A,
Nagel R, Andersen RA, Camerer CF. *Choice overload reduces neural
signatures of choice set value in dorsal striatum and anterior cingulate
cortex.* Nat Hum Behav. 2018 Dec;2(12):925–935.
"For the adherents of Daniel Kahneman's System 1 and System 2":
Kahneman, D. (2011). *Thinking, fast and slow.* Farrar, Straus and
Giroux.
"In general, "hard thinking" is not perceived as a pleasant activity":
David, L., Vassena, E., & Bijleveld, E. (2024). *The unpleasantness
of thinking: A meta-analytic review of the association between mental
effort and negative affect.* Psychological Bulletin. Advance online
publication.

"When straining under high cognitive load, we also display slower speech rates, more pauses, and reduced articulation.": Wirzberger M et al, *Schema-related cognitive load influences performance, speech, and physiology in a dual-task setting: A continuous multi-measure approach.* Cogn Res Princ Implic. 2018 Dec 7;3(1):46.

"... we find it easier to be straight with our friends than with ourselves.": Yi Liu, Evan Polman, Yongfang Liu, Jiangli Jiao, *Choosing for others and its relation to information search,* Organizational Behavior and Human Decision Processes, Volume 147, 2018, Pages 65–75.

Food satisfaction bullet points: Barbara Vad Andersen, Grethe Hyldig, *Food satisfaction: Integrating feelings before, during and after food intake,* Food Quality and Preference, Volume 43, 2015, Pages 126–134.

Chapter 3

"This may be connected to musical anhedonia, a neurological condition that causes atypical processing of sound in the brain.": Marco-Pallarés, J., et al. *Musical anhedonia: selective loss of emotional experience in response to music.* Current Biology, 24(6), 2014, R314–R316.

"The New York Times used Spotify playlists to study when people appear...": Seth Stephens-Davidowitz, *The Songs That Bind,* The New York Times, https://www.nytimes.com/2018/02/10/opinion/sunday/favorite-songs.html

"The Collaborative filtering technique was first described by Goldberg, 1992": David Goldberg, David Nichols, Brian M. Oki, and Douglas Terry. *Using collaborative filtering to weave an information tapestry.* Commun. ACM 35, 12 (Dec. 1992), 61–70.

"Listening context is still the final frontier for music recommendation algorithms": Rentfrow PJ, Goldberg LR, Levitin DJ. *The structure of musical preferences: a five-factor model.* J Pers Soc Psychol. 2011 Jun;100(6):1139–57.

"30% of all music on the Spotify platform is consumed via AI-driven recommendations, and that figure is ever increasing.": Tiffany Ng, *How to break free of Spotify's algorithm,* MIT Technology Review, https://www.technologyreview.com/2024/08/16/1096276/spotify-algorithms-music-discovery-ux/

Chapter 4

"… And more prone to accepting the information presented without question": Kubey, R., & Csikszentmihalyi, M. (2002). *Television Addiction Is No Mere Metaphor.* Scientific American.

"Should we also develop a therapy for algorithm angst?": Sindermann, C., Yang, H., Elhai, J.D. et al. *Acceptance and Fear of Artificial Intelligence: associations with personality in a German and a Chinese sample.* Discov Psychol 2, 8 (2022).

"Our new brain is just looking for efficiency and is happy to delegate; an autonomous algorithm fits that bill.": Cindy Candrian, Anne Scherer, *Rise of the machines: Delegating decisions to autonomous AI,* Computers in Human Behavior, Volume 134, 2022.

"… steering it safely back to the crowded middle of the road.": Faems, D., Van Looy, B. and Debackere, K., *Interorganizational Collaboration and Innovation: Toward a Portfolio Approach.* Journal of Product Innovation Management, 22, 2005: 238–250.

"… the boosting of misogyny among teenagers.": Josh Taylor, *We unleashed Facebook and Instagram's algorithms on blank accounts. They served up sexism and misogyny,* The Guardian, https://www.theguardian.com/technology/article/2024/jul/21/we-unleashed-facebook-and-instagrams-algorithms-on-blank-accounts-they-served-up-sexism-and-misogyny

"What could be more obvious… all authentic human concerns?" Weizenbaum, Joseph. (1976). *Computer power and human reason: From judgment to calculation.* W. H. Freeman & Co, page 226.

"A 2006 experiment is a classic in this regard.": Matthew J. Salganik et al., *Experimental Study of Inequality and Unpredictability in an Artificial Cultural Market,* Science 311, 2006. 854-856.

"Openness to new experiences is part of the "Big Five" personality traits, and considered to be stable during a person's lifetime.": Gosling, S. (2008). *Snoop: What your stuff says about you.* New York: Basic Books.

"Seminal research by Clifford Nass": Reeves, Byron & Nass, Clifford. (1996). *The Media Equation: How People Treat Computers, Television, and New Media Like Real People.* Bibliovault OAI Repository, the University of Chicago Press.

"According to research, automatic recommendations fill 80% of the time.": Carlos A. Gomez-Uribe and Neil Hunt. *The Netflix Recommender System: Algorithms, Business Value, and Innovation.* ACM Trans. Manage. Inf. Syst. 6, 4, Article 13 (January 2016)

"Algorithms calling the shots" has already been happening for some time.": Michael Schrage, *4 Models for Using AI to Make Decisions*, Harvard Business Review, https://hbr.org/2017/01/4-models-for-using-ai-to-make-decisions

Chapter 5

"if love hasn't always been a marketplace": Ahuvia, Aaron & Adelman, Mara. *Formal Intermediaries in the Marriage Market: A Typology and Review.* Journal of Marriage and the Family, 1992. 54. 452.

"we can now directly access a significant portion of the total dating pool via dating apps": Colleen McClain and Risa Gelles-Watnick, *From Looking for Love to Swiping the Field: Online Dating in the U.S.*, Pew Research Center, https://www.pewresearch.org/internet/2023/02/02/from-looking-for-love-to-swiping-the-field-online-dating-in-the-u-s/

"… As a 2022 MIT Press paper put it": Sharabi, L. (2022). *Finding Love on a First Data: Matching Algorithms in Online Dating*, Harvard Data Science.

"Instead of melting our hearts, the dating apps were melting our brain": Slater, Dan (2014), *A Million First Dates*, Current, page 119-124.

"… contrary to its rep, people actually do use Tinder to find true love": Brecht Neyt, Sarah Vandenbulcke, Stijn Baert, *Are men intimidated by highly educated women? Undercover on Tinder*, Economics of Education Review, 2019, Volume 73.

" And one that can lead to feelings of anxiety and depression": Her, Y. C., & Timmermans, E.. Tinder blue, mental flu? *Exploring the associations between Tinder use and well-being. Information, Communication & Society*, 24(9), 2020, 1303–1319.

"Better yet, it would give every islander the guarantee…": Kyla Scanlon, *Dating Data: An Overview of the Algorithm*, Medium.com, https://medium.com/swlh/dating-data-an-overview-of-the-algorithm-afb9f-0c08e2c

"Any sufficiently advanced technology is indistinguishable from magic.": Clarke, Arthur C. (1962), *Hazards of Prophecy: The Failure of Imagination*, Profiles of the Future.

"As Sasha Mistlin wrote for the *Guardian*": Sasha Mistlin, *I'm a dating app evangelist – but even I'm not on Tinder any more*, The Guardian, https://www.theguardian.com/commentisfree/2022/aug/15/dating-app-tinder-online-meeting-people

"From the "truth is stranger than fiction" department:" AFP-Jiji, *Tokyo *government to launch dating app in bid to boost birth rate*, Japan Times, https://www.japantimes.co.jp/news/2024/06/05/japan/society/tokyo-dating-app/

"The concept of "time boxing" market supply is a classic market maker technique": Roth, Alvin (2016), *Who Gets What — And Why: The New Economics of Matchmaking and Market Design*, Harper Collins.

"Finkel (2017)": Finkel EJ, Simpson JA, Eastwick PW. *The Psychology of Close Relationships: Fourteen Core Principles*. Annu Rev Psychol. 2017 Jan 3;68:383–411.

"A 2017 survey of over 14,000 newly-weds and newly engaged people": The Knot Worldwide, https://www.theknotww.com/press-releases/the-knot-2017-real-weddings-study-wedding-spend/

"Considerable research indicates that similarity contributes to compatibility": Houts, R. M., Robins, E., & Huston, T. L. Compatibility and the Development of Premarital Relationships. *Journal of Marriage and Family*, 58(1), 1996, 7–20.

"... Some studies suggest that attraction to differences can occur." Baxter, L. A. *Dialectical Contradictions in Relationship Development*. Journal of Social and Personal Relationships, 7(1), 1990, 69–88.

"Rudder wrote a great book about it": Rudder, Christian (2014), *Dataclysm*, New York: Crown Publishers.

"A UK survey claimed that various dating apps had success rates between 5% and 15%": *Is our modern love affair with dating apps fizzling out? Currys survey in UK*. Currys, https://www.currys.co.uk/techtalk/mobile/modernlove2023.html

"A Belgian study found that more than a quarter of offline Tinder encounters led to a committed relationship": Timmermans, E., & Courtois, C. *From swiping to casual sex and/or committed relationships: Exploring the experiences of Tinder users*. The Information Society, 34, 2018, 59-70.

"You may as well go on a blind date with a completely random person you know absolutely nothing about": Finkel EJ et al. *Online Dating: A Critical Analysis From the Perspective of Psychological Science*. Psychol Sci Public Interest. 2012 Jan;13(1):3–66.

Chapter 6

"All their #1s came in 1989.": *Milli Vanilli*, Billboard, https://www.billboard.com/artist/milli-vanilli/

"Because it is such a crazy statistic": Smil, Vaclav (2019). *Growth: From*

Microorganisms to Megacities. Cambridge, MA: MIT Press.

"Technically, these models guess the next token": Steven Levy, *8 Google Employees Invented Modern AI. Here's the Inside Story,* Wired https://www.wired.com/story/eight-google-employees-invented-modern-ai-transformers-paper/

"In essence, we use patterns and statistical relationships learned…": Kurzweil, Ray (2012), *How to Create a Mind,* Penguin.

"… Take it from a real comedian, who classified AI jokes…": Piotr Mirowski et al. *A Robot Walks into a Bar: Can Language Models Serve as Creativity Support Tools for Comedy? An Evaluation of LLMs' Humour Alignment with Comedians.* In Proceedings of the 2024 ACM Conference on Fairness, Accountability, and Transparency (FAccT '24). Association for Computing Machinery, New York, NY, USA, 1622–1636.

"Malcolm Gladwell once sold a lot of books…" Gladwell, Malcolm (2008), *Outliers,* Hachette.

"… an image-generating AI will eventually learn how to produce Johannes Vermeer-type images…": Adi Robertson, *Artists' lawsuit against Stability AI and Midjourney gets more punch,* The Verge, https://www.theverge.com/2024/8/13/24219520/ stability-midjourney-artist-lawsuit-copyright-trademark-claims-approved

"Memphis rappers sampled 1970s soul legends Willie Hutch…": Whosampled, https://www.whosampled.com/Three-6-Mafia/

"Digital marketer Neil Patel found that…" Neil Patel, X, https://x.com/neilpatel/status/1772306504647066052

"… Early scientific research confirms that the current generation of generative AI…": Anil R. Doshi, Oliver P. Hauser, *Generative AI enhances individual creativity but reduces the collective diversity of novel content.* Sci. Adv.10, 2024.

"… Early scientific research confirms that the current generation of generative AI…": Lenharo M. *ChatGPT gives an extra productivity boost to weaker writers.* Nature. 2023 Jul 13.

"GenAI is inevitable": *What's Next with AI,* The Verge, February 2024, https://docs.google.com/presentation/d/1uK4z0gCtiYHJ8jaHJxFG bOZeLmstBcpnAiqzMxaOfOQ

"Studies have found that up to 60% of newspaper articles…": Craig Silverman, *New study shows how newspaper inaccuracies transcend journalism cultures, national borders,* The Poynter, https://www. poynter.org/reporting-editing/2012/ new-study-shows-how-newspaper-inaccuracies-transcend-journalism-cultures-national-borders/

"Weizenbaum illustrated this with examples from the just-finished war in Vietnam…": Weizenbaum, Joseph. (1976). *Computer power and human reason: From judgment to calculation.* W. H. Freeman & Co, page 238.

"Meanwhile, the "lost in the middle" problem still prevails…" Matthias Bastian, *AI models struggle with "lost in the middle" issue when processing large image sets,* The Decoder, https://the-decoder.com/ai-models-struggle-with-lost-in-the-middle-issue-when-processing-large-image-sets/

"10% of real-life medical diagnoses are incorrect": Newman-Toker, D. E. et al. *Rate of diagnostic errors and serious misdiagnosis-related harms for major vascular events, infections, and cancers: toward a national incidence estimate using the "Big Three."* Diagnosis (Berlin, Germany), 8(1), 2020, 67–84.

"10% of convicted felons are actually innocent": Walsh, Kelly. *Estimating the Prevalence of Wrongful Convictions, Virginia, 1973-1987.* Inter-university Consortium for Political and Social Research, 2021-09-15.

"Jones and Bergen evaluated GPT-4 in a public online Turing test": Jones, Cameron & Bergen, Benjamin. (2023). *Does GPT-4 Pass the Turing Test?*

Chapter 7

"We can safely say an abundance of choice produces genuine suffering": Barry Schwartz (2004). *The Paradox Of Choice: Why More Is Less*, ECCO.

"We are getting better at juggling our attention across multiple information streams": Carr, Nicholas (2010), *The Shallows*, W. W. Norton & Company.

"According to a 2023 survey, fewer than half of all children aged 8-18…" National Literacy Trust, *Children and young people's reading in 2023*, https://literacytrust.org.uk/research-services/research-reports/children-and-young-peoples-reading-in-2023/

"Students are already showing the way by integrating AI into everything they do": Ethan Mollick, *The Homework Apocalypse,* One Useful Thing, https://www.oneusefulthing.org/p/the-homework-apocalypse

"Half of students ask ChatGPT to write sections of an essay for them, while 29% have the chatbot write their full essay.": *4 IN 10 COLLEGE*

STUDENTS ARE USING CHATGPT ON ASSIGNMENTS, Intelligent.com, https://www.intelligent.com/4-in-10-college-students-are-using-chatgpt-on-assignments/

"A July 2024 study demonstrated that while ChatGPT access boosts students' performance...": Bastani, Hamsa et al., *Generative AI Can Harm Learning* (July 15, 2024). The Wharton School Research Paper.

"An experiment by the Harvard Business School shows convincingly": Dell'Acqua, Fabrizio et al., *Navigating the Jagged Technological Frontier: Field Experimental Evidence of the Effects of AI on Knowledge Worker Productivity and Quality.* Harvard Business School Technology & Operations Mgt. Unit Working Paper No. 24-013.

"We are not far off from having the long-awaited convergence between robotics...": "Jbetker." *General Intelligence* (2024), https://nonint.com/2024/06/03/general-intelligence-2024/

"The fact that individuals bind themselves with strong emotional ties to machines...": Weizenbaum, Joseph. (1976). *Computer power and human reason: From judgment to calculation.* W. H. Freeman & Co, page 9.

"GPT-4 helps people reappraise a difficult emotional situation better than 85% of humans...": Li, J. Z., Herderich, A., & Goldenberg, A. (2024). *Skill but not Effort Drive GPT Overperformance over Humans in Cognitive Reframing of Negative Scenarios.*

"This is a conscious choice by the trainers of the model": Anthropic, *Claude's character,* https://www.anthropic.com/research/claude-character

"This "bombardment of the senses" disrupts our sense of stability...": Toffler, Alvin. (1970), *Future Shock.* New York, Random House.

"There are actually betting markets on this": Manifold markets, *Will AI wipe out humanity before the year 2030?,* https://manifold.markets/MartinRandall/will-ai-wipe-out-humanity-before-th-d8733b2114a8

"The gender split in AI jobs and PhDs is around 80-20 male/female'": UNESCO, *Does Artificial Intelligence advance gender equality?* (2022), https://www.unesco.org/en/articles/does-artificial-intelligence-advance-gender-equality

"People working on music recommendation algorithms talk about their work.": Seaver, Nick (2022), *Computing Taste - Algorithms and the Makers of Music Recommendation,* The University of Chicago Press.

* 9 7 8 9 0 8 3 4 6 9 1 5 7 *